Library of
Davidson College

RETURN TO
PUNJAB

RETURN TO PUNJAB

By
Prakash Tandon

UNIVERSITY OF CALIFORNIA PRESS
Berkeley • Los Angeles • London

University of California Press
Berkeley and Los Angeles, California
University of California Press, Ltd.
London, England
© 1981 by
The Regents of the University of California
Printed in the United States of America

1 2 3 4 5 6 7 8 9

Library of Congress Cataloging in Publication Data

Tandon, Prakash.
    Return to Punjab.

    1. Tandon, Prakash. 2. Businessmen—India—
Biography. I. Title.
HC432.5.T3A37   338'.04'0924 [B]   79-65766
ISBN 0-520-03990-4

TO
THE PUNJAB AND THE PUNJABIS

ACKNOWLEDGEMENTS

To Gärd, as before, for her support and impeccable sense of language; to Maya, Manu, and Gautam; to T. Thomas, and Amal Dutt; to John Thompson, Warren and Alice Ilchman, Leo Rose, Leroy Jones, N. C. B. Nath, I. Z. Bhatty, Prem Bhatia, G. D. Khosia, and many others for their advice on the manuscript. To those who deciphered my poor handwriting and helped with many drafts—G. D. Mathur, Thiagarajan, Padmanabhan, Ramdhan, D. D. Dhawan, V. Gopinathan, Balkrishna, and R. N. Sharma. To Luci Del Marle for both help with the manuscript and the cover graphic, and to Taya and Maurice Zinkin, with whom it all began.

CONTENTS

Acknowledgements	vii
Prologue	1
Chapter One UNILEVER	7
Two THE LAST VICEROY	13
Three NEW DELHI	24
Four UNIONS	36
Five AN INDIAN ROAD	47
Six KASHMIR	56
Seven GOVERNMENT AND BUSINESS	65
Eight INDIA'S WARS	75
Nine SHAREHOLDERS	85
Ten MAYA	93
Eleven HINDUSTAN STEEL	102
Twelve A NEW BUSINESS SCHOOL	115
Thirteen LOS ANGELES	134
Fourteen LEAVING LEVER	141
Fifteen MOSCOW	148
Sixteen STATE TRADING CORPORATION	155
Seventeen PORTRAIT OF A MINISTER	171
Eighteen PUNJAB NATIONAL BANK	185
Epilogue	203
Glossary	207

PROLOGUE

THIS is the third and last chapter of a story that began with the coming of the British to our part of the Punjab in 1852, when they fought their last battle outside the walls of our town of Gujrat. For ninety-five years they ruled over us. When they finally left and went back to their island, some stayed behind as traders. It was, after all, as traders that they had come to India in the first place three hundred years earlier; the century of empire was only an interlude.

My father had worked with the British for thirty years in their imperial days. I began my own career with them when their rule was slackening and they were reverting to commerce. For twenty-three years I learnt my trade in a British firm—that was the second chapter of the story. The pages that follow take it up when my employers, now grown into a large and prosperous manufacturing concern, asked me to take over their business in India with all its scattered factories and branches, and run it profitably for them for ten years.

PUNJABI CENTURY (1857–1947)

Gujrat was where our new history began in 1857. For generations before that the family moved between the rivers Jhelum and Chenab as they descended through the foothills into the plain of the Punjab. Our genealogies were inscribed for centuries in the books of our priests in the holy city of Hardwar on the banks of the Ganges, where after a death in the family someone would go to immerse the ashes and at the same time bring the record of marriages, births, and other events since the last visit up to date. This the pandit noted down in his long books covered with red muslin, folded at the middle and tied with a white string.

Of our more distant past we knew very little, apart from racial memory that ascribed our origin to the Aryans who came from somewhere north of the Himalayas. There was even a charming legend that we came from the vicinity of the north pole. At our weddings we still asked the couple to look up at the pole star above their heads.

PROLOGUE

After the chaos of a hundred years, when Moghuls, Marathas, Persians, Sikhs, and minor local satraps milled around in endless fighting, the British came with their fantastic faces that we thought looked like the bottoms of monkeys, and their yet more fantastic garb. After their defeat at Chelianwala, where my great-granduncle fought with the Sikh army, we made a final stand outside the gates of Gujrat. But the British brought peace, something we had only known in odd spells, and peace of a different kind, the result not of benign rule but of a system bent on producing order and the rule of law. There also came new communications, roads, postal service and telegraph; canals that brought water from the river to the fertile but parched land; education in schools and colleges that went far beyond the reading of scriptures in mosques and temples. At school we had to learn by heart the ten blessings of Angrezi Raj, the British rule.

We were slowly attracted out of our villages into the towns. My granduncle was the first to go from the village school to the new highschool in Gujrat, where an English headmaster taught the new language. A promising student, he was helped by the headmaster to enter the new university at Lahore to study law. Two years later he returned as the proud possessor of a *vakalat nama*—a licence to set up practice in the courts of Gujrat. My grandfather, a minor revenue officer in the new government, who had supported his orphan brother, must have been a proud man in his village; but he did not live long enough to see my father go even further.

My father, also orphaned young, was brought up by his uncle, and was in due course to help his younger brothers in the same way. One of them followed his uncle into law and practised in Gujrat. Father worked hard, and after high school he sat for the entrance examination to the new engineering college of Roorkee, the earliest of its kind in Asia, where they taught the new science of engineering canals, dams, roads, buildings, and railways.

Thus began the process of professionalization. Lawyers, doctors, engineers, civil servants, forest officers, teachers; they came from villages and small towns and spread all over the Punjab. Like the new communications network, they forged the old order, so far loosely knit together by custom and tradition, into a professional society. Lahore became its centre of higher education, with opportunities to practice in law and medicine, and to teach at the many colleges or serve in the government secretariats. Tradition

PROLOGUE

also attracted our young men to soldiering, and with the new rulers' armies they went to distant lands, from Flanders to Hong Kong. Energetic Sikh farmers went as far as California to farm, to Vancouver to lumber, and to Peking to police.

Few entered business and industry; it was not in our tradition. Professions and farming, with a little shopkeeping, were our main occupations. The Khatris had previously served as soldiers or minor officials; the senior positions had usually been closed to them. Now the scope for advancement was suddenly limited only in the higher reaches of administration, and even there openings gradually came. Thirsting for opportunity, like our rich soil that had waited for water and the plough, my father's generation sprouted quickly into an industrious and competent middle class. Into this class spread new ideas and values from the christianized Brahmo Samaj of Bengal and the Hindu reformist Arya Samaj of Western India. Never orthodox in the way of brahmanical Hinduism, our society laid itself open to these new ideas, while maintaining its basic culture. Throughout centuries of foreign conquest, we had drawn inward to maintain our identity without visible trappings that might offend our invaders. Dressed like Muslims, we spoke their language and tried to look indistinguishable. Now we took to the ways of the new rulers with the same wariness, readily though we adopted their professions; we even began to learn to live like them. Culturally we had been commuters for a long time, commuting daily from our Hindu Punjabi homes to the world of Muslim, Sikh, and now British culture.

BEYOND PUNJAB (1937–1960)

My own career should also have been in law or engineering, but in 1929 a further change was already on the way. Political ferment made government service less attractive, but new careers in industry were just opening up, and I chose to prepare for one of them. I went to England, where my elder brother was already studying mechanical and electrical engineering, and entered the University of Manchester to take a degree in commerce and serve articles for chartered accountancy. Upon my return eight years later, I joined the British firm of Unilever in their first attempt at Indianization.

It was curious that while the Indian Civil Service had begun the process of admitting Indians almost within a decade of its inception, as did subsequently all other government services, British

PROLOGUE

business was still tentative about admitting Indians three-quarters of a century later. While half the thousand officials of the ICS in 1937 were indigenous, British business and industry then had perhaps half a dozen Indians in their so-called "covenanted" ranks. Perhaps they were only following the tradition of our own businesses. To rise to a management position in an Indian firm you had to be a member of the family, caste, or region of India, and so it was with the British—though both were willing to take influence and parentage into account. The British would favourably consider an Oxford or Cambridge Blue, or the son of a judge or civil servant; to Indian business the Blue meant nothing, but being the son of a civil servant did.

I had no such claims. To the many firms I called on on my return from England I could only say that I had a degree in arts, another in commerce, a qualification in accounts, and had spent eight years in Europe. The head of an Indian shipping firm became upset at the thought that I might expect a salary on the level of the ICS. I protested that I had not asked for anything. The head of a British rubber tyre firm said that with my qualifications I might—*might*—get the job of the man sitting outside his door. In any case neither had anything to offer. The head of an international oil company thought the only qualifications relevant would be social ones. A friend of my father whose young son was struggling to start his own practice as a chartered accountant suggested I should leave Bombay and go as far away as possible!

Into this unsupportive environment I decided to settle. Some perversity attracted me to this cold city, Bombay, bursting with its new industrial and commercial growth. I took the only job offered me, which necessitated leaving the profession I had been trained for and starting in the advertising department for training in marketing research. It was carefully explained to me that the Englishman who was coming out to set up this new department had insisted that it should be staffed by Indians, with an Indian manager to organize and train Indian girls to do the field work among housewives, the customers for the firm's household products.

I joined as their first Indian manager, as diffident as they were. In fact it was the diffidence with which they offered me the job that attracted me. It was such a contrast to the confidence with which the others had rejected me. After eight years of pleasant but undirected life in England, I was eager to start work. In any case, market research was a job, and I needed one.

PROLOGUE

I stayed with the firm for over thirty years. They were long arduous years of mutual dedication to an idea, slowly testing and building the trust deep down, an experiment at all stages. The change from each stage to the next seemed as doubtful as it finally became inevitable: I wondered if they would make it, and they wondered if I should make it. For quite a long time, perhaps till the end, it had the quality of a love-hate relationship, but they made me their first indigenous chairman outside their home companies in England, Holland, and America. Interestingly, the first Indian chairman of a multinational corporation, J. M. Lal, appointed some months before me, was also a Punjabi. The whole process seemed remarkably similar to what my father used to tell me about his own experience and that of his senior colleagues who had joined the new services in the 1870s, when the ground was less familiar and the going must have been much harder.

RETURN TO PUNJAB (1961-1977)

In some ways Unilever gave me more responsibility and trust than they normally gave their own, but we were never close to each other. It was a part of my nature, and theirs. After eight years as chairman that never lacked excitement, I left them to join one of the corporations that Nehru had formed in his faith in socialism and public enterprise. From this international trading corporation I moved to a nationalized bank, an eighty-year-old Punjabi nationalist institution. Having left Punjab in 1929, I returned to it in 1972.

The whole story is one of a Punjabi family whose five generations lived through two momentous centuries of change—a family essentially no different from any other family of West Punjab, with a pattern of life that has endured through time, change, and strife. The British connection, significant in its own way, was just one of the many conquering waves that came and passed, each leaving a layer of influence, like the five rivers that have poured down water and mud interminably, and in so doing enriched our soil. Today, thirty years after Partition, our generation and the next have scattered all over India, mostly in the professions. My three children and their cousins, or their spouses, are in banking, the army, medicine, technology, accounting, and management, either in India or abroad. Curiously enough, they have all, despite their education in different parts of India, with some atavistic instinct married Punjabis, including our three, whose mother came from Sweden, while among the new all-India generation of professionals many marry outside the old boundaries.

A new Punjab has arisen in the heartland of the old eastern Punjab, with its name and traditions upheld. Now the granary, but still the old "sword arm" of India, it has already been involved in four wars; and its sons once again reach out to distant parts of the world. In a quarter of a century it has gained more than the vitality it temporarily lost—but, alas, it has only three rivers now.

Chapter One

UNILEVER

LEVER BROTHERS of Port Sunlight, near Liverpool, had exported soaps to India since 1875, and over the next half-century had built up their business till Sunlight became a household name, synonymous with soap, as later Dalda was with *vanaspati,* the vegetable cooking fat. They appointed Indian and European merchants as distributors in the port towns of Bombay, Calcutta, Madras, and Karachi, and through visiting salesmen and new forms of advertising and sampling developed a wholesale network that reached every town and village, the cost of which was usually paid for by resale of the empty wooden packing-cases their product came in. In the 1920s offices were opened in the port towns, followed by the setting up of companies and factories, which in the 1930s became full-fledged manufacturing and marketing concerns, fed with new systems and policies from Britain, and Lever's growing international operations. I had joined the company in 1937. In 1951, after many interesting years of travelling extensively and learning about the India of villages and towns, I became a director. I was made a member of the first board of the new Hindustan Lever in 1956, and vice-chairman in 1960. In 1961 Steve Turner, my chairman, had a heart attack. When it became clear after a few months that he would have to return home, I was invited to London for discussions, which turned out to be the ritual of my speeded-up appointment.

At Unilever House, sitting in the room of Robert Siddons, a member of the overseas committee responsible for India, I looked across the Thames, shimmering and busy under a bright June sun. On the other bank the city rose from the warehouses and municipal office buildings, the Royal Festival Hall tucked among them as a contrasting contemporary note. The view through the hazy rooftops to the green hills of Kent was similar to the one across the harbour to the hills beyond at which I had gazed from the Bombay office when John Rist offered me the job in 1937.

CHAPTER ONE

"Prakash," Robert began a little self-consciously, "we don't think Steve Turner can go back to India after his heart attack, and we would like to offer you the chairmanship."

"Thank you, Robert, I appreciate the trust," I replied.

This embarrassing ritual over, we began to discuss the details.

In the evening, Andrew Knox, chairman of the overseas committee, asked me to a drink at the Liberal Club. He was the last of his kind in the firm. At fifty-eight, he had already served it for forty-two years. His father had moved from the church to join Lord Leverhume in the early days of the business, and merged into the legend of the founder. Retiring, he left behind him his son Andrew, whom the founder must have trained with some personal care. Andrew had risen through the ranks at Port Sunlight, the home of the business, and subsequently at London in the new grandeur of Unilever House. For many years he visited India every winter (a cold-weather bird, as they used to call the businessmen who came from Europe at the beginning of winter), travelled through the country doing business, and took the P & O mail-boat back as the summer began. He became very deeply attached to India, and the Indian business in his eyes could do no wrong and deserved the best. I felt it an honour that he should have been associated with the decision to appoint me their first Indian chairman.

As we walked along the Thames Embankment, he talked about his past and the Indian business. He told me how it had been threatened with extinction when the Swadeshi movement's boycott of foreign goods brought it to a standstill in the 1920s—and yet that threat had given the business its new foundations. From an indenting business, it had grown over the next quarter-century to be one of the largest manufacturing houses in India. With all this Andrew had been closely associated.

In the Liberal Club we settled into deep leather chairs that could not have seated many Indians in the old days. He lifted his glass and took the plunge. "Prakash—we will have to say Prakash and Andrew now, for times have changed," he said. "In the old days we could have been Tandon and Knox, and got along pretty well, but today they will think we are not getting on well with each other if we continue to use surnames." He relaxed, having got over this onerous duty, and turned to our working relationship.

"It will be for you to keep us in touch with the business. I would like it to work in such a way that if someone stops me in the corridor and says, 'What is this we hear about India,' I should be able to say, 'I don't know, but if there is anything to it, we will no doubt hear from Mr. Tandon, and I will let you know. And if we don't hear from him, then it will not be worth bothering about.' We should prefer not to ask, but to let you tell us, how much and when you think necessary. There will, of course, be times when you will want to consult us. After all, it is not the same as working in London, where you can telephone or just walk across to Unilever House. Though you can phone from Bombay, somehow the distance makes it sound like a crisis, which can be misunderstood. So you will have to take most of your decisions by yourself. But when you do want a personal consultation—well, just put on your coat and hat and fly over."

Then he went on to warn me about the problems of the Indian business, and seemed to come out with long pent-up feelings about it. "Like too many things in India, things seem never to get a move on. There are always things happening the one way, to slow it down. Much less happens the other way, to speed it up. And there is always one more good reason that no one else had thought of before to make the government people take another look, just as something is getting done. You have an able government, but the ability seems to go into making more and more rules and producing more good reasons not to do things than anyone else I know of. It all baffles us. We get an interesting picture from here of our operations in many countries—new, developing, developed, old. Few I know have your ability. In South America, Africa, the East, near and far, there are few I have greater respect for, but you must learn to move faster, at the speed you are capable of, and not always be holding yourselves back.

"I wonder sometimes what stops you. It is not, as in some other countries, a lack of liking for business, for business is in your blood. Nowhere have I seen anything like your wholesale business, which for so little can do so much. At less than one percent they will store, finance, and deliver across long distances in dilapidated trucks and bullock carts. You can always rely on them to do the job. Our business is sound and well founded, and has the capacity for much greater growth. And yet, something seems to stand in the way.

"While your government is restrictive it is also permissive. In

CHAPTER ONE

the end you get your way, depending upon your perseverance. Let me not blame your government, for there is a lethargy in the business too. Even after your government has sanctioned a project, and we have approved of it, you seem to take ages to do it. What takes nine months to build elsewhere, takes you five years. Look at the office building that you began over three years ago; I wonder if I will ever enter it in my working life!"

Andrew was in a relentless mood. In the past he had discussed these issues with their own chairmen, but that was not the same as talking to me; I was both chairman and Indian, and could be held responsible for the sins of both company and country. It was for me to put them both right! I considered this a tall order, but I preferred to listen. In the afternoon, passing the office of Bonham-Carter on the Unilever directors' floor, I had knocked on his door. It was only a few years since I had made my coldness to Unilever clear to him and had turned away his feeler about my visiting England to attend a course at Henley Staff College. As I entered his room, he rushed across like an eager giant, pumped my hand up and down, and said, "Prakash, this is a great day for all of us—for Unilever, for the Indian company, and for me." It was their day, for their experiment with "Ization"—meaning indigenizing managerial talent up to the highest rungs of the ladder—was bearing its first significant fruit. My own feelings I would analyse later, on the long flight home.

There would be many hours alone to think. Now I let Andrew say all he had come to say. A good listener, he was not talkative by nature, but whatever he had to say he said, without apologizing for length or bluntness. He told me that he did not believe in dressing down a man in the newfangled way, used by some of his colleagues, of inviting him to lunch and letting him eat the food like poison till with the coffee they smoothly began to take him apart. "No, I call the man and tell him across the desk what I find wrong with him, and what he can do to put himself right with me. In the end they have been grateful because this leaves them with their self-respect. It also puts a little fight into them, if they have it in them," he went on.

He warned me that my problems would be more with my own people than with them. They found Indians very sensitive, and not an easy people to deal with. I remembered what an English writer of the twenties, Edward Thompson, had once said: an Indian is quick to register disappointment but slow to register satisfaction. Gärd, my Swedish wife, used to remark that nobody ever seemed to acknowledge a wedding present or open a gift for a new baby; it was just put aside impassively without a word of thanks. Yet a guest could make a blunt comment on your hospitality. A country cousin who paid us a visit said of our homemade ice cream, "In our Bahawalpur there were two kinds of ice cream—the four-anna kind and the two-anna kind. This is the two-anna ice cream."

"We can deal with each other with a directness that we cannot use with you without risking hurt," said Andrew. He gave me the example of his difficult relations with an English colleague, Paul Addis, whom I knew as an interesting man but one not easy to deal with. They did not care for each other, and in the end hardly spoke, which could not fail to be remarked upon in the company. So one day Andrew said to him, "Paul, you do not like me, and I have no great love for you, but it is not fair to the organisation because people are beginning to talk about it. We have to get on with each other." And they did, and even got to like each other, no doubt much to their mutual disgust.

I thought this an extreme example, but Andrew was an unusual person. He was a small, simple man, of a kind I had met in northern England in my student days, direct in speech, manner, and look. There was a completeness to him that made him totally predictable. He had one set of beliefs, a single faith, one manner, and was totally devoid of mannerisms. I have known him sad, overcome, happy, joyous, but always the same Andrew. His Scottish blood made him all the more wary as a Lancashireman. He would give when he believed it right, the right amount, no more and no less. I remembered him pulling up a waiter in a West End restaurant with, "No, my lad, you put the change down and I will decide what I give you."

We had two drinks and I went my way, thoroughly clear as to what was expected of me. With Andrew at least I would never be in doubt. After my farewell visit to Unilever in London seven years later, he wrote me that, though I hadn't said anything at our last meeting, he felt that I was leaving with something on my mind. I replied that in leaving the company to join a state enterprise, I felt what an Indian bride was traditionally said to feel when she leaves the shelter of her home to venture into an unknown world, not knowing how it will treat her. To this he replied:

CHAPTER ONE

If you feel that you have left home, I suppose I may claim to be one of your step-parents. An honourable position, and if you feel you need a word of encouragement, or even just a passing word of cheer, I hope you will always feel able to write "home" to

                                                Yours,
                                                Andrew

Chapter Two

THE LAST VICEROY

MY SALARY was fixed at a level to last me for ten years. It was modest by the standards of private industry in India, and carried practically no perquisites. Robert Siddons and I then proceeded to discuss plans for the new board. They thought that, given the big program and many new projects, I might retain Jim Davies, the technical director, as vice-chairman. I agreed. I also accepted the idea that, like the vice-chairman I had been before him, he should continue to keep his own department. Robert added that Lord Cole, the Unilever chairman, had hoped that Jim would stay in charge of the technical side, for otherwise he and I would get in each other's hair. Just then, Klijnstraa, a Dutch member of the overseas committee, also a giant of a man, joined us. He disagreed and put forth rather a novel view. As the first Indian chairman, I was likely to be called upon by the government and the community for many extramural commitments that I would not be able to refuse. He thought that for this I was also suited by nature. With all the new projects, Jim Davies would not have the time to be a real vice-chairman to me. So he must be kept free of all direct responsibility, and concentrate on being vice-chairman, to enable me to be the kind of chairman Klijnstraa thought I would have to be.

This altogether new idea had a logic that had just not occurred to us. Except at the Unilever centre, at the very top, this had not been tried in any company around the world. Till not so long ago a chairman regarded himself as responsible for running the business, instead of directing it through his board of directors. To have both a chairman and a vice-chairman with no direct responsibility, in a company that was, after all, not so large by world standards, was indeed new, and I found myself with an arrangement that was to have a profound effect on my life inside and out of the firm. A few words launched me on a type of career I had

CHAPTER TWO

not visualized. If the firm after my departure thought it an experiment of dubious value, and one they never repeated, it certainly enabled me to work out things in a way that gave me much unexpected and worthwhile experience.

In the evening there was a small dinner party, to which were invited members of the overseas committee and a few others whom I had known in India. Like all parties at which Andrew Knox was present, it was over early. There were no speeches; they just wished me well. That night I took a midnight BOAC Comet to Bombay, the beginning of an interminable series of Bombay-London-Bombay flights, always Air India on the way out and usually BOAC returning home—a kind of ritual gesture. The two airlines were interesting in their differences, one friendly, colourful, and informal in the mediocrity of its food and service; the other impeccable and coldly efficient. Not infrequently the young Air India hostesses and stewards would ask me about one or other of my children at college in Bombay; the English hostesses and the usually elderly and thin-haired stewards made you feel you were at the Savoy—you had paid to be there and you would get value for money, with little extras thrown in if a uniformed airline personage saw you up the gangway. Air India tried hard, but its boys and girls, used to servants in their homes, never learned to serve formally. They did not object; they just did not know how to. But it was their enthusiastic amateurishness that made the service attractive. On this occasion I was glad to have taken BOAC. I needed to be left alone, to sort out myself, and there was no one like the discreet English staff for troubling you as little as possible once they realized that that was how you wanted it.

I have always enjoyed flying, all the more since planes began to fly high and nonstop over long distances. Detached from earth, sheltered from its ever-insistent communication systems, high up there in the safety of withdrawal, I feel complete in myself; a feeling I can otherwise only experience in some inaccessible valley in the Himalayas. I am happiest alone, with myself; and up in the air there is a feeling of primeval aloneness. Nothing can happen except a sudden end, and time is whole, even though brittle. In this peace, through a night and a day, I sat with pencil and paper, and thought. Writing, even jotting down an odd point here and there, puts order into my thinking, as much as tidy surroundings do. And order frees my thoughts.

The company had decided on a large number of projects. I began to count, and it made an impressive list. New detergent-powder plants and modernization of the old soap plants; more glycerine capacity; new poultry and cattle-food plants; a new nickel catalyst plant; a new food-dehydration plant; a new research complex; a new plant for fine chemicals and perfumery; a new dairy and milk-processing factory ringed with fifty milk-collection and chilling centres spread over a radius of fifty miles; expansion of all four *vanaspati* factories; and a new head office building and a host of minor improvements and plant changes all over India. It was a programme running into many millions of rupees, and yet money was no problem—we had sufficient reserves. The problem was only one, government permissions—the many, many permissions needed just to be allowed to grow.

Why should permission to grow be the problem, I asked myself, when growth was what both the government and every Indian wanted so passionately? Could one not visit New Delhi and proudly announce one's intention to grow in a really big way to those to whom the power to authorize expansion belonged? I would arrive with an armful of plans and put them down on the table, one on top of the other, in a sizeable pile. For a single company the program we envisaged was quite formidable, especially as an earnest of the intentions of a foreign firm that wished to stay and identify itself with the country's economy. My spirits rose at the thought that as the first Indian chairman I would be starting at the threshold of so much development, the most extensive and diverse ever in the history of Hindustan Lever and of many other Unilever companies, or for that matter of the other companies in India then. But I had heard enough about the uncooperative attitude of government, not just towards foreign firms but to industry in general, to feel diffident. As a matter of principle, industrial growth seemed to be carefully pruned and curbed.

As I stepped out of the plane at Santa Cruz airport, Bombay's June heat and humidity, raised to the pre-monsoon crescendo, hit me in the face. The air was like steam, and carried the mixed odours of the buffalo stables of Andheri and the suburban shanties that were built on the marshes of the creek, where the tidal water mixed with refuse from the slaughterhouse and the open drainage had churned into a stagnant black liquid that seeped and oozed out of the mangrove swamps and thickets of lush grass. This was the early morning smell before the sun rose to bleach it out and the

CHAPTER TWO

breeze from the sea aerated the atmosphere. The terminal building was a chaos of officials, forms, declarations, certificates, stamps, and methodical searches, including an account of where each one of the past seven days had been spent; but it was a highly organized kind of chaos in which no control was missed out. Each authority—health, passport, prohibition, customs, foreign exchange—had to be fully satisfied, and each authority in turn had to fully satisfy its own audit, for whose every sustained objection a new control was introduced. As I was being shepherded out of this maze by an airline official, I saw Gärd, my wife, at the other end of the hall, looking eager and questioning.

Driving home on the new highway, the early morning defecators, each with a water can, usually made from an empty Quaker Oats or Dalda tin, were a strange sight for an international city. In our school English they were "answering the call of nature," an imagery understandable where nature called you out of the village into field or forest. Used to it from childhood in the open countryside of the Punjab, where after the cutting of the crops little privacy was left, the sight did not repel me much; but it did not belong to the modern cosmopolitan city known as the Gateway to India. The American architect Louis Kahn, who designed the Indian Institute of Management's impressive campus at Ahmedabad, raved over it. He called it the daily communion with nature. The state authorities, however, felt ashamed of this sight next door to the international airport being seen by foreign visitors as their first introduction to the country. There were protests from the tourist department, the Rotary clubs, and the elegant citizens of Bombay, less concerned about the lack of elementary sanitary facilities for the poor shanty dwellers than about their proximity to the airport. Plastered cement walls were erected on both sides of the road to hide the hutments, and some genius had them painted with cheerful folk pictures. The gregarious defecators, who enjoyed the sight of the traffic, moved to the road side of the walls. Here and there, wherever there was enough space left, newcomers put up more tin sheds and gunny-sack huts to take advantage of the wall. The municipality then built some flush latrines that nobody used, and at last everybody gave up—except the shanty dwellers. They continued to treat the area as their domain and to sit there every morning, preferring to face the highway and see the traffic go past.

Tired suddenly beyond words, I remembered Hoskyns-Abrahall, an earlier chairman, telling me how different and suddenly alone he had felt the first night after he succeeded Pettit as chairman. Every problem of the day before assumed different proportions, because it was now entirely his. In the middle of the night, he woke up oppressed, his heart palpitating, in a sweat, and sent for the doctor, who shrewdly gave him a sedative and sent him back to bed. He had been standing in for Pettit during his leave abroad, and had managed pretty well for two months. Yet when the letter came from London informing him that Pettit would be leaving India, and that they would like him to succeed, something happened, something changed. Till then, all the problems had ultimately been Pettit's; now they were all his. Something suddenly snapped—the dependence; the lifeline broke and he was all by himself.

Some years earlier, at a seminar, Hoskyns-Abrahall had remarked in his characteristic shy manner that a man at the top dearly loved to know how he was doing; yet, he thought, it was a temptation one had to resist. One chose loneliness if one chose the top, and had to be one's own best judge and severest critic.

An indifferent sleeper normally, the very first problem I faced contained its own remedy. Gärd told me afterward that but for a short break or two I had slept for twenty-two hours. I woke up no longer tired, and neither diffident nor confident—merely cool. Nor was I ever to experience that tiredness again, or elation or depression; just an aloneness always. On this even, detached note I was to continue for many years.

I was gradually to discover the deep anxieties that must have surrounded Turner, my predecessor, in steering the business through the currents. Questions were raised about each of his plans for expansion, motivated partly by the embarrassing position in which the government found itself on account of opposition to us by a leading Indian competitor. This company, Tata, had gathered the smaller manufacturers into an association whose only task seemed to be to oppose Lever. In the mid-1950s, they had begun to complain about Lever's size and growth, and had published advertisements to the effect that "the foreign firm" should be prevented from expanding further. This anti-Lever campaign was carried to the press, the public, and the government, sometimes in a bizarre form. In a dramatic gesture Naval Tata, a charmingly colourful personality, hired a Dakota plane and set out on a tour of India with his staff, holding meetings

CHAPTER TWO

with *vanaspati* and soap wholesalers, pleading with them not to patronize that "foreign firm." He invoked the "Swadeshi" spirit, and quoted Gandhiji on boycotting "foreign" products—even though they were now made in India. It had no effect on our sales, but he did get government worried enough to begin to raise objections to our plans for growth.

We heard some vivid descriptions of Naval's "Bharat Yatra" from salesmen and wholesalers in places like Patna and Amritsar, where a top-class Bombay Parsi, his Bombay Hindi laced with Parsi Gujarati and English, was something outside their experience. In later years, when we became good friends, Naval Tata and I had a good laugh about it.

In spite of all this effort, I think Tata did our business no harm. Nor did attacks in the press take any customers away from us. People were, if anything, on the rebound from Swadeshism. After years of shortages of imported consumer goods, and shoddy but expensive substitutes, they were glad to buy anything of quality, and were not interested in the fine distinction made between products manufactured in India by a foreign firm or an Indian firm. With the foreigner gone, boycott of foreign goods as a political protest no longer had meaning. But Tata did start something which in time was to grow bigger than they could ever have imagined— an economic outlook close to xenophobia and isolationism, shrinking our industrial and technological contacts abroad. When world technology began to travel freely across frontiers, we treated it warily; and while Russia signed an agreement with Fiat, we terminated one. Our terms to foreign investment became stricter, and frankly uninviting; we grew firmer in our belief that the answer to gaps in our technology was not to learn where we could, but to find out for ourselves, even at the cost of delay and obsolescence.

To protect Indian industry, duties had been progressively increased since the 1920s, till there was virtually a ban on imports. Industrial growth was planned in such a way that no new production could be sanctioned if unutilized capacity existed somewhere else. When Turner sought permission to expand, the government demurred on the grounds that the industry had surplus capacity which ought to be used before they could allow us to develop new capacity. It was a new kind of economic logic—that of the convoy; the fastest in an industry must wait till the slowest caught up.

Tata was not just a big industrial house. No ordinary firm, it was an institution of a kind that probably existed nowhere else in the world. They had pioneered India's industrialization, and struck new trails in virtually every direction—steel, textiles, chemicals, electronics, consultancy, insurance; they even started what was perhaps the first airline in Asia. They were patrons of science, culture, and social uplift, and had been in the vanguard of our nascent political life, contributing an early president to the Indian National Congress, as well as the first communist member to the British Parliament. Their prestige and influence were enhanced by the fact that they had not shied away from political protest at a time when protest was uncomfortable for a firm dependent on a foreign government. When at last we had our own government, one of Tata's first acts was to protest against a big firm growing bigger, little realizing that this was eventually to rebound against size as such. They thus started a bias against *all* large and successful industry.

I think there was also a reawakening in us of a feeling that is perhaps always close to our otherwise quite friendly attitude to foreigners. An Englishman who came to Bombay from Indonesia in 1955 told me that he was struck by the absence of the hostility he had felt in the streets of Jakarta, where the foreigner got sullen looks and was even edged off the pavement. I explained how in the worst days of the "Quit India" movement in 1942, Englishmen scattered in remote places had felt safe. Even in the parts of Bihar where for some time British law and order had ceased to exist, there were no cases of British families being attacked. Cases of insult to individual Englishmen in public were rare, let alone injury. Insults were usually the prerogative of our rulers. The freedom movement seldom took on a violent edge, despite provocation.

With independence, no longer voiceless and choiceless, we began to develop new relationships with foreigners. Politically, we opened missions all over the world. Socially, the very British and the Europeans who had kept their distance in the past were now glad to be made welcome. Young Indians, always venturesome, began to pour out by the thousands as students, doctors, nurses, and workers in any capacity in which they could learn or earn better abroad. But though extroverts abroad, at home we became defensive and sensitive, almost unconsciously at least mildly anti-Western, with a patronizing attitude towards Africans and fellow Asians. As I once told a foreigner, in India we are freely critical of

CHAPTER TWO

all we do—but don't you ever agree with us there! As the years passed, and hundreds of thousands of Indians worked and settled abroad, remitting hundreds of millions of rupees home, our regulations in respect to the few hundred foreigners who worked in India, mostly for multinational corporations, and the small fraction of the money coming in which they and their firms remitted out, became progressively tighter.

Steve Turner was caught between the growing customer demand on his production capacity and government's pressure on him not to expand. It was the kind of situation he was not cut out to meet. He cultivated no personal relations, as is the common approach in India, with our competitors, or with government secretaries and ministers, with whom he could have talked things over, explained his case, and come to some kind of compromise, as we always do in the long run. When he visited India in 1957, Lord Heyworth, the Unilever chairman, went all out to meet Tata, to understand their point of view. He spoke to J. R. D. Tata, and wondered whether the line adopted by them would not in the long run harm the interests of private industry in general. It might be Tata Oil Mills against the larger Hindustan Lever today, but inevitably this would come down to the smaller companies versus the larger. If Lever were "monopolists" today, Tata would be the "monopolists" of tomorrow. Did they have a basic faith in enterprise and competition? Why could they not do better? There was no mystery to our success.

Tata, cool and logical, a modern executive of the international kind, saw Heyworth's point, and the pressure did begin to lessen, but the line stuck with the authorities and was never relinquished. A chain reaction began that went only one way, ending twenty years later with the main activity of the large units in the soap industry being taken away from them and reserved for the small producers, at least in a government industrial policy statement.

Steve's departure was marked by a simple ceremony. I made a short speech, some others spoke, and he replied briefly. It was an occasion of pure sadness; few expected ever to see him again. But the directors' party at his flat that night was a cheerful affair. Here he let go, as did we all. He was totally relaxed and genuinely carried away by the occasion, his acid wit returning as the evening wore on. Next afternoon, the directors and their wives bade him a final goodbye in his flower-filled cabin on the homeward-bound Italian liner. This was the real farewell—a touching end to his

THE LAST VICEROY

twenty years in India. It was an end to an era; a transfer of power of its own kind; the departure of the last Unilever viceroy.

The day after Steve's departure from Bombay, I walked into the office building that I had first entered over twenty years before. The doorman, a Sikh ex-*havildar,* gave me his smartest salute, the liftmen beamed and stood aside, the sepoys bowed, the clerks stood at their desks and smiled sheepishly. As I walked into the boardroom, where the managers had assembled for my first "prayer meeting," as we called our weekly early-morning chit-chats, they stood up in discreet applause. Uncertainly I walked to Turner's chair and thanked them. It felt strange to be at the end of the board table up whose full length I had hesitatingly moved over the years. Steve's departure left me feeling like an uncertain ship's captain on his first voyage in command after the pilot has left. I thought of the time ten years back when I had joined the board. Twenty-four years had gone by since I had stepped on the first rung of the ladder.

From the boardroom I walked to the chairman's large hexagonal office. Its french windows and balconies looked out over Bombay harbour with its docks and ships, and the blue expanse of the bay. I looked across the desk, at Steve's empty leather chair, the dark brown carpet, the glass shelves of samples, the full-length portrait of Lord Leverhume, the founder, in his baronial regalia, made to look very patrician by Laslo. On another wall was Queen Elizabeth, with a "Portia look." Laslo and Annigoni had both done flattering jobs. Should I take them both away or add Gandhi and Nehru? It was a custom left behind by the British to hang the portraits of emperors and empresses in all government offices. Eventually I hit upon the idea of giving them both to my Welsh vice-chairman.

I pictured my predecessors. Shaw, my first managing director, sitting in this chair and telling me that the experiment they were embarking on could lead one way, to the ultimate in Indianization. The subsequent interviews, once to mumble a few words of sympathy over his wife's death, and next seeking permission for my own marriage, as was the custom in those days in British firms. It was all the more necessary to do so in my case because the British Legation in Stockholm had enquired of the authorities in Bombay whether I was in a position to support a European wife; a British police sergeant called on Shaw who, forewarned, gave me a "clearance." On another occasion, prompted by Hit-

CHAPTER TWO

ler's mounting successes in Europe, I had felt the urge to join in the war. But Shaw had laughed, and said that although things were going badly they would manage to win in the end, as they always did. There was no point therefore in my joining up. And later, being called in by Pettit, Shaw's successor, when he gave me my first chance in marketing. I remembered Pettit's constant encouragement over the years, often in face of my awkward and resisting ways, as if determined to prove his point that I would succeed.

Banerji, our chief medical officer, had nursed Steve Turner carefully during his last months in India. I called him to say that he was going to have an even tougher job with me, for the strains and stresses were going to be even more severe. I would do all I could to help him. Banerji took it all very seriously, and through the years we guarded my health together. At first I used to feel self-conscious, walking so frequently through the office to his room, wondering what the staff would think. "What's wrong with the chairman, always going to the doctor?" I would drop in for a checkup and chat, and it developed into an interesting, casual relationship, good humoured but with an underlying seriousness. He never made me feel as though I were under observation, and I never kept anything from him. I encouraged him to develop a similar relationship with others, the older men and those under special strain, but he found this less easy. Most people, he said, were on the defensive and regarded it as an intrusion. Some could have been the gainers. Banerji in fact taught me to come to terms with the stresses of the job, the long hours of work, the busy social schedule, the hardships of travel. Ours was a country in which a flight anywhere was most likely to start at dawn, and departures were rarely on time in an era of interminable strikes and delays, until a determined chairman of Indian Airlines put things right a decade later.

I envied the executives in the West their shorter hours, five-day week, regular holidays and, most of all, the relative lack of external pressure. The stresses they experienced were from within their organizations, not caused by the problems of their society. They led an orderly existence, with work and leisure in separate compartments. The telephone did not ring early in the morning and late in the evening on business, nor did people come to their houses to "pay their respects"—really to seek favours. This was a habit cultivated under the Raj. The British in their turn had acquired it from the Moghuls. It continues to flourish; some administrators and many heads of family businesses still hold "durbars" at home, especially on Sunday mornings. It all adds to the strain, especially the new, undelightful habit of holding seminars and conferences over the weekend to "save" working time.

Chapter Three

NEW DELHI

I ENVIED the chairman who came from outside, a stranger to all, unknown and untested, and free therefore to create new relationships. In an organization like this, which did not rely upon hierarchical assertion of authority, the chairman was just one of the directors, primus inter pares, with no powers of his own. He was only the chairman of a board that decided all matters of importance collectively. But to have been one of them for so long, and then one day to become their leader, was not easy, even though fortunately for me I had superseded no one. To assume the role of leader in a discussion which revealed differences that could sometimes be quite sharp, and try to bring about a compromise or, failing that, come to a decision acceptable to all, was hard at the beginning. Fortunately, the system of having a vice-chairman who, other things being equal, would succeed the chairman was a useful one. There was no break in continuity and no guessing. A year of vice-chairmanship and six months of acting chairmanship during Steve Turner's illness had, moreover, given my colleagues and others a feel of me, my ways and style, so different from Turner's, and especially my idiosyncracies.

My first problem with the board came soon enough, and appropriately for the Indian scene it was in union relations. There was trouble in one of our factories, where the union president had assaulted a worker who had openly disagreed with him. The factory manager wanted to take the obvious action of dismissing the man, but the state government intervened and the labour authority concerned asked us to let him off with an apology, making it known at the same time that, if we insisted upon dismissal, he might well be reinstated by them on appeal. I favoured accepting the man's apology and giving him a warning; for to have him reinstated would visibly weaken our authority. My colleagues all felt that such flagrant indiscipline could not be conducive to peace in a factory, and that if the state government interfered—well, never mind, we would at least have made our own position clear.

The board discussion went on, with positions hardening. While the directors were all on one side, the vice-chairman sensibly kept neutral, seemingly to protect my position. It was a Saturday afternoon, and eventually I decided to sleep on it and to resume on Monday. Jim Davies, the vice-chairman, followed me into my room and spoke bluntly but sympathetically.

"I see the reason for your hesitation, Prakash," he said. "You don't want the state government to reverse the decision, since that would undermine our authority within the factory. I personally would take a chance, at least letting it be known that dismissal was our straightforward answer to indiscipline. If we are overruled, let us be overruled; but let us not take less than the right and deserved action. However, the main thing is to act. Further discussion will only show our own internal division, and such things get known. Give your decision. They will accept it. They would have accepted it this afternoon."

"Thanks, Jim," I responded gratefully. "I needed that plain speaking. I found it difficult at our very first disagreement to overrule them all."

The board had anticipated my decision to accept the apology, and received it gracefully. No one demurred; they all understood. Curiously, the union man completely misinterpreted it and started boasting about it. Before long he repeated himself and left us with no choice. I was not worried about being overruled this time. He tried hard for years and brought pressure to bear, but we refused to take him back. He had had his chance.

It was nothing if not a blunt board of determined personalities. The two Englishmen were experienced, out to maintain the highest production standards, and themselves highly disciplined men. If at first they tended to treat bringing up the new chairman as almost a part of their Unilever job abroad, they were sensitive enough soon to realize that I was conscious of it.

Next I had to tackle the great problem that was to be my major preoccupation—dealing with "New Delhi," as the administration was referred to by business in Bombay. A new, quite complex relationship between government and business had developed over the years, ever since the British government first began directing industry during World War II and business growth started to depend upon government decisions. Before the war, when we

CHAPTER THREE

had only a small warehouse, Delhi had no importance to us. During the war our sub-office in Lahore was moved to Delhi, as we found a growing need to call on the central government secretariats, at first to get the odd import licence or arrange for defence supplies, and later to discuss price controls when they assumed importance. In 1944 planning for the post-war period brought in a new government policy for managing industrial growth, and the Delhi office acquired an important new role. Pettit, our chairman, who was deeply involved in getting a share in this growth, sometimes travelled twice in the same week to New Delhi—a twenty-four-hour train journey, invariably with interminable delays caused by heavy troop movements.

After the war New Delhi became the businessman's capital. There lay both patronage and permission, and as the first air services began their regular schedules, executives soon found themselves taking permanent suites at Delhi hotels. Some companies rented bungalows, called guest houses, where visiting senior executives stayed. Planning and development regulations proliferated and began to envelop industry. A stage was to be reached when for most conceivable things—allotment of raw materials; plant installation; shifting of existing plant to a new site; launching a new product or even a new package size; capitalization of reserves; bonus and new stock issues; debentures; large loans; staff retrenchment; import of foreign technicians and their terms of employment; appointment of directors and their terms; import of know-how; process technology; technological collaboration; the taking of young trainees, fresh from college if they happened to be closely related to a civil servant—permission had to be asked at New Delhi. It was safer in fact to ask before acting at all. As the administration expanded to cope with its every-growing task, procedures grew proportionately more complex, till the whole system was like a honeycomb. Permissions naturally took longer, as did executive visits, and the New Delhi offices grew ever bigger. Interestingly, it was not only private industry that opened offices to represent it in New Delhi, but also the state governments and public enterprises. Their problems were not basically dissimilar. Both largely consisted in dealing with procedures and delays and obtaining sanctions from the central government. The system at least had the merit of impartiality, for it dealt as slowly with its own state governments and public enterprises as it did with private industry and the public at large.

NEW DELHI

Dealing with New Delhi posed me a delicate task. Large companies had developed their relationships in different ways. Some had a Delhi director, usually chosen for his capacity to foster contacts. Others went a stage further, and appointed a retired Indian Civil Service (ICS) man, whose junior colleagues and former subordinates would provide convenient contacts for some years to come. He would also know the anatomy of decision making well, and be able to forecast the progress of the relevant file through the bureaucratic hierarchy. Some companies showed a predilection for employing politically well-connected sons and nephews with easy access to power. The interesting if not cynical part of this whole process was that mostly everybody got what they wanted, but had to go through a long-drawn-out drill that satisfied a series of impeccable desiderata of planning and procedure. If the request did not fit the framework, this added to the time needed. But little was ever denied. Everything merely went more slowly, and, as with a sluggish stream, proportionately less got through. There were of course those who got more and quicker results through their own devious ways. The large international firms and Indian companies of the professionally managed kind did not ask for more than their due, but matters that had been theirs to decide at the initiative and discretion of their management were now subject to prolonged negotiations. The time that should have gone into formulating policies went into procedures. Growth was thus painfully slow.

What made things more complex was the fact that the ministries worked independently of each other, with no system for coordinating problems that concerned more than one of them. Where the government should have done its own interministerial clearing, they expected one to go from ministry to ministry to get each clearance separately. At the end of the labyrinth, there was always the risk of an unexpected, innocent, casual comment on a file which could freeze everything, because no one would act finally until the road was cleared of the block, no matter how small or irrelevant.

I had only a distant acquaintance with this system. I knew no one in New Delhi. I had met one or two secretaries through Maurice and Taya Zinkin (he first a member of the ICS and then with Unilever, and she a prominent journalist), but so casually as not to be able to claim their acquaintance or even ring them up. To make contact with a ministerial secretary in the Indian govern-

CHAPTER THREE

ment is not like approaching even the most senior business executive, in Bombay or anywhere else in the world. You don't simply ring up and get through. Instead you explain to a suspicious and unconvinced personal assistant who you are and what your business is. If he does not recognize your name, the answer is invariably that the secretary is at a meeting—which, in fact, he is for most of the day—or has just left the room. Or, you are informed with perfect candour, he has gone to the toilet. If you leave your name and ask to be called back, you wait in vain; and so you keep trying, adding to the assistant's frustration and your own. But if it could take a week to contact someone on the telephone, it might take months to get a reply to a letter. Sometimes you did receive a prompt acknowledgment that the matter was receiving attention, and that was usually the end of the matter. There was a strange unconscious cynicism to it all.

No one therefore approached the secretariat in this way. At different levels the companies developed their own contacts between their Delhi representative and his personal assistants and the hierarchies of the bureaucracy. It was a curiously self-defeating process that helped no one but wasted a lot of time on all sides. The personal secretaries defended the ministerial secretaries from the barrage of visitors, who in turn argued that nothing happened unless they met the secretaries themselves; and so everybody met them.

With business so utterly dependent on New Delhi, and my utter innocence of its cocooned culture, I wondered how I would ever make any headway with my long list of projects, each needing more than one sanction. Perhaps I should also go in for a retired civil servant or someone with a name to represent us in the capital, a key to open doors. But my instincts held me back. Somehow it did not seem to fit in with our own style of management. I decided to leave the matter alone and to feel my way through, even though Unilever told me that in their Pakistan business they had for this purpose taken on a couple of prematurely retired English ICS officials.

With much trepidation I decided to take my first plunge and start the rounds, little knowing that New Delhi was to swallow me slowly until I would belong there. The first secretary I chose to meet was K. B. Lall, because I had heard so much about him from the Zinkins that I felt I almost knew him, and from their description he appeared to be somewhat of a character for a civil servant.

NEW DELHI

Lall was then joint secretary in the Ministry of Commerce and Industry. A Srivastava, he belonged to the Delhi Kayasth class, whose remarkable history ought one day to be told. A business caste, it comprises a large number of families—Narains, Lalls, Bahadurs, Dayals, Sahais, Srivastavas, Nathurs—all closely related through marriage, sharing wealth and influence and notoriously nepotistic. Settled in Delhi for centuries, they made their peace with each wave of invasion and each new dynasty, serving it in business and at court with a loyalty that was total while the dynasty lasted, and upon its eclipse as total again to its successors. They let the wave submerge them, but when the wave had passed and calm returned, like little rocks they came to the surface and reoccupied their traditional positions. The new dynasty needed money to pay troops, fight wars, and build new forts; business had to flourish to provide taxes and levies. The need was mutual. The Kayasths formed a financial system that could only be destroyed at the king's own peril. They no doubt had their ups and downs, but they bounced back each time and survived the violent change from the Moghuls to the British. Their traditional network encompassed key positions in the New Delhi of independent India.

Lall was a handsome, greying man in his forties, with an odd, sometimes mercurial mind and a mobile face, which could suddenly set when he was interested in what you said or when he came close to a decision. Yet he was curiously ponderous. Throughout our discussions he kept up a jovial facade of cultivated nonchalance, punctuated with much deliberate laughter and a complex, sometimes forced humour, the best part of it being the barbs he threw around. I explained that I was new on the job, new to Delhi, new to everything, and quite diffident in my newness. As I always played my cards face up, he could rest assured that my demands would be few and reasonable, and my advice, if ever sought, objective. Perhaps something about my open diffidence touched him. "Remember, you may find us indecisive and dilatory, but compared with the British civil servant you enjoy an advantage with us that is most worthwhile. When my British counterpart in Whitehall makes up his mind, it is made up; there is no further argument. But when we decide, if the decision does not suit you, you can always come back—and the door will be open," he said laughingly. "We remain indecisive even after we have decided."

CHAPTER THREE

Lall was an interesting example of a modern, British-trained civil servant—impeccable, suave, competent equally at procedure and solution, with the administrator's gift of shutting off his antennae to whatever he found it imprudent to perceive, and always determined to get what he wanted. He had the Kayasth flair for business and results, and a curiously complicated mind that in the face of a straight solution took a deliberately cautious detour. This was an interesting trait I was to find commonly among administrators—almost an instinct for taking a roundabout way and leaving no traces behind. This contradictory capacity to perceive without reacting, much less committing themselves, seemed a product of alien training, of a philosophical pragmatism of flexible values grafted on the Indian mind. I suppose this flexibility was a quality of ours that suited the British, who were themselves notable for it.

I began to understand the New Delhi bureaucracy and how it operated. The administrators, the Lalls included, were masters of power but slaves to their own basically suspicious and untrusting system. Where this extraordinary system had begun, and how it would ever end, was to me, as much as to them, an everlasting source of wonder. What E. M. Forster had called "the maniacal suspicion, that besetting Indian sin," had percolated the entire administration. We considered it a legacy from the British, part of their mistrust of their Indian subordinates' taking advantage of any permissiveness. This was facile, however, since we preserved it tenaciously and made it even more rigid and pervasive than what they left behind. It must have belonged to us, too. In many years in Delhi I was to ask this question again and again. There were many ingenious but unsatisfactory answers that left even the administrators themselves unconvinced. A section officer in charge of a few clerks was the first level to "note." The simplest form of hierarchical life, totally innocent of the technical, financial, or any other aspects of a problem, with knowledge only of precedents and a great adroitness at cautious negative supposition, such an official was entrusted with analyzing and commenting on cases complex far beyond his comprehension. He could cast them in a mould that could not be broken even by the secretary. This was something no one could explain. They all complained about the tyranny of the system, but all accepted it helplessly. It was not that they had become desensitized; it was worse—they had accepted it like Sindbad's Old Man of the Sea. As with poverty and dirt in India, there was a resigned acceptance that "it will always be with us." There was no fine impatience, just a complacent "It cannot be changed."

One of the more trying characteristics of the bureaucracy was its eel-like capacity for slithering out of its own decisions by means of a series of qualifications. Having once announced with a great flourish that to stimulate production a twenty-five percent expansion could be made in a firms' licensed capacity without government's sanction, provided there was no foreign exchange or substantial imported equipment involved, there came a clarifying circular letter, to the effect that,

> Expansion of capacity of existing units within certain limits has to be interpreted in the context of each specific industry and should not be understood as overriding all other considerations of policy. It is not the intention to relax all controls over expansion of industry.

The positive flourishes were in the brave announcements; the negative whimpers followed in the clarifications.

From the lowest level the file progressed upward, acquiring notes at each stage. But even an innocuous twist to an earlier notation as it rose up the ladder could damn a case in a way that the highest official, with all the power and conviction at his disposal, might not be able to undo. An innocent doubt once cast, a sceptical question lodged gently under the skin of the case, and no one could afford the risk of overruling, just in case the decision were to go wrong and a subsequent audit or a parliamentary committee were to ask why action had been taken without first dispelling the query that had been raised. The fact that out of a hundred decisions this was the only one that had gone wrong would be totally irrelevant, because they were examining only this particular instance of failure and not the many successes. It was no valid argument that this one failure had been compensated for many times. Why this failure? Why was notice not taken of the caution, the doubt, the question? The questioning could be relentless. It was no answer to say that anyone could raise a doubt, that anything could in retrospect have been done better. It was a system that could only breed fear, caution, and delay.

The system could also be made to work flexibly. The higher-up could call in the subordinate and carefully plant ideas for the note, and then each stage would echo them back, and one heard what one had tuned in for. Each level of the hierarchy built the case in a

CHAPTER THREE

given direction, precedents that suited were quoted, exceptions cited, and a welter of favourable arguments put forward, usually with some suitable but easily disposable doubts subtly cast for the sake of caution, out of which the higher-up chose the ones that suited him in writing out his own "balanced" note.

On my return I discussed the problem with my colleagues. We all felt that, despite our innocence, the right way with New Delhi was to deal direct—to convey the convictions behind our aims and efforts. For this Chandy, our legal director on the board, was well suited. But towards the end of 1961, after only a few months, Chandy left to head the new Indian Institute of Management at Calcutta. His experience in industry as an analyst and adviser, his intellect, and his pedagogic style, made him an ideal management academic, better than he was to fare later as an operator.

Chandy's unexpected departure was a great loss to me, and left a gap that had to be filled quickly. I decided to experiment and send a young man, Aspi Moddie, who had joined us late after a wartime career in the army and then in the new Indian Administrative Service.

As a district officer in Bihar, Moddie had made something of a name for himself as a young man of unusual initiative and thrust. He turned up in my office one day in 1952, a small compact man in his early thirties, with a cultivated crisp style. I asked him why he wanted to leave the administration, and he gave me a list of reasons, mainly centering on the difficulties of working in the districts under the new political masters. Stories had already begun to be told about these rulers and some of their ways of personal rule.

These were early days of power, and imitation of the earlier rulers varied from the naive to the ludicrous. There was one minister who sent the programme for his visit to a district town in advance: arrival at the station at 8:15 A.M., garlanding, reception at the town hall at 9 A.M., and so on, while the minister beamed and said they shouldn't have taken all that trouble. A police friend, who gave me the story, thought it was a good idea to have plain instructions so that the police could be lined up and the garlands kept moist in a basket. There was another minister who got upset because the red carpet wasn't long enough. The arrival of public figures in a cavalcade of motorcars, the national flag fluttering at the old British circuit house, where the police presented arms and took up positions on guard, struck familiar chords. Inside, delegations waited for favours from the district authorities with petitions, complaints, and offers of fealty.

Moddie's young ideals were shattered by interminable delays, red tape, vacillation, and, on the political level, much worse. Some of it was endemic to the administration—but, he said, a new hesitancy was creeping in. The administration had always been slow, running at its original mid-nineteenth-century speed. Backed by the system, however, it could be decisive as long as it acted to subserve the broad interests of the Raj. Now the system itself was tending to become intangible and amorphous, depending on the whims and interests of individual ministers. The supplicants in the circuit house would ask the minister to intercede with the administrator to release a man from jail and arrange for the criminal charge pending against him to be dropped, or to allot a scarce rationed commodity, sold at a premium in the open market, to someone who had no right to it. Such waywardness demoralized the administrators. When Moddie once told a superior that he proposed to act in a certain way, his senior agreed that he should go ahead, but added that if there was disapproval from the minister, Moddie would have to square it himself.

I told Moddie to go back. His reasons for leaving the administration were not good enough. The new era was not even five years old; much change had to take place, and it could not always be for the better. To quit so soon was to retreat in the face of the problem. He ought to give it a trial for another six months. Half a year later Moddie returned, however, determined to resign.

Moddie turned out to be an ideal choice for New Delhi, and did well in creating an understanding between us and government. He was different from other representatives in that he played his role in a low key. He did not throw parties and relied upon the strength of our case, neither giving nor receiving favours. His old Bihar colleagues, of whom there were quite a number at the centre, felt at ease with him in his new role.

As regards Chandy's replacement on the board, Unilever in London suggested that, on the assumption that I would stay as chairman for ten years till the retiring age of sixty, I might like to project the way I saw the board manned over the decade, and my likely successor. We had tacitly agreed that there would be two expatriate directors, out of the usual strength of eight, an Indian chairman, and preferably an Indian vice-chairman too. On these

CHAPTER THREE

premises, I prepared a plan for ten years, ending up with the question of who might succeed me—someone who would have to join the board in about 1965, be vice-chairman in 1968, and chairman in 1971, on my retirement.

A ten-year exercise of this kind was like playing a chess game, moving pieces forward or off the board till a winning piece reached the top; or like snakes-and-ladders, with some falling away and some lagging behind. It was exciting to think that the one who succeeded me might, all things being equal, remain head of the company till 1981. And it was likely that one of those we placed on our 'A' list, the pipeline to the board, before 1971, would be my successor's successor from 1981 to 1991! Thus in 1961 I was looking ahead thirty years, to a time when I would certainly not be around. Whatever the shape and activities of the company then, the most promising men would be trained in all kinds of testing situations, exposed to the latest in technical, financial, and managerial ideas all over the world, attend courses wherever advanced thinking was offered, and always be kept in line with the finest of their international colleagues, men running similar companies around the globe. Some day, under a world government, they might be able to move with complete ease from one country to another. It caught my imagination to be the architect of such a plan. There was always the risk, of course, that men so well groomed would be tempted away, and some of the best among them did indeed move to government.

The discussions in London brought up a droll point. "Supposing, Prakash, you were run over by a bus tomorrow, what should we do?" Ernest Woodruffe, later chairman of Unilever, asked me.

I proceeded to explain the possible immediate and subsequent moves.

"But supposing your successor got run over by a bus the day after?"

I explained the next set of moves. The exercise had so absorbed me that I must have done some hard thinking even at the subconscious level. We laughed when I said that we might leave it at the second catastrophe and not strain the laws of probability too much.

Seven years later, when I hurriedly asked to leave three years ahead of time, I suggested that Vasant Rajadhyaksha, who according to plan was to become vice-chairman just then and chairman in three years' time, be made chairman right away. The ten-year plan was compressed into seven, but it worked.

NEW DELHI

To me, this exercise had a special interest, because succession in India is a delicate subject, usually avoided till events overtake one and something has to be hastily done. I think it runs deep in our culture. When we were children, any hint of a guest's intention to depart was hushed up, something that must not be discussed. It was met by a family chorus of "Don't say anything like that. Haven't we made you comfortable in our poor home?" The guest's bed roll would be unpacked as ceremoniously as he had packed it, and he would shamefacedly have to wait for another chance to get away. It was the same with an allusion to death. A sensible man might want to make a will, or some arrangements with his sons about the division of the property in the event of his death. This would lead to loud protests from the family, asking him to withdraw his words, in the name of God. So the subject was dropped, and when death came there was bickering that often broke up hitherto united families.

Chapter Four

UNIONS

NINETEEN SIXTY-ONE was a wonderful year for India, the last of the halcyon years of the Nehru era, when everything went well and all the first fruits of the post-independence effort were beginning to ripen. The permissive Nehru policies of secularism, democracy, planning, and industrial growth created a world interest, both intellectual and material, in seeing an underdeveloped nation's bold experiments succeed. The upsurge in growth when the new planned projects were coming out of gestation and into production—the dams, steel plants, heavy engineering works, community development programmes, institutes of technology and management, the national chain of science laboratories, the new universities in towns that had barely possessed an intermediate college, two peaceful elections involving more people than the world had ever seen at the polls—gave the country a sense of initiative and confidence that it had not possessed for a thousand years. Industry boomed; Indian and foreign enterprises stood in line for permission to expand, start new plants and new joint ventures, pouring in whatever a project could absorb, with the public oversubscribing share issues fifteen to twenty times. Young Indians went to foreign universities, and were often snapped up by their well-endowed faculties and international agencies on the look-out for talent.

I learned to shuttle between Bombay and Delhi in the new Viscounts that cut the journey from the train's twenty-four hours, the De Havilland's eight, and the miracle of Dakota's five, to less than three hours. A pressurized cabin, hot meals, and air-conditioning made the journey pleasant. Each time there was a round of the ministries—finance, industry and commerce, food and agriculture, planning commission, petroleum and chemicals—giving clarifications, offering assurances that the project would hurt no one else's interests, raising foreign exchange. This was at the central level. Then there were the state government sanctions to be obtained for land, water, effluent, plant, buildings, boilers, raw materials, excise, and sales tax. And the financial institutions had to be approached to underwrite what government had agreed to.

This was also the year of a new long-term agreement with the union. Of late the unions in India had taken a leaf out of the freedom struggle, pressing their claims with protests, boycotts, hunger strikes, and demonstrations. The old slogans—Down with the British! Quit India! Injustice!—were all revived, but in a less tolerant and peaceful guise, accompanied by invective, calumny, and sometimes plain abuse. There were pen-down strikes, token or relay hunger strikes, where each person went without a meal, gate-demonstrations, processions and marches. The unions called them "peaceful," but they relied largely on yelling abuse and catcalls. Though there was no outright physical attack on management or facilities, the borderline was always a fine one. As with the Satyagrahas, occasional violence was met with, and a stage was reached in the late 1960s when, rather like in the 1942 Quit India movement, it became open and widespread. Even the term "peaceful" had its subtle and not so subtle nuances. A dense crowd in a manager's office, equipped with a high-pitched loudspeaker forcibly placed close to the manager's ears, blaring abuse hour after hour, and refusing to allow the manager to visit the toilet, was called peaceful. This kind of demonstration had its own name, *"gherao"*—to surround. Naturally the aggrieved protestors demonstrated in relays to maintain their own sanity and spirits.

Over the years, the trade unions had evolved a classic strategy and tactics of protest, which followed in essence the style of the Satyagraha campaigns. This was in fact to become our national style of protest over any issue on which anyone disagreed, individually or collectively, with an organization or the state. The unions perfected it in masterly fashion. Following the pattern of the letters to the Viceroy from the Congress party in the old days, a campaign always began with a letter from the union president to the company chairman, conveying his deep concern, which in turn reflected the deep concern of his followers, and the sincere hope that the issue would be resolved immediately through the chairman's personal intervention. The letter always ended on the note that, much as the union leader would like to, and was trying to, restrain the rank and file, he was afraid that unless full satisfaction of their just demands was forthcoming right away, they

CHAPTER FOUR

would be compelled to resort to direct action—another phrase borrowed from the political past. For this, management alone would be held responsible, he, the union president, having tried his best to avoid a clash. The letter often contained built-in anticipation of rejection, with demands pitched impossibly high and solutions demanded peremptorily, sometimes giving management only a few days, or even a few hours, in which to concede everything. Short of total acceptance, the door was shut. I once received a letter at midday giving me till four o'clock to concede all demands, and another at three regretting my callous dilatoriness! Punctually at four, hell descended in the shape of "peaceful protest"—though I did have the satisfaction of knowing that with equal punctuality it would be over, at least for that day, at five, to enable the demonstrators to go home.

Then there would begin a slow build-up, a gate meeting, some meetings with the management, inconclusive from the very start, and at last the sudden declaration that, despite all efforts, negotiations had broken down because of management's intransigence, leaving the leadership with no choice but a "peaceful struggle." There would be lunch-time gate meetings, black mourning badges, refusals to accept the morning and afternoon cup of tea, pen-down strikes for ten minutes at stated intervals, silent stand-up protests at the desks, and whatever else the leadership's ingenuity could muster as weapons. The fairest management was lumped together with the least fair.

There was the lighter side as well. We had an Englishman with us on a two-year spell to organize our new cattle-food compounding business. Robinson was a charming, old-fashioned young man, the best description of him being Edwardian. He had Edwardian ways and manners, and already wore a cut of clothes that was later to become the rage. The story spread that one afternoon, when the staff in the main hall was in the midst of a silent stand-up protest, Robinson was found standing solemnly among them, his head bowed and hands folded as though at a graveside. When everyone stood to attention, bowed, with hands folded in protest just as his tea tray arrived, Robinson, new to the country, thought that somebody had suddenly died or that perhaps it was the anniversary of some tragic event, so he hastily followed suit. To his dismay everyone began to titter, but he let that pass as another incomprehensible custom. He had seen a Hindu funeral with clanging cymbals and bells and strangely cheerful singing. But mourning was mourning. It took all sorts to make a world!

On another occasion—this was some years later in the State Trading Corporation of India—I had invited some pressmen to lunch, and in the meantime a flash protest had blown up over some minor issue. I received a letter by special messenger late at night, informing me that,

> It is most unfortunate that despite our just demand for the withdrawal of management's unilateral action, you have not acceded to our request and even thought it fit to ignore it and throw a luncheon party, on Monday the 7th at a hotel. We strongly resent this callousness, and have decided in our own humble way to observe a mass hunger strike in the office throughout the office hours on that day. So, while you will be at the luncheon party, we will all be foregoing our lunch in the office and even be skipping our tea and snacks as a mark of our heart-felt protest throughout the day, with prayers for a better understanding to dawn on the management.

Each protest meeting reached a higher pitch despite various attempts at negotiation, and soon the decision to "struggle and fight to the end" was announced. We never had a strike and always managed to reach an agreement, since the union basically trusted the management, which because it was fair could afford to be firm. The contest had nevertheless become a ritual that had to be gone through with, because the gains at the end had always to be perceived as being "won" by the leadership, which had to prove itself. Otherwise someone else took over, promising more drama and better struggle.

The struggle mobilized an ingenious array of weapons that brought out the Indian love of drama and pageantry—it was like a wedding, a funeral, and a *mohalla* quarrel all rolled into one. There would be a cheerleader, who had to demonstrate his capacity to coin rhythmic and alliterative slogans; there would be banners, placards, cartoons; often an effigy would be burnt like King Ravana at Dussehra, with a mock funeral and marches along the thoroughfares to attract public notice. As one went further north, the proceedings became lustier, bordering on bawdiness and reaching a level of pure mudslinging.

A competent Punjabi union leader might organize a *siapa*—the old Punjabi custom in which a death was celebrated for several days by women gathering in a circle each morning, stripped to the waist and with their thighs uncovered. Following the *siapa*

CHAPTER FOUR

leader's rhythmic, doleful chants, they would beat their breasts and thighs with both hands. Under a good, experienced leader this could reach a crescendo, with the women beating themselves black and blue but dutifully returning the next morning. A real *siapa* was usually reserved for an early death, especially that of a son. A union *siapa* was for management, usually for the chairman.

Yet pure hatred or pure violence was rare, at least in the Punjab. There was an underlying robust Punjabi humour, and a basic kindness in the mutual relationship. Nor was respect, provided one had once commanded it, ever really lost. As if to reassure management, odd individuals would drop in throughout the struggle to tell you that what they said was not necessarily how they felt. But this was not so in the East, where the flame of hatred could burn fiercely, with none of the innocuous ribaldry of the North. Violence was always close to the surface there, and protests had altogether different political and emotional roots. An English manager was once bodily lifted up and thrown into a furnace.

Filthy or otherwise, the abuse hurled by the union at management was in interesting contrast to the language expected from the latter, which had to be impeccable. While conducting a disciplinary enquiry, our branch manager in Delhi was once asked by the union representative for yet another adjournment. "I am afraid I cannot go on postponing the enquiry interminably," he responded. "If Mr. X has not been able to prepare his case despite the ample time he has had, that is his funeral. I propose going ahead with the enquiry." We paid a stiff price. All hell was let loose. The branch manager was accused of prejudice; he had used unpardonable language; he wanted to see the poor man's funeral; he wanted to destroy the union. We were taken to court, and even upon appeal we lost. We has used intemperate language. This after all the union cursing and mock funerals for management.

Reaching my first long-term union agreement was a trial of strength. There were heightened expectations of the first Indian chairman. The schedule of demands was a document of such perfection that, due in January, it was not ready till July. It was a model of welfare, absorbing the company's entire profit before tax, leaving the management with the challenge of starting all over again to rebuild profits. In the interminable list of demands, nothing was missing except payment without work. This in any case was not necessary, because legislation permitted a person to be away from work, either with pay, on half pay, or without pay, for 180 days every year; and meanwhile they could work elsewhere.

The whole system of confrontation and struggle seemed out of place in the context of our poverty and needs. Perhaps it had been necessary once, when management was ruthless, but it was unseemly and crude as a weapon. In India we now had perhaps the world's most protective legislation, and in a company like ours the difference in take-home pay between myself and my driver was barely three-to-one after tax. What we needed was something that would put the collective shoulder behind the wheel, at least for a few years. Negotiations, yes; as tough and as hard as they could be, with much homework to challenge management. I remembered the union leaders at Harvard, with whom I had shared a course in advanced management, how they pored over company financial statements, working out profitability, costs, and resources, employing ratios to see where there was room to get more out of management. They did not rely on slogans and lung power but backed their struggle with knowledge and cogent argument. How much easier, I felt, management's task was in India, in one way—yet how much more difficult in another.

Once again the demonstrations had a lighter side. The factory union was trying to force us to rehire some workers who had rushed the security personnel at a shop to force the unwilling workers inside to come out. They sent notice that they would march in a procession to our suburb and hold the usual "peaceful" demonstration outside our house late in the evening, allowing for the time it took me to get home, and asked if I could please cooperate by being in. The personnel director felt that this must be discouraged and that I ought to stay away that evening and inform them that I refused to cooperate. Reluctantly, because I felt that it might be misunderstood as shying away, I decided to go to an evening cinema show. My wife was both amused and delighted. It must have been years since she had seen a film in my company. So, with a feeling of having been trapped, I sat through the film, which was actually quite good, with Ava Gardner to look at. The demonstrators had meanwhile checked on me and decided to call it off; but the next week they sent word again. This time I told personnel that I must face it and get it over with.

A strange sight met me when I reached home. The usual peace in the quiet, leafy lane at the end of our drive was shattered. Some bewildered children had collected to look at the crowd, while the

CHAPTER FOUR

frightened neighbours had shut their windows for safety but had their noses pressed to the panes. As my car swung in, the noise subsided dramatically into a hushed silence. I decided to run the gauntlet by walking up the drive. The crowd separated politely; I waved and saluted with joined hands, forced a smile and went on, apparently to their surprise. It was only when I reached the top of the flight of steps leading to the house that they recovered, but they now decided to stop the demonstration. They asked Bakshi, our driver, who was almost a member of the family, to convey to me that they would like to send up a delegation. I said I would certainly be glad to meet them, but there must be no more than two or three representatives; and I would be equally glad if they chose to continue with their demonstration. No, came the answer, they did not wish to shout but would rather discuss things.

Slowly, awkwardly, a long line of a dozen men and women came up the garden steps. Apparently they had not been able to keep the numbers down. We all sat there solemnly, not knowing where to start. They looked at each other like shy school children. Eventually I opened the conversation. We discussed everything—conditions in the factory, the backlog of problems, the rising cost of living, inflation, and a good deal else connected with life and work came up. As I was quite relaxed and in no hurry, the talk went on for well over an hour. A Christian girl from our suburb was especially lively. Finally we shook hands and agreed that, while the matter would be examined carefully, we were all behind the firm despite such differences as were bound to arise now and again.

But the aftermath was unexpected and amusing. These were the days of prohibition in Bombay, and ours was a suburb of Christian and Koli fishermen, notorious for illicit distilling and bootlegging. Most of the demonstrators were people from the locality who had found it convenient to join the procession on their way home from work. As our discussion was going on, the crowd below, who had agreed not to shout, became restive. Some of the locals invited others to visit the neighbouring huts for a drink, and in the hour or so of waiting they drank quite a lot, so that when they reassembled to hear the delegation's report, some of them were quite high. As the delegation had not much news to give, the followers began to barrack them, and there was a free-for-all. Disgusted, the crowd began to stray back to the huts, and decided in future to resort to the more conventional and convenient form of half-hour demonstrations at the factory gate.

UNIONS

My first encounter with a colourful union personality came a few years later. George Fernandes, later to become the union minister of industry in the Janata government and then the rising star of Bombay, was to succeed the strongest leader the city had known, S. K. Patil. Fernandes had been trying to take over our Bombay factory union, which was one of the few in the main industrial area of Sewri that he did not control. The union had had a varied career, having tried every political shade, even complete independence. Starting as a company union, it broke away because the more than three thousand factory workers could neither be led by the four hundred clerks at the head office nor lead them. In turn the socialists, the communists, and the Congress party were tried.

Under the Maharashtra government rules, a new union could not be challenged until it had had a year in which to prove itself, but George Fernandes was much too impatient and considered the prohibition a meaningless formality, because he was convinced that if a poll were taken he would win hands down. He was nothing if not confident, and when the time came, he did indeed win. After that there was no holding him back. He started firing one broadside after another, seizing on small issues and making big causes of them. He wrote me brief, staccato letters, each more urgent than the last. Peace was endangered, there was a threat of complete breakdown; and if things got out of hand, which he was convinced would happen very soon, the responsibility would all be mine. He built up to a crescendo, and delivered an ultimatum: unless he and I met, the situation would blow up—for which the responsibility would all be mine. I wrote back and invited him for a chat and a cup of tea with me.

Fernandes walked in briskly, a self-assured, handsome, well-set man. He looked surprised at my office. It was a bare room in cream and light mauve, with a bare desk. There were none of the usual excrescences and appurtenances denoting a chairman's office. And I walked forward to meet him in a bush shirt and *chappals,* which seemed to surprise him most of all. I took him to the low chairs by the wall and asked him to sit down.

"You are surprised at my dress and the office, Mr. Fernandes?" I enquired.

"Yes. I expected to see one of those large offices, with a couple of peons outside, and you in one of those Bombay chairman's dark suits, collar and tie, and with a patronizing manner," he

CHAPTER FOUR

replied. "Instead your office looks simple, and you look so relaxed, dressed just like me."

I told him that I had learned to wear a bush shirt and *chappals* on my visits to Delhi in the summer. I had discovered that when I passed the guards outside the ministries, they invariably stopped me and asked for my permit if I was dressed in the usual Bombay businessman's suit and tie. But if I was in a bush shirt, they took me for at least a secretary, if not a modern deputy minister, and saluted and let me pass. Besides, it was the most sensible way to dress in the hot weather. At home, I said, I always wore *kurta* pyjamas, and that was even more comfortable. He asked why I couldn't wear them at the office too. I said I had often thought of it, but had rejected the idea for practical reasons. Our staff here, in contrast to other offices, was reasonably well turned out. If not smart, they were at least neatly and tidily dressed. What I was afraid of was that, once I wore something as informal as *kurta* pyjamas, it would be a signal to them to come dressed anyhow they pleased, and the variety of clothing might conceivably be quite something: pyjamas—perhaps striped; *dhoti; mundu; lungi;* shorts; jeans; in fact it might be pure sartorial chaos. Fernandes laughed and conceded that at least it was not snobbery on my part.

"Mr. Fernandes," I said, "I am glad to see you. I have heard so much about you. Please tell me, which unions do you control in Bombay?" He laughed self-consciously and said, "It would be easier if you asked which I didn't control—I have all the government offices, both central and state, transport, the oil industry, the rubber companies, dock workers, taxi drivers, hotels and restaurants, and many others. And now also yours, as I told you a year ago when you preferred to stand on a legal formality."

"I appreciate that, but let me assure you we will observe the same legal formality in your case, when the time comes!" I replied. This we did, in fact, because a new union followed after he left Bombay for Delhi.

Fernandes laughed again, and went on to explain that what gave him power with Bombay labour was that he could speak fluently to them in Konkani, Marathi, Gujarati, Hindi, and English, which no other union leader could. They felt at ease wih him.

"Tell me, how do you manage to control such a vast spread—an empire, I was going to say," I continued. "I am quite interested in how one runs an organization which most of the time lives to struggle." I told him about my own experience at the

UNIONS

Harvard Business School, where the second line of union leadership, handpicked by their organizations in the United States and Europe, were trained for three months, mostly in financial, production, and marketing management, as well as in industrial relations. The idea was to give them a thorough grounding in general management, so as both to be able to run their own organizations better and to understand what made their adversaries tick. Instead, we in India have only demonstrations and attrition, which do achieve something but not nearly enough to force management into greater efficiencies.

We discussed the need for training generally, whether of men who managed a company or led a union, and I suggested we might run a training course for one of his groups. He thought that this was a good idea—but who would pay for it? I said that of course it should not be misunderstood as charity or, worse, an attempt at indoctrination. If he felt it would do his men good, the union would have to pay for it. That was worth thinking over, he replied, but suggested we get down to the crisis at the factory.

"That, Mr. Fernandes, I suggest we leave to your union men and our personnel management," I replied. "I don't believe in looking over the shoulders of our men when they are negotiating, as I am sure you don't either. But if there is an occasion when you would like to discuss an issue directly with us, the personnel director and I will be glad to have a chat with you and your colleagues. As things are, why don't you let the men sort it out? My door is always open, but let us confine our discussions to general matters of policy or to insuperable problems."

He went to see the personnel director and remarked to him, "Whew, that was sophisticated."

Next year Fernandes got elected to Parliament in a most dramatic victory over S. K. Patil, the Bombay veteran, who had spent vast sums of money, even hiring an airplane with streamers, while Fernandes knocked at each voter's door. Fernandes shifted his activities to Delhi, where somehow he did not make his mark. I met him at a F)tary meeting in Bombay and asked him about it, and his answer was interesting. "In Parliament today you need to behave in a special way to make your mark," he said. "If I really do my homework and study a subject to make a well-reasoned, thoughtful speech, then all the press will report is, 'Mr. Fernandes also spoke.' But if I fulminate and accuse, refuse to sit down, and generally show great agitation—well, the next day in the press

CHAPTER FOUR

Mr. Fernandes will hit the headlines. Our press, its readers, and even my colleagues are only interested in display and excitement."

I found this strange coming from George Fernandes, because I had thought he would be good at this and enjoy it, but apparently things were different in Parliament. He loved excitement, crowds and battle, but there was some innate niceness about him. Excepting once—when a strike got out of hand, the men rushed some expensive and complex atomic-power-generation machinery, and the subsequent police firing left some ten persons dead—his struggles in those days were always highly charged but peaceful. His greatest triumph was the first Bombay Bandh, when he brought a bustling city of eight million people to a standstill. Nothing stirred, except the police on duty, and the demonstrators. What this achieved was another matter, but it proved his power. He was tough, but avoided rough tactics. He fought clean, and managed to keep the Bombay strikes orderly. Of course, Bombay had a tradition of decency, but his power at one time was so absolute that he could have changed it in any way he wanted to and have made it into the nightmare that Calcutta became.

As the year 1961 drew towards its close, everything in India somehow looked good, especially to me. Perhaps the exhilaration of tackling my problems by myself gave the times a more shining edge. But it was indeed a year of successes: Nehru's India vindicating its stand on secularism, neutrality, democracy, and planning. There was, of course, a cloud the size of a hand over the Himalayas, but with a peaceful border and friendship sworn and resworn in the name of a brotherhood spanning two thousand years of history, everyone was certain that only the ignorant or the politically perverse could suspect the Chinese of hostile intentions. The rumours about Aksai Chin and the Chinese building a road were dismissed. A junior army officer who asked Krishna Menon, then the defense minister and the co-architect of our foreign policy, whether irrespective of our relations with China we could, purely from a defence angle, leave such a long border unguarded, drew down on his head a wrathful harangue on history, neutrality, British imperialism, American perfidy, and many other things of which a young officer should have been aware.

That autumn, inasmuch as my affairs were going fairly smoothly, I decided to take my annual holiday in Kashmir. It was a little late in the year, but we decided to try it as a change from spring and summer.

Chapter Five

AN INDIAN ROAD

SINCE 1953 the family had visited Kashmir every year. From the very beginning, we made the journey of fifteen hundred miles by road, an experience which was a great education, especially for the children. When the children began their schooling in Mussoorie and Dehra Dun, the journey increased to one of nearly two thousand miles, covering a considerable part of the country, with a variety of people, towns, landscapes, flora and fauna that showed the diversity and unity of India. And over the years, as we repeated the journey, we saw two sides of India, one growing and one static.

At a lonely spot, somewhere in north Maharashtra, where a road took off to a small town eighteen miles away, an enterprising person had installed a Burmah-Shell filling station that was open twenty-four hours a day. At night the proprietor slept on a string cot with a hurricane lamp by his side, getting up hastily at the sound of a truck pulling in. During the day he maintained the place, cooked his food, and passed the time chatting with the truck drivers.

Soon someone else saw an opening and arrived with a bullock cart loaded with bamboo poles, matting, some rickety wooden benches, and pots and pans, and set up a cook shop. First he provided only hot syrupy tea, but as his business grew he also served simple meals of *chapatis* and *dal,* to which he presently added vegetables, and eventually a meat dish. Soon he was serving complete meals, and one day an impressive signboard went up advertising "The New Highway Hotel & Restaurant—Hot Vegetarian and Non-Vegetarian Meals. Rice Plate Is Ready." Now you could get hardboiled eggs, biscuits, and coloured aerated drinks, and for the drivers who wanted a few hours' sleep there were *charpoys* in the open, under the stars at night and under the *neem* tree during the day, with a hand pump for water, and a dry privy.

CHAPTER FIVE

The "hotel" (with the stress on the first syllable) had come a long way from the original tea-stall.

When the Malayali vulcanizer in the next town heard about it, he sent his assistant to explore, and soon he too arrived with a truckload of tyres and tubes and a vulcanizing outfit. The Malayalis from Kerala had spread everywhere with their tire and tube shops. Along the thousand miles from Bombay to Agra, vulcanizing was synonymous with Kerala. The vulcanizer could do almost anything to a tube and a tyre, except make them; and if a truck had need at night, he would gladly get up from his sleep. He never complained if the truck was in a hurry, though he naturally grumbled if he was awakened in the name of an emergency and the driver then went to sleep at the "hotel" for the night. The filling station progressively turned into a garage with cleaning and servicing facilities and some spare parts. Before long a young mechanic from a neighbouring town offered to work there on his own; the garage men welcomed this, as it provided one more reason for trucks to stop.

The drivers were pretty good crisis mechanics themselves, of course, and, short of a total breakdown, they could do virtually anything with wire, string, and Sunlight soap (which, mixed with grit and dust, did an ideal job on leaking petrol pipe joints). But they only overhauled their vehicles at the roadside when there was a total breakdown and the truck came to a stop, because preventive maintenance was not in their vocabulary. Then they would put stones around the truck, which was left exactly where it had broken down, often in the middle of the road. The driver would look philosophically under the hood or chassis, and decide on the course of action to be taken. He would leave his mate, usually called the *"kleender,"* to guard the truck, and thumb a lift in another truck to the nearest filling station, there to discuss the matter with the mechanic, who returned with him for a further examination. If the breakdown was serious, they would proceed to the nearest town, buy the necessary parts, and perhaps bring back a more knowledgeable mechanic. The three of them would then get down to the job, sometimes taking the whole engine away for a complete overhaul.

Repairs completed, the driver started up again, with no more thought for maintenance until the next breakdown. Foresight was not in his nature. The very couplets in Urdu or Hindi that were written on the back of the trucks, with gaily painted festoons of

AN INDIAN ROAD

flowers and scenes of lakes, snowy mountains, and pine forests, summed up their drivers' fatalism. *What can happen when in God's care? No storm can blow out the lamp that He protects. May you with the evil eye have your face blackened.* Added to this were friendly slogans and salutations: *O.K.; Bye-Bye; Ta Ta; Use dipper at night; God protect; We shall meet again.* They were totally nerveless drivers. Aldous Huxley called them the most unmechanical in the world. They grossly overloaded their trucks, drove them tirelessly for days and nights on end, and ate and drank heartily. Rarely could one travel for more than a hundred miles without seeing a wreck, not infrequently two trucks in a headlong collision, lying in the most preposterous positions. There must have been a deity for truck drivers who protected them from even more wrecks and casualties. And indeed along the roads there were small temples where drivers prayed for their ill-deserved safety.

The hotel "sublet" a corner to a *pan-bidiwalls,* who prepared the *pan,* sold cigarettes and matches and some popular soaps. In due course a *kirana* merchant joined the community and dispensed a variety of foodstuffs, soaps, hair oils, toffee, biscuits, fruit juices, and other things that passing motorists and bus passengers might be tempted to buy.

In addition to the Shell inspector, salesmen began to visit the community. The first among them, as always, was the Brooke Bond man, trading in the tea-stall variety of tea, which could be brewed over and over again, the strength of the brew ever improving. Then came the Wimco man with matches, and after him the Sunlight man.

In the space of a few years, I saw this outpost transformed into a flourishing community of shopkeepers. After ten years had passed, it was a small township of a few hundred people. It could not be termed a village, as no farmers lived there. It was a settlement of shops and services, dependent entirely on the road, and on the initiative of the inhabitants. This is how growth and "urbanization" took place. The catalysts were a new road, a crossroads or a T-junction; buses and trucks; a filling station. The rest could be left to the enterprise of small men, whose businesses sprang up like mushrooms overnight. They needed no help, only the opportunity. Their ancestors had sought it in many distant parts of the world.

Like all new growth in India, it was haphazard and unsightly, with an air of transience; but this was misleading. It arose out of

CHAPTER FIVE

poverty and reflected the best these people could do with their meagre resources. One could not, however, mistake the initiative behind such growth, the upward thrust of the seed to the surface of an inhospitable soil.

In contrast, the green, well-tended housing colonies of the new public-sector factories along the road made one wonder. There villages were suddenly raised to urban standards, comparable in amenities to anywhere else in the world, with schools, hospitals, clubs, swimming pools, shopping arcades, community centres, and wide, well-lit roads fringed with lawns and trees. Might it not have been better, one wondered, if all this money had been made available to many times the number of people in the shape of opportunities? The small entrepreneurs could have been left to sort out their own affairs for at least one generation, until their productive capacity had acquired its own momentum, carrying with it new life for them and employment for others. The haphazard growth bore no comparison to these colonies, but it was self-created and self-sustained. Each lakh spent on it would have multiplied faster than crores spent on the public sector. If one petrol pump and the passing trucks could create so much employment, how much more would the saved crores have done? Roads and trucks were the fastest catalysts. New growth could, of course, also have come from surpluses produced by the new state ventures, but in those days they rarely produced a surplus. Mostly they drew in more and more funds just to keep going. But I suppose it was a question of how one saw the priorities.

When the road left Maharashtra to enter Madhya Pradesh, not only its rutted, ill-maintained surface changed but also its character. It now crossed the Vindhyachal, which divides Hindustan from the Deccan. In the hot summer, the landscape of scrub-covered hills, gnarled thorn and teak, and dry riverbeds had a rugged grandeur. In the early summer the drab colours were shot through with a blaze of flowering trees. Undulating valleys and plateaus alternated for several hundred miles, till the road dipped down into the flat, uninteresting alluvial plain of the north.

On our return in July, the dry and dusty land was transformed. The sky was now a washed-out blue, with fat clouds moving north to their annual rendezvous with the Himalayas. Sometimes they travelled in lazy groups, sometimes like the vast expanse of an attacking army, eagerly awaited by the soil for its liberation. At the violent onslaught of the rain, the dry earth sighed with hissing steam and softened under the downpour, and soon innumerable little gurgling streams gave voice to her satisfaction. The sunburnt land was now a happy green. The watercourses rushed to merge into rivulets and rivers, and ultimately into the sacred Godavari or Narmada, or the Chambal, which empties into the holy Yamuna, and finally into the sea. One or the other of the rivers was bound to be in flood and to have washed over, if not swept away, the bridge. No matter how high and strong the bridges, the rivers threatened them each year. And because of the way some of them were built by the contractors, they were all too ready to give way. Feast or famine was the fate of the land: rivers dry or swollen, earth scorched or lush, scrub or crops, mud huts or palaces, straggling *pi* dogs or bounding deer. There were violent contrasts, too, among the people.

On our way north in the heat of May, the road was gay with wedding parties going from one village to another, women and children packed into bullock carts and the men walking. Before the rains break, there is not much for the farmers to do, so there is leisure to celebrate. The people of the fertile plains are of sturdy Jat or Rajput stock, the men in red turbans and the women in red and yellow. But sometimes we met a different kind of wedding party. They were the forest people, the Bhils, of a different racial origin, the earliest inhabitants of the land. Small and lean as a result of endemic disease and chronic malnutrition, but wiry and sinewy, they were nonetheless beautiful. Their graceful, small-breasted women, walking behind the men, were decked out with jewelry of brass and copper, and occasionally of silver. The men wore their hair down to the neck, and each carried a bow and arrows. I took these to be mere symbols, but when I stopped a Bhil and asked him, he shyly told me otherwise. To demonstrate, he held himself as taut as his bow, pulled the string, and let go the steel-shafted arrow. It flew with a fine zing and hit a hard *dhak* tree, where the head dug deep. He pulled it out and let me feel its weight. It was doubtless a killer. I asked if he would sell me his bow and arrows, and in my indiscretion offered a fair sum, but he politely shook his head and with a smile walked away. A bystander explained that Bhil's weapon was part of his male pride, which money would not tempt him to part with.

We came across a strange Indian dream in the forests at Shivpuri, a small market town that a maharaja of Gwalior had tried to develop into a summer resort. This plateau, with stray showers in

CHAPTER FIVE

the dry weather, was much cooler than his capital in the plains. In the forest he had laid out roads, built a palace, villas, and offices to accommodate his court and retinue. There was a lake with a boathouse, gardens, and a family temple. But the maharaja died before his dream materialized further. Most of the buildings were never completed; some were ready but never occupied. Strangely the forest people have not availed themselves of the magnificent accommodation at their disposal, whether from fear of ghosts or awe of the old rulers, and yet they would worship at the private temple of the maharaja.

For some twelve years we made our annual pilgrimage to Kashmir, usually going up in the heat and returning in the rains. We never rushed the hot part of the journey. Setting out before the first light of dawn, we stopped at midday for lunch and a rest, started again in the afternoon, and looked for a quiet *dak* bungalow before dark. We would settle in for the night, organize a meal, and then go to sleep in the open, a lovely sleep in the cool night air, where the only sound was some jackal's far-off cry.

Through the years we evolved our own system of grading the bungalows. Our five stars went to those way down on the official rating, where very few people ever stopped. They were built of brick and tile, and always clean; there were bucketsful of cool well water, and the *chowkidar* was visibly pleased to have guests. On our black list were the new, garishly painted cement and concrete bungalows in district towns. They were generally dirty, and if they boasted the so-called modern comforts, these were usually out of order. It was, in any case, difficult to get in at the bigger places, where the rooms were occupied by government officials, often by some minister holding his local durbar. In fact, such bungalows were closed to the public, with police guards posted outside, when a minister was expected.

The narrow strip of road rolled on for a thousand miles to Delhi, through the vast and timeless landscape, broken by clusters of mud huts with thatched or tiled roofs; small temples and mosques; old, congested cities; ancient forts; palace ruins far from anywhere. There were also new townships with suburban housing and all the signs of growth, ugly but alive.

Away from the towns in the fifties, the road still teemed with wildlife. It was not uncommon to see *neelgai,* wild boar, and big herds of deer. But, sadly, India's freedom began to take its toll. In the British days, gun licences had been issued sparingly. While

AN INDIAN ROAD

hunting had been the preserve of a few maharajas and high officials, at least wild life was spared. Independence brought indiscriminate freedom to kill, so that Indian wildlife is now nearing extinction. It is lucky that peacocks are sacred, and still cross the roads in the early morning, rending the air with their raucous love calls.

Sometimes by the road we saw small encampments of a few families, with carts whose shape strongly resembled the ancient fighting chariot. The carts were heavily studded, but there were no horses. These folk are like gypsies, and live like gypsies the world over, parking their caravans near prosperous habitations and plying their trade of ironsmith. The chariot, which has a small tent as its superstructure, contains their possessions. They live in the open, build little mud ovens, and create a kind of permanence that in fact is transitory. One day they suddenly move on, leaving behind some debris and cold ashes. How they pulled their heavy carts away always puzzled me.

They are known as Lohanas, from *loha,* iron; and legend has it that they came originally from Chittor in Rajasthan. When Chittorgarh fort was taken by Akbar after a long and bitter siege, their ancestors left and vowed to wander about and not return until the conquerors had left Chittor. The Moghuls went, and the British went, and the government of the new state of Rajasthan in a flamboyantly imaginative gesture decided to fulfil the old pledge. Some hundred of Lohanas were collected at the foot of Chittorgarh. Led by Nehru on horseback, they marched in procession up to the fort and were ceremoniously conducted into their ancestral home. Two pieces of fractured history were thus joined together; but when the speeches and celebrations were over, the Lohanas again took to the road that had been their home for twenty generations, returning to the only life they knew.

After Delhi, the road got slightly wider and acquired a more prosperous look. The fields were better cultivated, the people sturdier and better dressed. But the greatest changes were the absence of bullock carts; the number of buses and trucks—including, of course, the wrecks; and the numerous tubewells and tractors. The wedding parties traveled in buses or in trailers hitched to tractors. One rarely saw a horse. All the main towns had new roads bypassing them. The inner cities had remained unchanged, but with the population increased ten and twentyfold they teemed with people and traffic. I liked the feel of their vital chaos. Proba-

CHAPTER FIVE

bly because I come from there, I always enjoy driving through the Punjab and feeling its vigor and progress. The home life of the Punjabi still had some of the old timelessness about it, but not his working life. In the two hundred and fifty miles from Delhi to Amritsar, one saw more that was new than in all the thousand miles south of Delhi.

One also saw unmistakable signs of the widening base of bureaucracy along the way. In the twelve hundred miles from Bombay to Pathankot some hundreds of road blocks for freight trucks made their appearance in the space of fifteen years. Some of the new revenue from this source went to the state, but much was shared out along the line. Truckers overloaded their vehicles dangerously, transporting contraband like wheat, sugar, or cement from areas of surplus to those of scarcity—traffic that had to be "regularized." The contraband still moved, but to the mutual interest of those who carried and those who regulated—and, also it was said, of those who legislated. There were also points that checked licences and permits, and others that only checked who passed. The arm of regulation reached out with an insatiable appetite. But here, too, initiative was at work, and the important check points also became growth points, with filling stations and shops that took care of the checkers and the checked on the implicit understanding that trucks would be held up long enough for their business. One wondered how long the system would endure before the roads became fit for any Indian to travel and transport goods freely. The Grand Trunk Road was the road on which Kipling's Kim travelled, where he observed the nefarious and colourful activities of his time. The road was full of interest still.

One realized how people in towns and country reflected their positions in society in their hours of work. In the summer, by seven in the morning, all those who lived by the sweat of their brow were at work; by eight, the small shopkeepers had lifted their shutters; and well before nine all shops and businesses were open; but it was only after ten that there were signs of the rulers stirring in the government offices, post offices, and later the nationalized banks and insurance offices. Anything to do with administration did not really settle down to work before half past ten. It was the reverse in the evening, when the administration stopped work between four and five, and shopkeepers by eight, while the toilers worked as late as they usefully could. In the winter, administration hours became shorter still, and much time

AN INDIAN ROAD

was spent in front of the offices basking in the sun or sipping tea while supplicants waited patiently.

This road from the coast to Kashmir was an education in itself. In its variety—of climate, from coastal damp heat to snowy peaks; of vegetation, from the thorny scrub of the Vindhyas to the juniper and dwarf birches of Pissu Ghati; of people, equally varied from the small, compact Maratha farmers to the large, bearded Gujars—it presented an interesting vertical cross section of India. To me, only too conscious of the power of New Delhi, the abundant signs of a powerful administration, slothful and wasteful of resources, were in marked contrast to the enterprise of the people with meagre means.

Chapter Six

KASHMIR

AFTER AMRITSAR, one became conscious that the border with Pakistan was nearby. East Punjab was now as the Northwest Frontier of the old Punjab had been. There was a military presence about. After recent harvesting, the fields were empty for troops and tanks to conduct their spring manoeuvres. At Pathankot, now a garrison town, one at last left the plains of India behind and began to climb into the Himalayas along the three hundred miles of road to the valley of Kashmir. It ran almost flat as far as Jammu, skirting the foothills and crossing innumerable dry rivers, which could in a few hours become raging torrents. From this point on one never forgot the proximity of Pakistan. The road often overlooked its contiguous parts, in which I had been brought up, still evocative of nostalgia. Not many miles away was what would always remain home, though unreachable and closed to me for ever.

The road from Jammu to Kashmir, then the only link except for an uncertain daily flight, was a miracle of engineering tenacity. Like the trucks on the Bombay-Delhi road, it used to rupture a number of times every year; each time it was hastily repaired to permit the impatient, piled-up traffic to move. At every major breakdown there was talk of a new alignment which would avoid the crumbling mountainsides of the first range and build on the safe rock of the inner ranges. Each year the engineers, a bit too pleased with the tough repair job, no doubt ably and speedily done, seemed to begrudge the trouble of having to start on a new road altogether.

This road was really an old bridle path, which at best had been good for *tongas*. The real main road had originally been the one from Rawalpindi to Srinagar. When Pakistan attacked the Kashmir valley, the bridle path had been hastily made serviceable for heavy military traffic, and when peace returned there, too much has been spent on it to discard it. There had, in fact, been a third road, the one used by the Moghuls, which went up from my home town of Gujrat to the Pir Panjal range about the Kashmir valley; but this too had been left behind in Pakistan.

From Jammu the road climbs to about four thousand feet and then descends to less than two thousand. Once more it ascends tortuously, to seven thousand feet, and then promptly dips down to two thousand again. A final climb to nine thousand feet—to descend at last to the five-thousand-foot-high valley of Kashmir through the bleak Banihal pass—was eliminated when the Germans built an all-weather tunnel four thousand feet below.

Nothing was ever again quite so exciting as our first sight of the Kashmir valley in April 1953, when after a freezing night in a bungalow we drove through the short brick-and-wood tunnel near the top of the Banihal at nine thousand feet, and saw the wondrous valley deep below. The sun shone on the huge snow walls on either side of the road and on the inundated rice fields, a glittering silver and blue. But for the clumps of trees that were visible, it would have looked like the vast lake that it once used to be.

In April the road was crowded with convoys of army trucks and with Bakarwals driving their goats up to the mountain pastures. Bakarwal means goatman; his cousin, the Gujar, is a cattleman. Both are Muslims. In winter, the Gujars and their animals huddle together in low huts made of stone and mud and cut into the hill slope, which makes the back wall. From above you hardly notice their grass and poppy-covered roofs. In summer, they drive their cattle up to higher pastures and live in tents under the pines, with pine twigs for mattresses. It is lovely when the sun shines, but miserable in the rain. Their clothes are dark and drab like their mud huts, but their hawklike faces are handsome. So are their women, who wear sombre but harmonious colours, usually black and dark red—a long embroidered *kurta,* flared *salwar,* and sturdy spurred shoes. Their quaint red and black caps, with long ear-flaps down to the shoulders, seem like relics of the helmets the men wore as warriors long ago. Their hair style of innumerable intricately woven plaits is not conducive to frequent washing.

There is something sad about the Gujars, as if the memory of their lost glory has stayed with them. Once they came to India from the plains of Central Asia as proud conquerors on horseback and formed a dynasty. The present state of Gujarat is named after

CHAPTER SIX

them, as is my home city in West Punjab. Driven from the plains of the Punjab by subsequent waves of conquerors, they went with their herds into the mountains of Kashmir. But they kept their language, a melodious Punjabi, purer than that spoken in the plains today.

The Gujars are a hospitable people and will unhesitatingly offer you bread, made from the sweet maize they grow on the hillsides. They never beg. Once at a Gujar camp when a woman came up to us and begged, the Gujars hurriedly said, "She is a Moghul." Her ancestors must have been camp followers of Jenhangir or Shah Jehan when their huge holiday camps moved into the valley, but she still did not belong, and the Gujars looked down on her for her lack of pride.

The Kashmir Muslims themselves live in the valleys as farmers, traders, and artisans. Men, women, and children all wear a loose wide-sleeved embroidered robe, reaching below the knees, over the baggy *salwar*. It is a comfortable dress in all weathers, for in winter they pull in their arms for warmth, letting the sleeves hang loose, and even their individual central heating system, the *kangri*, a little basket containing live coals, is carried inside their robes. For holiday best, their robes are in brilliant colours with rich embroidery. The Pandit women used to wear a dress very like the habit of European nuns, though in bright colours. The colour is disappearing, and now you rarely see some old woman in traditional dress. The young have all gone over to the sari, and the middle-class Muslim women to the *salwar kameez*. Some of the gaiety of a Srinagar Sunday also seems to have disappeared.

On the first warm spring Sunday, all Srinagar picnics in the Moghul gardens by the lake, Nishat, Shalimar, and Chashma Shahi. It is still too early for tourists. The Plains people have a lesson to learn from the Kashmiris, who sit quietly on the lawns and enjoy the sunshine and the flowers, the playing fountains and the birds, without making the raucous noises so familiar elsewhere in India. They open wicker baskets and make tea in samovars, eat their hard biscuits and whatever else they have brought, and when they depart leave nothing behind; litter and noise are the contribution of outside visitors. The emperor Jehangir, who built the gardens and planted the majestic *chenar* trees, would be pleased to see how well the Kashmiris maintain them.

Kashmiris are handsome and fair, with the charming courtesy of speech and manners that is the Muslim rulers' legacy. They are also very hard-working, and utilize all the resources of soil and water. Every little patch is cultivated; every stream is diverted into laboriously built channels; every man, woman, and child toils in this market garden that is the valley. Women and children gather the lake weed, and on a floating mass of it soil is heaped and vegetables are sown. As one crop follows another, more soil is formed. These are their floating fields. Patches are sold and bought, and it is a curious sight to see a field being towed away by its buyer. Eventually they anchor the fields by planting trees whose roots will reach the bottom, and consequently the lake is shrinking. As elsewhere in India, the pressure of population is eroding the environment. The Woolar and Dal lakes are now only half the size they were when I first visited them in the 1920s, and in a few generations this unique heritage will be lost.

Snow-peaked mountains slope to the confluence of two streams in the small valley of Pahlgam. Every year people from all over India come here in August for the festival of Raksha Bandhan. Rich and poor, city folk and peasants, young and old, including a gathering of *sadhus,* they throng the single street of the town and the forest paths. Their features and garments bespeak wherever they come from, Kohima or Kanyakumari, Cuttack or Keshod. They are mostly Hindu, with a sprinkling of tourists of other faiths. They have come together for the Amarnath Yatra; most out of faith and religious fervour, others for adventure and the beauty of the trek.

One morning, a mile-long caravan begins the arduous climb through woods noisy with the chatter of the descending Shishnag river. Walking, clutching their ponies, or carried in litters, the pilgrims arrive at their first stop, a little plateau called Chandan Wadi, valley of sandalwood—though only pine grows there. On one side is the snow bridge, and the many who have never seen snow rush down to feel it. The children throw snowballs till hunger drives them to the cook shops, and cold and fatigue into the tents. A whole little town of shops and tents exists just for one week in the year.

The next day, the procession winds its way across the snow bridge and up the arduous thousand-foot climb of Pissu Ghati, a region of birches, shimmering silvery trunks against the blue sky. On the tissue-thin flakes of their bark, *bhoj patra,* the holy Vedas were written. The chill increases, the birches become smaller and give way to tiny juniper bushes. Once past the tree line, nothing

CHAPTER SIX

breaks the contour of the overwhelming landscape. But along the path now blooms the miracle of the short mountain summer, poppies and irises in yellow and blue and a gay carpet of a hundred kinds of tiny flowers. The only inhabitants are shining black ravens and whistling marmots, who sit on their hindlegs and stare curiously at the invasion of their domain.

The second camp site overlooks the awesome, green Shishnag lake. The pious bathe amongst its ice floes, but most shiver even at a wash in the streamlet which trickles past the camp. Plains people huddle together to keep warm at twelve thousand feet. By now strangers have got to know each other. Kerala folk join Punjabis, and in Hindi or English they talk about the journey, their homes and their daily lives, discovering the common heritage of their ancient land.

The air gets thinner and colder, the path more fearsome, clinging to the rock over abysses of two thousand feet. The third night is spent at Panch Tarni, where five icy streams defy bridging. Next morning, the day of the festival, the pilgrims have only a few fairly easy miles to go to the famous cave. Here, at thirteen thousand feet, lies their destination, a long way from anywhere, accessible only for the three months into which spring, summer, and autumn are hastily compressed before the snows close in. Inside the enormous cave, in the soft colours of opal, pink, blue, green, and mauve, the sacred ice lingam stands perfectly formed. Its sides melt smoothly into a hem of ice, which the pilgrims cover with wild flowers. Some feel a mystic ecstasy at the sight they have longed to see, others are struck by its strange beauty; but in all there is a feeling of purity that cleanses the soul. And they look hopefully for the legendary pigeons, said to be incarnations of Shiv and Parvati.

Here is the unity of diverse India. Here people meet, some in faith and others to find solace and inspiration in the vision of their origin and the majesty of their God. But here too, alas, a mountain road is making its way inexorably forward, and soon cars and trucks and buses spewing smoke will shatter the peace and pollute the clean air of the mountains and valleys, and the annual Yatra will become a day's return trip. We will have progress.

Among Kashmir's mixed population of different ethnic groups, the oldest are the Kashmiri Brahmins, whose learning and culture go back to before the building of the old sun temple of Martand, near Srinagar. After the waves of Muslim invasion, as Kashmir changed hands from one dynasty to another, they remained quiescent for centuries, until in the British era they came into their own again and spread into the Punjab and Uttar Pradesh, always in letters, the professions, and politics. After independence, they rose in stature, and have provided India with talent and leadership.

Curiously, those who were converted to Islam shared none of their characteristics. Where the Brahmins were celebrated for erudition, the Muslims went in for farming, cattle herding, and handicrafts—something to do, perhaps, with their caste origins. Even under the Moghuls, Sikhs, and Dogras, it was generally the Brahmins who were prominently the officials. It is a curious quirk of our indestructible caste system that throughout a thousand years of Muslim rule, the Brahmins who remained Brahmins, willing to suffer indignities and refusing to take the softer option of embracing the conquerors' religion, managed to retain their pre-eminence in a social order which failed to raise the hewers of wood and drawers of water, the tillers and the artisans, above the stations to which they had belonged before they adopted the rulers' faith. They remained, as today, where they had been before. It was the same under the Sikhs and the Christian British as under the Muslims. It is the same in the Punjab. The *kami*—meaning, literally, the worker, and actually a term for society's helot—be he Hindu, Muslim, Sikh, or Christian, is still where he always was, unless he manages to submerge himself in the urban anonymity of a modern profession. In the most tolerant society of them all, the Sikh, where all are equal before the Guru, the Harijan converts are still referred to as Mazhabi Sikhs, Sikhs who have merely adopted the religion.

The Kashmiri Muslims are among the world's greatest arts-and-crafts workers. European travellers introduced them to new crafts—papier-mâché, crocheting, crewel tapestry, petit point—but all continued in the traditional patterns the Moghuls had brought with them, the Persian delicacy of colour and line in painting, embroidery, and wood carving. But though great artists in wood, they suffer from the artistic temperament and have no time to learn carpentry; hence their furniture is always poorly joined. Their character has the natural naiveté of the artist—euphoric, optimistic, often unpractical, and bound to tradition.

Their tourist department was the most likeably euphoric of all, making the tallest promises and giving the shortest measure of reality. It never tired of quoting the couplet attributed to Jehangir:

CHAPTER SIX

"If there is a paradise on earth, it is this, it is this, it is this." My managerial mind was fascinated by their plans for new roads, bridges, resorts, playgrounds, ski slopes, cable cars, and modern, centrally heated winter hotels. One was always asked, "How does Kashmir compare with Switzerland? Is it not far more beautiful? We will make it even better than Switzerland." As we always came fully equipped, and needed only a couple of bare rooms, we generally resisted the blandishments of the director of tourism. "This time you must stay at our latest Swiss chalets, which beat anything they have in Switzerland," he would say. It hurt him that I preferred an old forest bungalow in the pine wood. To please him we once went to a Swiss chalet, prepared from experience for the worst, and it was worse than we had expected.

The wooden huts had only their borrowed shape in common with their Swiss prototypes; all else was the product of indigenous talent. They did not even have the utilitarian beauty of the old forest huts. The natural deal wood, which Kashmiris usually leave unpainted to acquire a satin-smooth patina, had been garishly painted. None of the hinges or locks were properly fitted, and broken windows had not been replaced because of the administrative problems involved. The boasted "sanitary" had not yet been fitted, but was lying on the bathroom floor. The forest and the stream which had to serve as toilet instead were a good ten minutes' walk away, as the huts had been built in the middle of a meadow.

To those of us who knew Kashmir well, it was a strange sort of progress from the old timbered huts of the British forest officers. They had built them in the forest, protected from cold winds, near a perennial spring or stream. Given a slope, there might even be running water in the hut. The rooms were small and cosy, easily heated by the open fireplaces. No lack of fuel! But in the "Swiss chalet," exposed to the winds of heaven, there was not a single fireplace. Somebody hadn't noticed them in Switzerland, or the prototypes were centrally heated. On a rainy day, it was miserable. Since there was supposed to be electricity, for which there was only the wiring so far, there were not even enough lanterns provided.

Such signs of "planning" were fast multiplying all over Kashmir in the fifties, as money poured in to raise the living standards of the people and improve tourist amenities. The waste was impartial—the locals got no better deal than the tourists. More lakhs were budgeted than were spent, and more lakhs spent than actually put to work. To compensate for the lack of results, more plans were made and more budgets prepared. I also spent time looking at their industrializing process, which involved large amounts spent on new plants and projects. Some of these never worked, others only fitfully, but there was no dearth of optimism. The whole face of Kashmir was going to be transformed!

Many years later a team of management experts turned up. They left behind them an elegantly bound and phrased report that advocated management accounting to men who had still to learn their debits and credits; an information and control system and modern communications to an organization that ran on dog-eared files; restructuring, performance budgeting, and appraisal; and proposal to institute a cadre of committed and competent managers. This report had no visible results, except that its author was invited to Harvard University to propound on the growth, constraints, and solutions to problems of a developing society, and ended up with the United Nations doing good to other developing countries.

With each year's journey from Bombay to Kashmir, I learnt more about the contrast between the vigour of unplanned initiative and the often weak results of planned growth. It was the difference between a sturdy weed and a wilting, overbred plant. One saw the squandering of planned effort and the careful husbanding of the small self-created opportunities. While a thriving population had grown up around that multiplier of non-directed growth, the filling station, the well-planned factories and their manicured estates had a forlorn look.

These were early days, though, for drawing conclusions. Why was it that casual seeds brought growth, while careful sowing resulted in a constant drain on resources and bore no fruit? The village community hall, opened by a minister, often remained unused; instead the villagers congregated outside tea shops, listening to their radios and making their own comments. And yet to tackle such the vast problem of development, some planning was necessary, if only to provide the road, build trucks, and supply fuel. How else was that crossroads going to sprout? The question was how to marry the sturdy, ruggedly individualistic initiative of old with the discipline of modern planning, not to make one exploitative and the other ineffective. Would we learn the answer with time?

CHAPTER SIX

Kashmir was full of new government departments and their outposts—departments of sericulture, flood control, improved agricultural practice, cooperation, animal husbandry, poultry farming, industrial development, fisheries, soil research—all intended to promote new growth in a society that had been static and impoverished for centuries, but all rather ineffective. Many years later, I was invited to serve on a committee to review Kashmir's development over the past twenty-five years. As I listened to the problems, there was a familiar ring to it all. Were solutions always to be so far behind?

Kashmir represented a compressed version of the problem of institution-building everywhere in India and a blown-up version of contemporary Delhi, where budget-oriented institutions sprouted and flourished in breathtaking variety. Where a hospital would have served, an institution for the study of the history of Indian medicine was sponsored instead. It also served!

Chapter Seven

GOVERNMENT AND BUSINESS

NINETEEN SIXTY-TWO marked my first full year as chairman of Hindustan Lever, and with the union contract behind me I devoted all my attention to New Delhi. If government was difficult and ponderous, Unilever was sensitive and suspicious. If government felt they were doing the company a favour in accepting its plans for expansion, Unilever did not see it that way, and felt instead that the price for that favour was unfair and high—and so between them I was like the *dhobi*'s proverbial dog that belongs neither to the house nor to the *ghat*.

Negotiations with New Delhi dragged a lengthy course, while the file moved from point to point, backwards and forwards, occasionally only forwards. Then it went to the ministries in the state capitals concerned—Uttar Pradesh, Bengal, Madras, Maharashtra. In our rounds of the ministries we sometimes passed the same point again and again, till, like the bullock at the Persian wheel, we were familiar with each point of the circle; but at least the bullock's eyes are mercifully covered so that he does not grow dizzy. The negotiations took nine years altogether.

A trip to Delhi always induced a sick feeling deep inside me. The daily Viscount left at dawn, after a restless night during which I contemplated the early-morning alarm and wondered what new problems lay in store, what surprises, what setbacks. Indian Airlines was experiencing delays as a result of strikes, go-slows, and technical troubles, which were to add hours of philosophical waiting at the airport to the waiting for the file. The reasons for both could be equally trivial. I once sat for three hours at Palam airport because an air-hostess on the inward flight had "insulted" the pilot, who had reprimanded her for not serving his tea promptly. He refused to fly back unless she apologized or was offloaded. The girl said she was busy serving passengers, so why should she apologize; and if she was offloaded, the other girls

CHAPTER SEVEN

would join her. The girls were adamant and so was the pilot. One waited patiently. Ultimately a new crew was collected, and we boarded the plane hours late, wondering if the offloaded captain, his mates, and the girls had all collected their overtime, and whether these hours of argument had been clocked into their month's flying hours.

These were also the years when pilots, who would not have soiled their hands carrying their own cup of tea, were declared "workmen" by a court and given all the privileges of workers under the Industrial Disputes Act. They could now ask for a "living wage"—a charming euphemism for a wage (plus tax-free perquisites denied to others under the tax rules) many times higher than the highest salary in the civil service. Soon they learned to work to rule, which was worse and meant yet more delays. One began to find them an unlovable sight as a class of prima donnas, associating them with predictable delays for unpredictable reasons. The engineers had not yet learned to be workers, but they soon were to do so. The only heroes were the least privileged commercial staff and the passengers. Even the loaders had their go-slow tantrums.

In Delhi the next morning, Aspi Moddie would come to my room at the hotel which was my second home and give me the latest intelligence about the file. "Ramachandran," his personal assistant, had his antennae out and had learned from "Ramaswamy," the personal assistant of a minister's secretary, that according to the information he had received from "Ramadurai," the personal assistant of the secretary in another ministry, that was where the file now reposed. After a note by the undersecretary, the file had gone to the joint secretary, who was waiting for the return from tour of the additional secretary, before it would go up to the secretary. The note might raise a new issue, potentially as frustrating as it was ingenious. It was no use asking to be trusted, for trust was not what the system was built upon. It was best in such cases to go back to the originator of the query, and appeal to his superior knowledge for guidance. He knew so much, and we so little. We, after all, were only investors risking capital, while he was guiding the nation's economy.

Sometimes the objection was trifling; then it needed the most careful consideration. At least, one had to be wary and treat it gingerly for fear of upsetting some serious-minded but limited enthusiast. With one such I had a harrowing experience trying to learn the first principles of financial management and marketing, which he propounded generously for my benefit. It was hard to reason with him and impossible to argue; one learned with some difficulty that one could not afford to argue with a bad idea. Although one continued to agree neutrally, one had to remain persistent in non-acceptance. The one with the power always knew better, He who has the stick, his is the buffalo, as our Punjabi proverb says.

I pondered this system left behind by the "heaven-born" ICS of the nineteenth century. Lampooned by Kipling and helplessly abhorred by the administrator today, a century later, the system's only strength seemed to lie in its predictable negativity. Time as an expense in the shape of rising prices and delayed production was not its concern. Spawned a century earlier, it had not learned the cost of delays in an era of inflation, when prices of equipment rose monthly. Yet one could see the administrator's point, because a decision taken quickly could lay him open to suspicions of unreasonable haste. Why was the decision taken so hurriedly? Why was the file so slim? What was the motive? There was no national crisis, no emergency. Why then this unseemly haste? The onus of proving his innocence lay with the poor administrator who had acted expeditiously.

There were those in industry who met the system's hurdles in subterranean ways through their Delhi representatives, working quietly and assiduously at all levels to ensure the smooth and speedy passage of the file. I once heard fragments of a conversation between a great Indian businessman and a minion of his, one of the many men he employed solely to smooth the path of the file. I had taken Lord Cole, the chairman of Unilever, to meet this tycoon, and as he spoke to us in English, he kept up a steady conversation on the side with this man, in a dialect of Hindi that I could at least make sense of.

"When is he arriving?"
"I see, by the seven o'clock flight."
"Will you meet him?"
"So you have it arranged, and the file will be on his table tomorrow."
"Do you think he will decide tomorrow?"
"I see, you have it settled."
"Do you think there is likely to be a hitch?"
"Well, I know you will manage it."

CHAPTER SEVEN

"Or else, let me know—but soon!"

Someone told me later of the same businessman that where it took us years to obtain a given licence, it would have taken him as many months. And then he would have had the theoretical right to block our way, because he had been granted licensed capacity that would, under our system of planning, take care of the market. Whether he went ahead to build that capacity, and how long he took over it, was not relevant. He could thus thwart tomorrow's competitors as well as today's. This became known as pre-empting capacity.

As was usual with the system—something that K. B. Lall had tried to teach me but that I had by now despaired of—the break always came, but unexpectedly. The tangled skein suddenly showed signs of untangling. I got a message that L. K. Jha, previously secretary in the commerce ministry and now secretary in the economic affairs department in the ministry of finance, had called an interministerial meeting to discuss all our proposals and finalize everything. Would I attend it? I was suddenly so elated that I forgave the system its years of delays, and even blessed it. In my euphoria, I felt as if it was deliberately designed to put one's proposals through an ordeal to ensure that we made no hasty mistakes and to chisel and hone each in turn to trim it of all unnecessary expense.

Jha was known popularly as "L. K.," a custom originating with the British, who did not call their Indian colleagues by their first names, either because they found them difficult or because using first names would have implied a familiarity which they preferred to avoid. A tall, handsome man, he made his presence felt from the moment one entered his office, and was remarkable for the quality, rare among Indians, of being a good listener. As I got to know him over the years, I came to admire him all the more. I could ring him up for a ten-minute appointment and take literally ten minutes, sometimes even less. Though without K. B. Lall's expansiveness and bubbling humour, Jha got down to business straightaway, and his face literally moulded itself into an expression that was all attention. As the presentation came to the first important issue, one of his eyes opened a shade wider and fixed itself on you with compelling attention. In the end, he would sum up his understanding of what you had said, and give his views openly and tersely; there was never any equivocation.

He belonged to the prewar generation of the ICS. Each was an individual, though they all had the stamp of a basic prototype. Dharma Vira, Bhoothalingam, Dandekar, Ranganathan, Lall, Shankar, of the ones I got to know well at work, were all men of great ability, and each one was a character. They were the system's rare problem solvers. One could tell them apart from the type of professional executives in industry, especially those in the multinational corporations. Yet they were essentially professional executives from the same Indian matrix. The difference lay in their wide powers and authority, which went back to the days of the Raj. They were the givers, and everyone else, even the highest executives in industry, was a supplicant. One was conscious of their power as one entered their large offices past obsequious entourages.

When I went to the meeting, I met with a bevy of secretaries. I was alone, and this perhaps gave me a subtle advantage, but I felt a little nervous as a supplicant asking for economic grants. How easy life would be, I felt, if one stopped growing and simply profited from a stagnation which assured the comfort of shortages and hence high profits. Jha came straight to the point. Our projects were all growth promoters and foreign-exchange savers, but we were a foreign company, repatriating dividends, and the government would like to take this opportunity to ask us to dilute our foreign holdings and increase Indian participation. He continued: even the reduced shareholding would mean higher overall profits and no diminution of Unilever's control. He would therefore make us an offer. The government would grant our requests to expand existing plants and to build new ones, in return for a reduction in our Unilever shareholdings in favour of the Indian shareholders; with great punctilio he corrected himself—he meant, resident shareholders. After all, he added with sardonic humour, an Englishman resident in India had rights equal to an Indian shareholder. (We, who owned property in most parts of the world, were soon to pass a law restricting foreigners from owning it in India.) I agreed on the percentage, and Jha was pleased. The formalities of fixing the price of the issue to Indian shareholders would follow in due course, though he thought the price of the shares might be around thirty-five rupees. I returned to the hotel, where I began typing out a letter to Unilever. A major catastrophe was to follow.

Not long before, I had met a senior civil servant, Bhoothalingam, who had reminisced about the beginnings of Indianization of the capital of foreign companies. In 1955, he observed, govern-

CHAPTER SEVEN

ment had approached two of the largest British companies, Anglo-Dutch Shell and Lever, and asked them to convert themselves into Indian public limited companies with a small Indian shareholding. They were both alarmed, but while Unilever had agreed, Shell had refused, saying that it could make better use of its scarce capital elsewhere in the world. Bhoothalingam wondered what the shape of the foreign oil companies might have been had they accepted the suggestion, which the government then genuinely saw as being as much in their interest as in that of the Indian investing public.

On a subsequent visit to London I asked John Hoskyns-Abrahall, who had been chairman in India at the time and was now on the Unilever board, about the matter. Yes, he said, H. V. R. Iengar, the commerce secretary, had called on him with a suggestion from his minister to the effect that Lever should consider going Indian. It had done well out of the country and had a good future, but there was a rising national sentiment that wanted to see foreign companies in India adopt an Indian look. And of course, Iengar added significantly, its future prosperity was dependent on the government's granting import and other licences and permits. Hoskyns-Abrahall had heard out this hitherto undreamt of proposition with great aplomb but, he confessed, "you could have knocked me over with a feather." However, he thanked Iengar for displaying such solicitude for Lever! Later when I spoke to Lord Heyworth, then Unilever's chairman, he remarked that it was the first suggestion of its kind that the company had had from anywhere in the world; but, as he had told his colleagues, it was a sign of the times, and if similar propositions were going to come from other developing countries, it was time they examined its implications.

The Dutch chairman saw things differently. If they entertained this suggestion from India, they would receive similar ones from all the developing countries. It should be turned down firmly and clearly, so as to nip economic nationalism in the bud. Heyworth had countered that if such propositions were indeed going to come from other countries, India was the best place to consider it. The experience would be worthwhile. India would always be reasonable, which was more than he could say of many other nations.

I also discussed the matter with David Mudie, chairman of Shell in India. He had had a similar offer from Iengar, and had recommended it to his headquarters in London. The proposal was turned down flat: they would take their money elsewhere. Mudie agreed that, had they accepted, who knew but what the course of events might have been different. As it was, their expansion and diversification were doomed. In fact, the Indian government set up its own oil company, which grew rapidly, while Shell, Esso, and Caltex stagnated before being taken over twenty years later.

The reply from Unilever, London, to Jha's offer was unexpectedly sharp and brief. They were deeply concerned at my recommendation. Jasper Knight, the finance director, was flying to India immediately, accompanied by John Short, senior partner in Cooper Brothers, the Unilever auditors. Would I please arrange meetings with the government?

Knight's visit, arranged without consulting me, seemed to take things out of my hands. Short's joining Knight to emphasize the "shareholders' interest," I felt, added a ludicrous touch to the heavy hand with which Unilever had decided to deal with the situation. My first reaction was to tell them to handle it all themselves. I would be glad to withdraw altogether to save them the embarrassment of having to undo my tentative agreement, which admittedly was tacit and subject to their concurrence but nevertheless was an acceptance of the government's viewpoint by the man on the spot. It might be better, in the circumstances, for Unilever to reopen negotiations alone on the track that suited them. I was filled with cold disgust at this overreaction. They could at least have discussed the matter with me, if need be have asked me to "put on my hat and coat and fly over to London." To send a team out seemed unnecessary at this stage. It implied that Unilever was alarmed by the government's proposal and, worse, that by my ready agreement, without putting up a fight on their behalf, I had showed little or no concern. And if this was how I had begun, where would I end? When I thought of these negotiations, the wisdom of Andrew Knox seemed illusory. The trust, the delegation of responsibility, and all the theory one had heard about and discussed at Unilever conferences and elsewhere seemed remote.

A quiet exit from what seemed an unpromising beginning was tempting. But a withdrawal was all too easy; also, it was a soft option when one had been trained on hard choices. It was understandable, too, if Unilever felt diffident about me. They had long considered me something of a problem, in view of my internal struggle of conflicting loyalties, even though they had "found my

CHAPTER SEVEN

conduct always quite unexceptionable." In retrospect I could understand why London now suddenly took fright. The doubts about me that they had waived when they handed the company over to me must have revived in a suspect situation. It was early for Indianization; they could have waited and appointed one more expatriate chairman, and yet they had preferred not to, and had appointed me. This crisis must have reawakened their fears. I was, after all, not one of them. I decided in the end to handle the matter coolly, and telexed back welcoming the visit; it would give Knight an opportunity to meet government officials and get a personal feel of things. Such problems might arise again in the future. It was best, therefore, to meet this one with all possible care.

With Knight and Short, we got down to discussions straightaway. Knight was wary and defensive, and Short trailed behind him like Stan Laurel. At the first opportunity I tackled Knight. I said I could understand Unilever's anxiety—but did he really feel that their interests were not being looked after by me in a way that would inspire confidence? He admitted they had that feeling, and thought it best to be open about it. They did not much mind government driving a bargain on equity, but did object very much to being asked to shed theirs so cheaply. At this rate, they would have to lower their shareholdings at an unrealistic price each time they wanted to expand, so that theoretically they might in the end find themselves dispossessed for a song. This prospect was totally unacceptable to them. And, he told me frankly, they did wonder whether I felt the way they did. He had brought John Short along as they had many thousands of shareholders all over Europe, and now in America, and thought their auditors should be included to represent the shareholders' interests. He hoped I agreed with him.

Yes and no, I said. In the West they would never be asked to dilute their capital, and therefore this sequence of events would not occur, but this was India, where policies were likely to be different, though that was not to say mulcting or confiscatory. India was still a profitable investment for them. They would, however, have to adjust themselves to Indian aspirations that were both political and economic, with a touch of emotion thrown in. They might come across the same situation in some other developing countries, but with less reasonableness and security. I went on to say that the government reasoned that expansion would bring them—I somehow could not say "us" to Knight because his attitude made me feel an outsider—greater overall profits than before, so that a dilution of equity would mean no loss and would probably result in increased earnings in the long run. Shareholders in India possessed an equity in such gains by virtue of the market. I felt convinced that government would not have offered this deal to another company. There had recently been cases of foreign companies accepting a much lower price than ours. I thought that in their own best interests they should accept. Otherwise, I feared, reopening the subject might harden positions. I could, however, assure him that if that was the position they chose to adopt, I would be with them.

The discussions began disastrously at the very first meeting with the controller of capital issues. After presentation of Knight's arguments, both exploded. The controller proceeded to explain at some length a jumble of financial reasoning, and this particularly galled Knight. There followed a heated discussion. While Knight quoted the U.S. Securities Exchange Commission and the City of London, the young, eloquent controller quoted from American textbooks on finance, and when he raised his voice, Knight quivered. We met many others, but made no headway. I let Knight handle it in his own way. In the end I told him, with a touch of unkindness, that he should by now know the government's views, and that it looked to me like a question of retrieving a lost position. He would have to leave me to handle it. Knight and Short left at the end of the week in disgust, and I returned to Bombay wondering how I would be able to save the situation.

On his return to London, Knight wrote Jha a tough letter, expressing his disappointment. It ended on a clumsy note to the effect that if there was no agreement on the issue, Unilever might have to reconsider their policy of further investment, greatly as they would deplore this. Some foreign companies they knew were already reconsidering their positions. Had the letter been addressed to the young controller, it would have torn the whole thing. Jha was a seasoned civil servant, more polished and cooler than Knight. Years afterwards, as our ambassador in Washington, he performed the delicate task of handling an angry Nixon and his administration over the third India-Pakistan war with skill and patience, and subsequently as governor of Kashmir assisted in Sheikh Abdullah's return from exile. Now he ignored the letter,

CHAPTER SEVEN

and instead discussed where we were heading next in a practical way.

My trips to Delhi resumed, now with the support of Jha's broad shoulders. He was very understanding, and felt that our agreement should stand in respect to both the extent to which Unilever would transfer its equity shareholding and the price at which we should offer it to the Indian shareholders. Eventually we all agreed, and I put the details before a special meeting of the shareholders in India to get their imprimatur. This was a delicate job, for even if Unilever held 90 percent of the shares, use of force majeure would have created a new crisis. The press, the stock exchange, and the shareholders already considered the price of the shares too high, and forcing a vote would have won us only a hollow victory. Though the agreement somehow went through at the shareholders' meeting, it was not without protest.

The year was coming to an end, and at last it looked as if my problems might soon be over. My love of results had made me introduce a weekly profit-and-loss account, ready every Tuesday afternoon. The results for 1962 had been mounting steadily: production, sales, and profits went up and up. In a developing country, good results give one a satisfaction all its own. With this alone, I felt I could face the angry shareholders. And then out of the clear Himalayan autumn skies came a bolt from the blue.

I was in Srinagar relaxing for a week-end with Ernest Woodruffe, Unilever's vice-chairman, and his wife Enid. They had only recently been married, and had come to India virtually on their honeymoon. Gärd and I accompanied them to Delhi and beyond. At Srinagar he told me one evening that he had heard that China had attacked India. Our first reaction was that it was no more than another border skirmish—that someone's picket had penetrated too deep. But it turned out to be much more, a short but full-scale war, of a kind that was to become typical of this part of the world in the years to follow. It brought to an end the first phase of Indian independence.

Chapter Eight

INDIA'S WARS

NINETEEN SIXTY-TWO was a testing time for the country. The uninterrupted progress of many years reached a watershed, marking the beginning of the end of the Nehru era. We had long pursued a policy of critical neutrality in the West, an appreciative neutrality in the East, and had made uncertain attempts at leadership in the Third World. In the early fifties, the world had taken some notice of Nehru's political stance and held him in respect. Even China had changed its attitude radically since the Korean War, when it had called India the lackey and running dog of American imperialism. In a world where no one trusted anyone else, Nehru, speaking for one of the poorest of countries, based his leadership on moral authority alone. This was something new for a head of state without conventional strength. For the West, Nehru combined a Western intellect and sensitivity with an Eastern message of peace. Those who were sick of wars and colonialism needed a neutral friend, a bridge to the communist world, and an example of modernity to the developing nations, to whom Nehru was a beacon signalling independence. In India we took pride in the friends Nehru made abroad and the return visits of foreign leaders. Among those who came to India were Bulganin and Khrushchev, Tito, Chou En-lai and, by a pleasant irony of fate, the queen of England, who but for the altered course of history would have come as our empress, and would certainly not have received the spontaneous welcome she did.

One of those who influenced Nehru in his predilection for neutrality was the first Czech ambassador, Bohuslav Kratochvil, who came to India in 1949. Returning home from England on the S. S. *Jal Jawahar,* the first Indian-owned passenger ship on the U.K. run, we got to know him and his wife. They had both been in German concentration camps, but talked very little about this experience, from which she seemed to have recovered well, but he only partially.

CHAPTER EIGHT

His assignment to India, a welcome break, was to a great extent a step into the unknown, and through me Kratochvil sought to get a feel of the new India. He asked me questions on Indian history and politics. He wanted to know about Nehru, and for this he had a source in the author Reginald Reynolds, a member of a pacifist group going to India for a conference who twenty years earlier had spent a year in Gandhiji's ashram.

A European intellectual and a socialist by conviction, Kratochvil was on a mission to the world's largest nascent democracy, which had also chosen socialism. He felt that his own country, European in its industrial and social culture, had something to offer India as a bridge to the Eastern bloc, while India also held the promise for the Czechs of a bridge to the Western bloc. The two sides of Europe could not stay divided forever, and socialism was bound to spread over the West, though probably not in its Eastern form. In case of a confrontation, India would be trusted by both sides to help in a disengagement.

In New Delhi, I dropped in on the Kratochvils occasionally, and he sometimes visited us in Bombay. Bohuslav told me how he had got close to Nehru, with whose intellectual make-up he had much in common. He talked about the fast-moving events in a world that was forming new alignments, and the role that India and Nehru ought to play. The new American hard line was distasteful to his European mind, while he could understand the Russian hard line as a reaction to the war and to American policies. No other country, he argued, had the strength to stand up to America.

Slowly there came a change. Boha was not so sure of his ground anymore; he no longer seemed acceptable to his own government. Prague had sent a new man to the embassy whose only function seemed to be to watch the ambassador. Eventually he told Nehru that he was going to quit his post and settle in England, where he might serve his country better than if he remained in India, thus possibly embarrassing Nehru.

Boha, his wife, and child managed to leave the embassy unnoticed; we saw them in Bombay, and waved goodbye from Ballard Pier. The news of the first defection of a prominent East European broke soon afterwards, and the press swarmed after them when the ship reached Aden. In London he settled into a small job, and there he eventually died in relative obscurity, one of the endless stream of men without a country that wars leave behind.

INDIA'S WARS

I believe Kratochvil had an influence on the shaping of Nehru's policy of neutrality, which he ultimately and unsuccessfully tried to modify. Perhaps Boha on his side felt too intellectually committed to be an apostate, even though the system in the end rejected him.

Nineteen sixty-two was the culmination of everything that Nehru had sedulously built up over the past fifteen years. It was the year in which his three policies—of democracy, secularism, and planned growth—were seemingly all bearing fruit. In fact, his every success had begun to raise the question of who would succeed him—a healthy sign. He must latterly have been asking that question himself. Once, thinking aloud, he expressed a desire to retire. The impulse went no further, but that did not stop people from asking the question he had asked himself.

Some years earlier, in 1953, I had met Louis Fischer, an American journalist who had written an engaging book on Gandhi, and he told me that he had just received a cable from his New York paper saying, "Cable two hundred words after Nehru what?" After a Roosevelt, a Truman; after a Churchill, an Attlee, he explained. According to this logic, if, by the time Nehru went, democracy had taken root in India, as Fischer thought it had, he would be followed by someone very unlike him, unspectacular, uncomplex, with no flair for international affairs or great projects, someone who would get on with all the day-to-day matters, the little things that Nehru was not interested in. Without realizing it he had outlined the type that in fact did succeed—Shastri.

Democracy had indeed taken root as Fischer hoped, as the test of the subsequent three wars, droughts and famines, two rapid successions, and the Emergency were to show. Whatever the occasional problems created by religious differences, Nehru had firmly headed us away from a theocratic state, the basis on which India had been partitioned. Numerous projects in the public and private sectors were coming out of gestation. Industrial growth reached 11 percent for the first and the last time. There was confidence abroad in the road we had taken, neither to the extreme right nor to the left. Many watching China and India must have felt gratified that the Indian path, too, seemed to be leading somewhere.

But something had already begun to happen. Our policy had begun to waver, and our reactions to contradict each other. In 1956 there was the expected reaction to the Anglo-French action in Suez, but Nehru unexpectedly held back over Russian action in

CHAPTER EIGHT

Hungary. Over Tibet he was ambivalent. Torn between historical logic and emotion, he threw away Tibet and lowered India's northern guard—as if to prove that Tibet's neutrality was a creation of British imperialism. There were other growing ambivalences, too, that could not be sorted out, presumably because while logic pointed one way or the other, emotion drew him in only one direction, to the Eastern bloc. After Tibet, there followed the Chinese movements in Aksai Chin, which we generously tried to ignore, or to settle through negotiations as we had always advocated, which did not work in the face of hard new realities. In the end we had to fight a war, which we were pushed into by the Chinese on the one hand and by our political and military advisers—Krishna Menon and his amenable, overpromoted chief of staff—on the other.

We knew very little about the Chinese. The only ones ever seen outside of Chinatown in Calcutta had been cloth peddlers on bicycles, who disappeared during World War II. Except for Hiuen Tsang and Fa Hien, who travelled in India centuries ago, they had never been featured in our school history books. Nehru's "historical brotherliness" made no impact, and it would have been better if Chinese friendship had been put to the people on some other basis, such as a good-neighbour policy, or community of interests with a people also making a heroic effort to rise out of centuries of poverty.

The rupture caused considerable bewilderment, more perhaps to Nehru and Krishna Menon than to the people. Our patience with the Chinese was wearing thin, the leadership declared. Despite our friendliest persuasion and repeated demands, they were nibbling deeper into our territory. We were now told that our brothers, erstwhile disciples of Buddha, seemed to understand only force—for once, when one of our pickets deep in Ladakh stood up to them, they retreated. If they continued their incursions, we might be pushed to act, though our forces were limited by comparison and concentrated against the wrong enemy, and our men were supplied with inadequate equipment. In the meantime we prepared erudite notes proving our claim to the usurped area, quoting *shlokas* from the Vedas in our favour, and even basing it on the old British boundary, the MacMahon Line. Nothing worked, neither erudition nor protests nor heroic noises. In the end, an inexperienced, quixotic chief of staff threatened to throw the Chinese out, and rushed to the area to assume personal command of the troops. That worked in a way, because the Chinese struck, and hard. Like the hordes of Jenghiz Khan, they swarmed down the passes and rolled us as far back as it suited them. We were outmanned, outgunned, and outflanked. And then as swiftly as they had come, having achieved whatever they had set out to, they declared that they were going back.

Reactions differed, but there was a common denominator: "And we called them brothers!" It perhaps did not occur to us that the faith in "two thousand years of friendship" was of our own creation, an idea we had foisted on them; or that in their realism the Chinese should not have been expected to overlook their own interests merely because we had cast the mantle of brotherliness—*"bhai bhai"*—upon them.

We are emotional, forever looking for objects on which to pin our extravagant expectations. We give what we can, but we certainly expect a lot, and we are often all too soon disappointed and disenchanted. I do not think we realize sufficiently how much our society conditions us to expect and receive. Our caste and joint-family system inculcate a belief in our fundamental rights irrespective of our capacity to return. Once I asked an English visitor sitting next to me on a plane what he thought of us. His answer was curiously direct. "What one does for you, you regard as your right and accept casually. What one cannot do for you upsets you greatly. One is judged not by the lot one may have done but by the little that one may not have been able to do. If only you occasionally showed some appreciation for what was done; sometimes even generously ignored what could not be done—or, better still, thanked one for at least trying—what a difference it would make! If only you had a simple common word for thanks; but you have to say it in English." We both laughed.

To our credit, India soon bounced back, and the memory of the Chinese invasion faded more quickly than was the case with similar incidents in many other parts of the world. We are not given to nursing grievances. Joint-family living teaches one not to sulk for long. The loss of distant, stony territory in the frozen wastes of the Himalayas, a mere speck compared to the fertile plains of Pakistan that we had left behind in the East and West, was soon forgotten. Adhering to our own logic, we even cont'nued to support China's entry into the United Nations. Had China but made a bold conciliatory gesture, we would have been *bhais* again.

One did wonder, though, whither our neutrality was leading

CHAPTER EIGHT

us, for at one stage we had severed relations with something like a billion of the world's people. While other nations that strongly, even violently, disagreed with each other, still maintained a reasonable degree of contact, we broke off relations with China, Taiwan, Pakistan, Portugal, South Africa, and Israel. Instead of cultivating benign patience and tolerance of all points of view, agreeing with some and disagreeing with others but taking sides with none, neutrality led us into a stance that was neither in our character nor belonged to our history. We have not traditionally held the past against others. When the British left, we parted with almost lachrymose ceremonial, and adopted and even improved on the trappings they had left behind: the viceroy's palace, complete with aides-de-camp and bodyguards, the coach and horses, bugles, "The Last Post," and "Abide With Me." In starched, immaculate whiteness, the new rulers learnt to walk stiffly past guards of honour. There was no rancour against those who till yesterday had been called oppressors and exploiters, and their conduct as rulers we now often treasured and faithfully followed. How could we, then, not be friends with a third of the world's population? Why did neutrality, which should have been benign and tolerant, make us as brittle as Westerners, who tend to see things in a stronger light where we usually manage to forget and compromise? In the past, we had minded our own business, but now neutrality had led us into a self-righteous posture: those who did not see things our way were in the wrong.

There was a certain amount of overreaction for a time, some necessary and some avoidable. Some who had approved of Nehru's policies for fifteen years now found them all wrong; some began rushing in small circles as if preparing to fight the war backwards. Nehru soon fell ill; typically one realized only from a photograph in a London paper that the illness was serious. The day after his stroke, our papers said that he was taking a slight illness as an opportunity to rest after months of overwork and strain, sitting in the afternoon sun and relaxing. The shock was considerable, for of all the architects of reborn India he was the second greatest, and now the only one alive.

The Chinese withdrew, their objective, as they saw it, presumably achieved. Left at that, it would probably have done the country and its economy no particular harm—if only, having failed to react in time, we had not overreacted afterwards. If the brief invasion gave a jolt to our ego, economic overreaction affected the foundations of new growth. This, some argued, was just what the Chinese had hoped for and expected us to do. Their calculation might have been that it would not only bring India down a notch or two in the estimation of the world, and especially of the developing nations, but also make us tie our economy in a knot. We went into a phase of brahmanical self-mortification and self-denial. Instead of strengthening the economy as a basis for a stronger defence, we began to tighten things up; impermissiveness took over in the name of conservation of resources. Just when we should have relaxed to produce more, we closed up. The finance minister was given the task of raising the necessary resources for doubling defence expenditure, and he set to work with a characteristic single-mindedness. Instead of spreading the burden over two or three years, the budget came down on the economy like a sledge hammer.

This was not our only war; there were three more, all with Pakistan. We Punjabis had accepted Partition in disbelief. Only when the flames began to singe us personally and mass evacuations began, from *mohallas* to city centres, and then to large evacuation camps where people were herded into guarded trucks, did we come to regard it as a reality. The convoys moved towards the main artery of the Punjab, the Grand Trunk Road; for countless centuries the path of the invader's sword and torch, the ancient road was now full of soldiers ferrying their own across the new border.

When all this was over, twelve million people had been evacuated to new homes. As the flames began to subside and the strangers settled down to a new life, our first war broke out. Again the Grand Trunk Road was full of military convoys moving to and fro, this time defending Jammu and Kashmir against Pakistan's so-called raiders, whose first waves were followed by professional armies as they erupted into a chaos of rape and looting. Then a real war began, the bulk of the men on both sides again being Punjabis. The cease-fire came after a weary eighteen months of fighting in the snows of the Himalayas; at times it was the highest war ever fought.

After the war, new roads and canals were constructed, and in sixteen years of peace the Punjab's face began to change. Many of the new farmers had left behind lands that their efforts had enriched in Pakistan. Their grandfathers, who had been tempted

CHAPTER EIGHT

away from their farms in East Punjab over a half century before with the promise of as much land as they wanted in the canal colonies, had marvelled at the combination of virgin soil and flowing waters. Today the refugee grandsons, back on the old soil, marvelled at the new canals from the Bhakra dam. When the water flowed for the first time through the new brick-and-cement, polythene-lined Nangal canals, the refugee farmers danced with joy, though old people who had heard of the upstream power stations feared that the water had lost its power to nourish the soil when the electricity, the *"bijli,"* had been taken out of it. By the 1960s, the Punjab was again flourishing agriculturally and producing surpluses of wheat, and even rice, of which it was very proud. It was once more the granary of India, besides inevitably being its sword arm and its historic no-man's-land.

In 1965, in the pleasant month of December, my wife and I returned to our Punjab. We had been invited by the Pakistan Lever company to visit them for a week. Relations between the two countries were steadily improving, and the many Punjabis who had visited Lahore and beyond had returned full of praise for Pakistan's achievements and the untouched beauty of Lahore. A Harvard group of economists went further, and found more right with Pakistan than with India. Its industry, agriculture, and exports were doing well at a time when India's pace, after the China war, was beginning to flag.

From Karachi, where at eighteen I had first seen the sea and sailed to England, we took a train to Bahawalpur state, where I had grown up under the mediaeval rule of a nawab in whose capital city the roads had been closed and men warned to stay indoors when the heavily veiled royal ladies were driven from one palace to another in equally heavily wrapped Rolls Royces. Aziz, an old trainee from the Indian firm who was now a director of the partitioned Pakistani half of the business, and his wife, provided us with discreet company in Lahore, ready to look the other way if something attracted my reminiscent gaze.

One evening I left Falleti's Hotel and stepped into the Lahore I had known as an adolescent by way of the Mall with its untouched late nineteenth-century buildings, a mixture of late Persian and British colonial, past the old bronze Sikh gun and the statue of Lawrence. The inscription to the effect that he had been willing to serve (or was it to govern?) with both the pen and the sword was in the early days of national awakening read as a blunt reminder of the conquest. I walked through the Gol Bagh, laid out in a circle, where out in the sun or under the shrubs and trees one studied during the cool months, up the slope past the Victorian Gothic of Government College, from where I had seen field-hockey players leave for the Olympics at Amsterdam in 1928. The world championship gave them no great thrill, for the world did not then know how to play hockey; many of them lived to see the day when an Indian team could not even get into the finals. At the Shahalmi gate I left the British city, and entered the old city ascribed to Rama's son Lava. The ambitious young widow of Ranjit Singh, Jindan Kaur, had literally handed over the keys to Henry Lawrence without a fight. I found it to the credit of those whose Lahore it was today that both the old and the new parts were left untouched, and had escaped the ugly growth that was enveloping the Delhis of Shahjahan and Lutyens. Here in old Lahore no modern traffic entered the narrow bazaars and lanes, with their overhanging carved-wood balconies. From the busy streets and *mandis* I nostalgically walked through the famous Hira Mandi, the diamond market, though a little too early in the evening for its bright lights, painted faces, and kohled eyes. The Pathan, Kashmiri, Dogra, Chamba, Kulu, Sindhi, and pure Jat Punjabi girls were still busy with their toilet after the siesta that had refreshed them for what they hoped would be a long night of singing, dancing, and love with old, young, and adolescents alike. From the Lahori gate I walked through Anarkali, the busiest, most prosperous bazaar of Lahore, with its brightly lit shops and restaurants, still the great attraction for all Punjabis. From there I returned slowly to Falleti's by way of the back of the Mall.

Next day we drove to Gujrat, eighty miles from Lahore, where I had gone to school and college. Around the old walled town time had stood still. Apart from some new suburbs, it was untouched. We stopped at the gate whence a narrow lane ran to the *mohalla* and the lane in which we had lived. Some doubt, discreetly encouraged by the man who accompanied us, prevented me from going inside the city, and after literally performing the proverbial Punjabi ritual of "touching" Gujrat, we returned to Lahore. From the Grand Trunk Road I caught a last glimpse of Gujrat through the sunset dust and the *shisham* trees by the wayside, a view I had seen so often when going to the river Chenab at Besakhi, the weathered, dark-brown mass of the fortress rising like a flat-topped cone in the city. Pakistan was busy with its

CHAPTER EIGHT

forthcoming elections, and all seemed peaceful. It came clearly to me that Partition was forever; there was no going back. All I met with, everything I saw, made it clear that the new Punjab was a purely Muslim land in which its Hindus had no place.

The skirmishes on the border of Rajasthan in the early summer months of 1965 seemed an ordinary affair. We did not realize that they were the prelude to a full-scale war. After the rains, the border between our Punjab and Jammu and their land was aflame again. It was serious this time, with squadrons of tanks and planes and army divisions engaged after the fashion of a blitzkrieg. It was strange in the security of Bombay to hear in the news the familiar names of canals, villages, towns, and suburbs, now pounded by tanks and planes. Shalimar gardens, Ichhogil canal, associated only with picnics by flowing water; the banks of the river Sutlej, where people used to gather for the bacchanalian spring festival of Besakhi; the reed marshes, the home of water birds—all were now the graveyards of disabled tanks. The war seemed a desecration of that peaceful countryside. The heroic announcements on the radio that our brave troops and their tanks, led by a Punjabi general, were reaching the suburbs of Lahore gave me a sick and hollow feeling deep inside. Would he shell the city, the Mall, the Government College, the *mohallas* and *mandis?* When he was forced back over the canal, it would not have made sense to a Bombay man if he had heard me say, "Thank the god who looked after Lahore."

As if all this was not enough, there was a third war five years later, in 1971, and again the borders of Punjab and Jammu were a battlefield. Again tanks and planes pounded our villages and towns. These recurring short wars did not, however, leave permanent scars, since we did not make vendettas of them. Though they drained precious resources that should have gone into growth, nothing held back the Punjab.

Chapter Nine

SHAREHOLDERS

ON THE first day of March 1962, I was flying back from Lucknow to Delhi with Aspi Moddie. The national budget had, as customary, been presented on the evening of the last day of February. The headlines screamed. I read quickly through Finance Minister Moraji Desai's preamble with an apprehension that built to a crescendo as I came to the crunch, the new taxes. It was a tough budget that sought, in the aftermath of the Chinese war, to raise large new revenues. I skipped over the personal taxes, quite unconcerned about how the budget might affect me personally, and hurried on to the corporate taxes, making mental calculations at a furious rate. "Oh no!" I found myself saying audibly. The profitability of the business, built up with such loving care through the year, adding each week's figures to the last, was shattered. My first full year's work lay in splinters, and I wondered what it would take to restore it. It seemed hopeless.

What had been imposed in personal taxation was probably a worse blow, but that seemed not to matter; what mattered was what happened to the company one was responsible for. My mind momentarily wandered back to the utter surprise of a shareholder at the last annual general meeting when he discovered that neither I nor the directors owned a single share in the company. "But what is your stake in the company, Mr. Chairman, if you own nothing of it?" he had asked. I now sadly recalled my answer— my professional pride in seeing the company and his interest in it prosper. I do not think he believed, any more than did a minister I worked under some years later, that one could be devoted to an organization, its growth and profitability, with a professionalism that excluded one's own interests.

As I grappled with the figures and their impact, a horrible thought came to me, at first slowly and then in a blinding flash. The thirty-five rupees as a rights value of the shares that I had

85

CHAPTER NINE

fought so hard to get from the government, and that we were now going to offer to the Indian shareholder, were now history. It would no longer be fair or relevant to charge this amount in the new circumstances. In fact the stock market would make its own judgment during the day and place a much lower value on the shares. Share values indeed dropped, and precipitously. By evening the stock exchange had to be closed.

Was growth, I wondered, forever going to run against a strong headwind, when surely it should have the wind behind it? Would one be fighting for it all the time? But there was no time to philosophize. Back in my room at the Ashoka Hotel, which I had left only a day earlier feeling generally satisfied with life, I returned to the fray. Aspi and I began to figure out the future. As after a flood or fire, one had to make a quick beginning somewhere. We felt the first and the right thing was immediately to withdraw the rights offer, so that the shareholders would be left in no doubt. We had many thousands of small shareholders who had implicit trust in us. If approached at thirty-five rupees, many would take up their rights at that price even now, despite the changed circumstances, trusting us to have offered them good value. Many would not even read the market quotations and, even if they did, the uninitiated would think we were expecting our shares to rise. We pored over a long coded cable to Unilever stating our views, and sent it off.

London reacted quickly and well. No delegation came flying over this time; instead Robert Siddons told me, in a long-distance call, that they were as shocked as I was, and asked if I would come to London to discuss the situation. They were not agreeable to my suggestion that we withdraw the offer, since it would look like weakness on our part in the eyes of both the government and the shareholders. I was satisfied, inasmuch as this time at least they were asking me to put on my hat and coat and fly over! All right, I told Robert. I would be over the following week, as soon as I had worked out the implications of a new plan and sounded out New Delhi. Back I went to L. K. Jha, and placed my views before him. To go to the market with thirty-five rupees under these circumstances would be immoral. We would have to withdraw the offer, and would return with a new plan as soon as things had settled down. In the meantime, we would state our intention of going ahead with the core of our expansion plans, though in a phased manner.

SHAREHOLDERS

Jha liked the idea, and I assured him in a letter on the same day that we had hope and faith that, despite the burdens arising out of the emergency and the new taxation, we would be able to press on with our plans. To show trust in the government and the economy, we would go right ahead when many were hesitating, however understandably. Jha also liked the financial arrangements I suggested. In principle, he was agreeable; but of course he had the government to consult and I had Unilever. In my heart I forgave the system for my past experience of it—even blessed it for such decisiveness.

I took the midnight Air India flight to London. When I arrived, there was more than the usual driver with a Unilever placard in his hand waiting for me at the exit of the air terminal; there was a young man who wondered if I could go straight to Unilever House for a meeting they had fixed for eleven o'clock. It was now half past nine. After a night flight of fourteen hours, the idea of meeting straightaway was sensible. I would be able to get the preliminary round of discussions over with, and sleep the evening and night through. Throughout that day I realized that whatever my intellectual capacity for a top position, my ability to take strain, both physical and mental, was at least a qualification of some order.

As it was, I felt more alert as the day progressed, and we decided to talk things through, so that I could see the special committee of the two chairmen, George Cole and Frits Temple, and the vice-chairman, Ernest Woodruffe, the next day, and leave the day after. Andrew Knox, chairman of the overseas committee, with a personal knowledge of India extending over forty years, agreed that we must go ahead, but he was sad at the turn things had taken. "It can only create more problems for you," he observed. "You are overreacting, and maybe you should not oblige the Chinese by responding this way. Anyway I am sure the special committee will accept your proposals, particularly as you have cut out the frills and dropped some of the projects, such as buying a biscuit company."

If Frits Temple had expected all this when he had questioned Lord Heyworth's judgment seven years before, at least he did not say, "I told you so." Lord Cole was anxious to proceed; compared with some of the hazards on his old African beat, the Indian budget was reasonable. If Unilever had any reservations about going ahead exactly as originally planned, my earnestness about

CHAPTER NINE

finding a way that suited both Hindustan Lever and the government must have made them withdraw them. Jasper Knight was silent this time, while I was vocal and insistent.

I felt sad this time at leaving Europe, which after its difficult early post-war years was now filled with vitality. I had never seen it so confident; a far cry from the Europe of the Great Depression; from Europe sliding into a war it did not want to fight but could not avoid; from Europe after the war, still in a state of trauma. Now it bustled with healthy activity, as it coalesced into the Common Market, with its back, one hoped, forever turned to wars. Europe was in an exhilarating mood of expansion and affluence, the ill effects of which had not yet hit it. We too had not long before been full of optimism. Now, after the Chinese "incident," as it was being called, we were suddenly in a suicidal "Johar" mood where economic policy was concerned. This should have been a time to build eagerly, freely, and confidently, instead of piling up new restrictions, quotas, and cutbacks, and strewing ashes on our heads. Europeans—the victorious, the vanquished, and the neutrals alike—were hitching their wagons to the stars, while we were digging ourselves into the ground. The early confidence of the Nehru era had given way to gloom, and he himself must have felt distraught and confused. The only one who looked confident and purposeful in midst of all this was Morarji Desai. Upright, austere, severe, and with a streak of self-righteousness, he went about the process of carrying out his brief with visible satisfaction. "This hurts me more than it hurts you," was his attitude. "Later Nehru blamed me, but that was his brief to me, and I did it. Why could he not have told me otherwise?" he said some years afterwards, when he was out of power.

In Delhi on my next visit, Aspi said there had been new trouble. Someone had twitted Desai in Parliament that, as an instance of the havoc his budget had caused, the chairman of Hindustan Lever had dashed off to London to tell his principals to drop all expansion plans. When I went to see L. K. Jha he said, yes, Desai had misunderstood the purpose of my visit to Unilever in London, which in fact was to persuade them not to proceed with the rights issue. Desai thought that, as his challenger in Parliament had charged, I had gone to ask Unilever to drop all plans for growth in India. I decided to speak to Morarji, and asked Jha if he would mind my telling the minister that I had seen him, and that he had agreed with my plans. Jha said he would not.

SHAREHOLDERS

Morarji's personal secretary, Tonpe, one of the kindest and mildest of men, who had long served his chief with great loyalty, saw my predicament and arranged a meeting practically without notice. He told me I could have precisely the time it took Morarji to travel by car from his office in Parliament to the Congress House, where he had a meeting. As the minister got into the car, Tonpe hustled me into it. Morarji sat in a corner, withdrawn into himself, engrossed in the file before him. Never had I felt so remote from someone a mere foot away.

"Yes, what have you to say?" he asked.

"I will wait, sir, till you have read your papers," I replied.

"No, I can do both, read and listen to you. Go ahead!" he said.

It was a disconcerting experience to talk to such a forbidding presence—if, in its remoteness, it could be called a presence. His face had a granite calm, and his voice was cold and resonant. There was something compelling about him. You could not but admire him, at least for being all of a piece.

"I came to see you because I believe there was some misunderstanding about the moves I made," I began.

"No, there is no misunderstanding about it," he replied. "You are entitled to act as you think best, but don't come to me for anything. I will have nothing to do with it."

"But this is exactly the misunderstanding," I persevered. "You have a feeling that I have acted wrongly. If you knew the position correctly, you would not think so. What I did was right, and the only possible decision in the interests of our Indian shareholders. I have discussed the matter with your secretary, and he agrees with me."

He suddenly turned from his file and looked at me with the first flicker of interest. "Oh, you have spoken to Jha—and he thinks yours was the right step?"

"Yes, sir," I answered. "He would be glad to explain it to you."

While Morarji had a reputation for being inflexible, his fairness and decisiveness as an administrator were also admitted, and those who had served under him always spoke highly of his trusting, supportive nature. But to one who had never met him before, this was not visible in a flash. The car reached its destination. As I left him he almost smiled, saying that he would have a word with the secretary. I gave myself a sixty-forty chance, because although he had heard me out, he was not known to change his mind easily. I

CHAPTER NINE

decided to leave things alone and await results. A couple of days later, I was at a farewell party at the flat of our vice-chairman, Jim Davies, when there was a call from New Delhi.

"Prakashji, this is Aspi here," Moddie's voice said. "I thought I would mention to you that I have got an appointment with Morarji Desai tomorrow to follow up our case and see if I can clinch it. Do you mind? I think I can manage it."

This shook me, since it was quite contrary to my intention of leaving Morarji alone, in case he felt I was pressuring him. Moddie's quick follow-up might irritate him; and yet I could not say no at this stage. He sounded as though he was raring to go, and I did not want to hold him back. I had to decide quickly.

"Yes, Aspi, by all means—and good luck," I replied. "I am sure he will listen to you."

A triumphant telex came from Aspi the following evening, saying matters were all settled; we could go right ahead with our plans. That night I slept long and well; in fact, good sleep was becoming a habit with me as stress mounted. Next day I took stock of things. What a victory, I thought, to be allowed to grow!

The final test came at the special meeting when I had to put the proposal to the shareholders for approval. We had expected a stormy meeting, but never so stormy as it turned out. Our new building, Hindustan Lever House, had its own auditorium, which was packed to overflowing. In the front row were all the familiar faces of the professional shareholders who went from one meeting to another. They were mostly old Parsis, with a few Gujaratis, to whom this was something to do in an otherwise dull retirement. At most places, they were given a big tea; at some, a gift of the company's products or a gift coupon. There was one among them who was always against everything we did, and I had to be very careful with him. He could hit out at any level that suited him, and many a great chairman had fallen victim to his ingenious, well-timed, sometimes quite unscrupulous blows.

There was a tension in the auditorium. When I walked up to the dais and bowed to the familiar faces in the front row, their smiles in return were wan. Speech followed speech, each battening on the criticisms of the one before. Some of the old Parsis waxed eloquent. How dare this foreign firm act so high-handedly, now that the empire no longer existed and the British ruled neither the waves nor India? First they had exploited the country and now they mulcted their Indian shareholders! Such treatment of the

SHAREHOLDERS

poor, underdeveloped, and downtrodden was a new and ugly form of imperialist exploitation. To this refrain the speeches went on.

Only two people were silent, my special shareholder and I. I said I was in no hurry and would like everyone to have his say, at any length he liked, because the subject was so important that I did not want discussion curbed. Eventually, after many had spoken twice and thrice, they demanded that I answer. I turned to our shareholder and suggested that surely he also had something to say. He said no, he would rather hear me reply to what had already been asked. The general strength of their feelings, in his opinion, must have registered well enough on me by now. This brought great applause. Without saying much, he had said enough.

It was ironic that, having persuaded first Jasper Knight and Unilever, then the government and my friend the controller of capital issues, and finally Morarji Desai, I now had to face the shareholders' suspicions. How isolated one can be! Unilever felt that I had let them down; Morarji felt I had let down the national cause in an emergency; and the shareholders made no bones about my having joined in Unilever's "exploitation." The company had, of course, sent me their proxy, for use if I had to decide by putting the matter to a vote, but this was what I dreaded most. To fail to convince the three hundred shareholders present, to have them vote unanimously against the resolution, and then to call for a poll and use the brute strength of the company's 90 percent to carry the resolution and the day seemed wrong.

I rose on leaden feet and began to explain that Unilever had made a generous gesture in not taking up the share of the rights due to them, but that they did not see why the other shareholders should not pay a fair price, especially at this juncture. The money thus received would strengthen the general reserves of Hindustan Lever, in which they, too, had a stake. In fact, it would be improper for the present shareholders in their own selfish interest to deprive future shareholders of a fair price and accretion to reserves. The profits belonged to the company, not just to those who happened to be shareholders today; a company existed in perpetuity. I went on to explain the whole record of Hindustan Lever, an enviable one of growth and fairness. We, the board members, had voluntarily refrained from buying shares, because our inside knowledge would give us an unfair advantage over the shareholders. In light of the

CHAPTER NINE

company's record, how could one be so misunderstood? I ended by saying that if, today, they were paying a few rupees extra, they would gain as much and more through increased future returns on a greatly expanded and strengthened asset. I was confident of our future and their share in it. Finally, after four hours of discussion, I appealed to them to unite in support of the management, and then called for a vote on the following motion: To make the rights issue at the price agreed upon with the government and regarded as high by the shareholders.

There was complete unanimity, except for "the" shareholder, who alone refrained, and while normally few bother to raise their hands, that night a forest went up when I asked who was for the motion. As I walked out of the hall, the old Scotsman who was the head of our firm of solicitors came up to me and said very kindly, "Today the mantle of that great chairman of Bombay, Sir Purshotamdas Thakurdas, should fall on your shoulders." I felt touched, but a trifle embarrassed. I had really pulled out all the stops.

Chapter Ten

MAYA

IN 1964 our eldest child, Maya, who had finished college, got married. When our children were small, my wife had been anxious that they should grow up as ordinary Indian children, without any feeling of being different from other youngsters because of having a foreign-born mother, and in this she succeeded well. In the early years, before we moved into a house of our own, we shared the ground floor of a rented house with a Punjabi couple, whose only son was like a fourth child to us. Their rooms were always full of Punjabi relations with children. We, too, kept open house, Indian style. The top floor was occupied by the owners, a Muslim joint family, where the children were also welcome. None of the women of the house spoke English. Gärd spoke only Hindi to the children, and she also had the Scandinavian idea that they should not be sent to school at an early age, which was regarded as strange in a country where children learn to spell and do sums at the age of four. So when she took them to Sweden in the summer of 1948, only Maya, aged seven, who had been to convent school in Bandra for a year and had learned English as a second language, could communicate with strangers. All three nevertheless played happily with Swedish children, and soon learned Swedish. At the end of their five months' stay they were fluent, but once back home they forgot it just as quickly. Gärd saw no point in their keeping up a language that was not likely to be of any practical value but would make them feel alien. Besides, now that Hindi was firmly established as their own language, they had to learn English.

Schooling in India has always presented a problem, traceable basically to the language conflict and our inability to establish a lingua franca. Most good schools in a town such as Bombay were run by Christian missions, and although India was independent, education in them was not yet geared to this fact. Geography still

CHAPTER TEN

started with the British Isles, and in the history books "we" meant the British. Indian schools, on the other hand, taught either in Gujarati or in Marathi, which made it difficult for children to move from one part of India to another. When Maya was nine, we sent her to Woodstock in Mussoorie, of which we had had good reports. A coeducational school, founded in the mid-nineteenth century for children of American missionaries, it had a reputation for good academic standards and strict American Protestant upbringing, while being nonetheless sufficiently secular and permissive in its own way. Generations of American children from all over India and neighbouring countries had studied there. I once met an American who fifty years earlier had gone to school there from Malaya, a fortnight's journey by rail, road, and sea. With the advent of international air traffic, children came to the Himalayas from the oil fields of the Persian Gulf. In the cold and snows of winter, the school was closed for three months.

Maya was a confident child, quite excited to begin with about this new adventure and all her new clothes. She had never had so many at one time, and was particularly entranced with all the woollies. Woodstock had no uniforms, unless one counted blue jeans with patched knees, something still outside Maya's experience. Into her black japanned tin trunk went clothes and toiletries and a generous supply of goodies. But on the day before leaving, she said she didn't want to go. "Then," said Gärd, "we shall unpack the trunk and lock up the woollies you don't need in Bombay." This made Maya reconsider her decision. Her younger brothers teased her, but were told to mind their own business. Their time would come, and then they would snivel like babies.

Next day at Bombay central station Maya boarded the coach reserved for the Woodstock party, with an eye firmly on her trunk. We waved goodbye, and she joined the boys and girls who were to be her companions for two days and two nights in the train, and for many years at school. That was the end of the Maya we had known, and as the Frontier Mail pulled away and her face faded into the phosphorescent darkness of the platform, I wondered whether separating the young from home was really an intelligent form of upbringing.

The decision to send her away to school was largely mine. Gärd, not being Anglo-Saxon, did not believe in boarding-school education; she saw no sense in separating young children from their parents. But she accepted my decision patiently, as she did so many of my incomprehensible actions. Boarding school was a British institution that had served British needs and culture. In India the British had built schools in the salubrious mountains, though they had always preferred to send their children to England if possible, even though doing so had often meant lifelong separation. There are pathetic references to the joys of childhood denied in the diaries of mothers quietly pining for their young ones, whom they were to meet years later as grown strangers. The system eventually developed a caste distinction. To the hill schools went the children of parents who either had settled in India, were of mixed descent, or were associated with the military. Only during the 1939–45 war did the upper-class British send their children to school in India. Run on British public-school lines, these hill schools taught Indian children to fit into life in India after a fashion.

The reasons weighing with me were the climate and the problem of daily commuting by bus or train from our suburb to one of the good schools in the city. There were convent schools in Bandra, and Maya had been to two of them, but their teaching methods seemed old-fashioned and uninspiring. To be fair, the period was one of transition. Independence and the new idea of secularism demanded adjustments, whereas these schools provided an education that centred on the Bible and Britain.

Gärd readily saw the benefit of Woodstock's higher standards of teaching, and from her own experience thoroughly approved of coeducation. But there were risks involved, for although Woodstock provided Hindi and Indian history for the Indian pupils, it was really meant to equip children for life in America. It was no more secular than Catholic education. Some teachers were broad-minded, with an interest in things Indian; others were very rigid in their Christian Protestant faith.

Maya took to her new school from the beginning. Her mind opened wide to Woodstock's teachings and ways. She was thoroughly happy, and made good friends with American girls and boys. She seemed to be developing very well in these surroundings, but as she entered her teens I noticed a growing alienation from Indian culture. Her accent, outlook, and ways, her conversation and interests, all began to point in one direction—to a continuation into an American life. It would have been hard to define what Indian culture was then, or for that matter is today, some twenty years later; but, whatever it was, Maya was growing into

CHAPTER TEN

an American girl whom nobody would have called Indian. She was becoming like the other girls at Woodstock, where most were American.

American culture, as I was to discover later, has a stronger pull than any other. I have known Indians who have lived in England for a lifetime, and yet their ways and accent have remained Indian; they could return to India and remain unnoticed. Not so those who have lived in America. American culture is infectious and insistent, and permeates others easily. It is a culture generous in giving itself, with none of the involuntary holding back of the British or the European. Two years at Woodstock had more influence on Maya than British-style public schools had on the Indian boys who were sent there. Many considered me somewhat British, with a frank withdrawal in the face of emotion and a self-control that to some bordered on unconcern, if not callousness. With most people there was a gulf that only I, not they, could bridge. Perhaps I was made that way, and the eight impressionable years of my youth in England had merely accentuated it. And yet, while the stamp of this culture on me was one of cold aloofness, on Maya the American stamp was one of warmth and open friendliness. It jarred, at times, but never froze one out. Whatever their comparative merits, why should I grudge Maya the stamp of a culture foreign to India, when the one I had acquired was equally alien?

I asked myself what I really feared. Was it lest Maya exchange an unidentifiable Indian culture for an identifiable American one? For that matter, was there an Indian culture? If so, what was it? The question baffled me. We did not even speak a language of our own, except to illiterates and children. To anyone even moderately literate, we spoke in English; and even when we spoke in an Indian language, our speech was spattered with English words and whole English sentences. We particularly needed English to express emotions or sophisticated thinking. We did not lack expressive equivalents in our own language, but when speaking English we used Punjabi and when speaking Punjabi we used English, so much so that a stranger could easily grasp the gist of the conversation.

What else did our culture contain? Few of us read books in any language; sadly, few ever read. Popular reading, outside of the English dailies, used to be *Reader's Digest;* now it is also *Time* magazine, and possibly *The Economist* or an Indian weekly; but it seldom goes beyond current affairs. In the arts, painting had switched from a revival of the Ajanta, Rajput, and Kangra styles to the European impressionists, later to give way to the nonobjective and abstract. Sculpture was confined mostly to diminutive statues of Gandhi, complete with glasses, and later of Nehru, to fit a small, crowded city's main *chowk* and suit the modest municipal purse. The most charming of all was a diminutive statue of Lal Bahadur Shastri, himself of small stature, with a garland in his hand and a Gnat aircraft hovering over his head, no doubt commemorating his 1965 Pakistan war. Sometimes the statues were covered with aluminium paint to give them durability, like the Gandhi statue at Bombay's Juhu Beach. This was in contrast to our consistently removing all statues left behind by the British of their generals, governors, and monarchs. Indian upper-class homes at the time were dull imitations of Europe. The renaissance of Indian handicrafts was just beginning; all else was Swiss cuckoo clocks and Japanese calendars. Under the British, the middle classes had acquired a patchwork culture reminiscent of E. M. Forster's description of Indian guests at an Englishman's tea-party. European dress, he wrote, was like leprosy on them, a patch here and a patch there.

Our culture, so called, has always baffled and also bothered me, especially as I have lived and worked in an international environment most of my life. By nature I am a good learner, with a high degree of imitativeness and an approach bordering on perfectionism. When I went to England at the age of eighteen, I gave myself over to English ways without hesitation or reservation, and without passing judgement as most foreigners living abroad do. I was going to live there for many years, so I decided to like English food, manners, music, and art; in fact I adopted everything, for better or worse. In the end, I could not see any trace of an Indian left in me. Upon my return home, it so happened that I joined a firm of the British north country, where I had lived during the formative years of my youth; consequently I fitted in perfectly. Before I lost it, my Lancashire accent even made some of my expatriate associates from Warrington and Liverpool homesick. But after Gärd came from Sweden to marry me, there was a change. I split in two: one half worked with the British, and the other half withdrew inwards.

As the first Indian among a large number of British managers, I stood out. While at work I learned fast and imitatively, totally absorbing their approach and style; socially I was completely out-

CHAPTER TEN

side their lives. In the office contact or familiarity with my peers was confined to work, with a few pleasantries occasionally exchanged. This enforced isolation was useful because it helped me to take to the learning process as if obsessed and to recrystallize in me what had originally been Punjabi but had become diffused over the years. Born and bred in the heart of the Punjab, West Punjab was all the India I had known. Now living in Bombay and travelling extensively gave me my first introduction to India. The Punjab was not India but a historical no-man's-land, only vaguely sharing India's culture. Punjabi culture was adept at survival, rising to heights of any kind only when misfortune laid it low, and I think some such atavistic change begin in me. Beneath the international, British exterior the Punjabi core began to revive.

Had I not worked in this foreign environment, but joined the government or an Indian firm, I believe I would have developed differently. Instead of becoming two distinct halves, I would have developed into a mélange of the kind E. M. Forster described. English and Punjabi would have fluently woven in and out of the same sentences like colours in bleeding Madras cloth, and I would have acquired an approach equally confused, as I was to find years later when I joined a government-administered business.

My friends Maurice and Taya Zinkin had lived in India until Partition, when Maurice left the civil service, and had returned after he joined Unilever. Possessing an insatiable appetite for knowledge of the country and its people, they engaged me in long conversations, remarking that I displayed a sensitive, though instinctive, understanding of things Indian. Despite my Punjabi core, I had apparently acquired more knowledge of India than the usual westernized Indian. They found our talks on the Punjab of special interest. To Maurice, who had begun his career in the ICS in Maharashtra, the Maharashtrians were the finest people of India, endowed with the austerity and keen mind of the Jews and a brahmanical tradition that matched his own rabbinical inheritance. As he began to see the Punjabis through my eyes and learn something about them, however, he grudgingly began to admire them too, albeit not nearly so much as Maharashtrians.

In discussing the Punjab and the Punjabis, I discovered that I had inherited a memory. For, after all, I had lived there for barely the first eighteen years of my life, mostly in lonely canal colonies and small towns; neither had I read anything in Punjabi. Watching people and their customs—the rituals of birth, marriage, and death, their lives of selfless, generous help and vicious intrigues—must have made a deep impression on me in my youth. I came to feel that I had inherited a cumulative racial memory of a sort. The Zinkins began first to suggest, and then to insist, that I write down all I could recall, before my memory dimmed and knowledge of the past died with the generation which the great Partition had exiled to every part of India. How much would my children know of how their forefathers had lived in a world now totally erased by Pakistan?

I was confused by the problem of Maya's Americanization and de-Indianization. Unfortunately, for me the Americanization was more obvious than the de-Indianization because the former was clearer than the latter. I also asked myself whether, in preventing Woodstock and its American culture from permeating Maya's mind, I was not also excluding their values, which were wholesome and better than anything our Indian schools could then give her. Just when a thousand years of Muslim hegemony had at last begun to produce a common Hindu-Muslim culture, the British had arrived with new and totally unfamiliar concepts. And whereas through the centuries of hard Muslim rule we had managed to retain our essential core, under the benign British we paradoxically began to lose it and to turn into a hotchpotch.

Thus my thoughts oscillated. There was nothing wrong in itself with what I thought was not good for Maya. And what I could give her in its place was unidentifiable and no better. When I broached the subject with her, she reacted sharply.

"Why, why should I change my school?" she demanded. "I am happy, I have good friends, I am doing well at my studies, the teaching is good. What have you got against it?"

I said I had nothing against the school. It was a good school, she was doing well, and I liked all her friends.

"Then?"

"Maya, it isn't easy to explain, but I'll try," I said.

I told her how I felt about her avid absorption of American culture, which was unfitting her for life in India. She would thrive if she went to America like the other girls. But when she left school one day to return to an Indian environment, she would have to readjust, and this readjustment would be more difficult and painful the longer it was postponed. She had derived a lot from her school, and these foundation years would prove useful to her, but now she needed an Indian orientation. She should move to a purely Indian school, such as the Maharani Gayatri Devi in Jaipur. This had originally been a school for girls of the Rajput princely families, but was now a good public school for Indian girls, under a new English principal.

Maya kept asking me to specify the American culture that I objected to. I did my best to convince her that I was not prejudiced, but that the American ways—let us forget culture—that she had assimilated were so different from our own that she would stand out like a foreigner. Perhaps in a country with a well-defined culture, one could be bicultural, as many Europeans were. There were Hollanders in Unilever who were as British as they were Dutch. But our case was different. Contemporary Indian culture, however one defined it, lacked the strength to withstand something as vigorous as American culture, and Maya had not yet found an Indian core.

Reluctantly she agreed to give the new school a trial. As she was a little late for the start of the term, I took her by train to Jaipur myself. Something of a hedonist, she enjoyed the luxury of air-conditioned travel as a start to a new life. She would be ahead of the other girls, who did not have her experience of international surroundings. The principal, who extended the unexpected courtesy of meeting us at the station, understood Maya's predicament and went out of her way to put her at ease.

Next evening, when I went to the school to take her out to dinner, Maya ran impatiently to the car. In a long red woollen coat, blue shirt, and a white *salwar,* her dark brown pigtails plaited with black cords, she looked so different. She talked excitedly about the school, the different systems, and how the girls were awed by her experiences. She stayed there three years and finished well, topping the list in Rajasthan in the Cambridge senior examinations. For this she got a gold medal, endowed by a local businessman, which she complained was wafer thin. Twenty-five years later she wrote me from Washington that, excellent though the schools there were, she wanted to send her nine-year-old daughter Ayesha to school in India. In view of her own experience, she felt it was the best thing to do.

With her brothers, Manu and Gautam, there was no such problem. They both went to Doon School at Dehra Dun, where there were only Indian boys, and they grew up entirely as Indians of their own kind. After college in Bombay, Maya married a Punjabi, by coincidence from Gujrat; his family's home had in fact been in the next *mohalla* to ours. He worked for an American bank, and later joined the World Bank in Washington. As for Manu, after taking a commerce degree in Bombay, he went to London to do his articles in chartered accountancy but, quite unlike me, did not like England at all. As have thousands of Indians now living in England, he met with racial prejudice, understandable perhaps, but no more tolerable for that reason. Gautam joined one of the old cavalry regiments of the Indian army. Both married Punjabi girls.

Chapter Eleven

HINDUSTAN STEEL

HIHDUSTAN STEEL, India's first and largest public enterprise, established in 1961, was having teething troubles. Its new, dynamic minister, C. Subramaniam, thought that its board should include an experienced manager who could help to introduce a management culture into its administrative style of operation. He invited me to join the board as a non-executive director. This provided my first experience of serving on the board of a major company in the public sector. Hindustan Steel operated four large steel mills, which specialized in a range of products, coal and iron-ore mines, and a fertilizer plant. It was large by any standards, with the added complexity that the plants had been built in collaboration with four countries. The Russians built a plant at Bhillai, the British at Durgapur, the Germans at Rourkela, and the Japanese an alloy-steel plant at Durgapur. Each country was responsible for building and handing over a going concern. If to all this industrial and cultural diversity was added the naiveté, indeed utter innocence of anything to do with steel or management, of some of those on our side who negotiated, coordinated, and ultimately ran the mills when they were handed over, confusion of a rare order may be imagined.

One story, which I at first considered apocryphal, turned out to be so true that one's mind boggled at the reality. Our chairman, who was retired from the civil service, went on a visit to the United States at the invitation of U.S. Steel. Its president, as the head of the world's largest steel company, decided to take personal notice of the visit of the chairman of the developing world's largest steel complex. He arranged a special flight to one of their plants to create an opportunity for a personal chat. No matter how much the American probed into Hindustan Steel's workings, he drew a blank from our chairman. He was genuinely interested in the operations of a steel complex in a country like India and in its technology, which was at least in one respect of the latest, especially as talks were going on then about the next and largest plant to be set up with U.S. collaboration. Our chairman, neither a steel man nor particularly sensitive to new technology and its operational performance in the Indian context, gave short, simple answers. Fortunately he did not talk authoritatively about things of which he knew nothing, a not uncommon trait of ours. Exasperated, the U.S. Steel president gave up, politely remarking, "Mr. Chairman, you are the most relaxed chairman of a steel company I have had the pleasure of meeting."

"Yes, yes," said the chairman happily, when I asked him about this incident. "He really was very impressed with my calm, relaxed way. He expected I would be tense and overwrought like high-powered American top executives. I am, as you know, a very relaxed person." And, as if to illustrate this, he sucked at his briar pipe.

Those responsible for the negotiating and planning were drawn from the administration. They came from the Indian Civil Service, the Indian Audit and Accounts Service, and the Indian Railways. The ICS men led the teams, helped by the finance men, whose expertise was not really in finance but in audit and control, in rules and regulations. The technicians were railway men, mechanical, electrical, signals, and construction engineers. An occasional metallurgical scientist or someone from industry assisted. I think there were emotional blocks in both the government and the private steel industry. The latter had two plants, one of them particularly successful. Government, setting up in competition with the private sector, was not anxious to learn from it, nor were the private firms anxious to teach the government anything. It was interesting that we asked foreign private industry, but not our own, for help.

The sensible thing would have been to do a clean job like the British government—to nationalize the two private steel firms, Tata and Indian Iron, learn to run them well, use them as nuclei, expanded and diversified, and then build new ones. Or else we should have given the private plants freedom to expand and diversify, to stand or fall in competition with the public-sector plants. This too would have made sense, but there was an ideological contradiction at work here, stemming from our tender-mindedness, which always creates problems. Letting private concerns exist without the freedom to thrive did as much harm to Tata and

CHAPTER ELEVEN

Indian Iron as it did to Hindustan Steel. In fact, Indian Iron declined to such an extent that the government had to take it over a decade and a half later instead of doing so when it was in full health. Fifteen valuable years were thus lost.

The men who did come from the private steel plants were not always of top quality, and required to work under civil servants who were unappreciative of if not oblivious to their skills and contribution, the best of them left in disgust. To man the new mills, we sent hundreds of young, newly graduated engineers to steel companies in the United States, the United Kingdom, Germany, and the Soviet Union for nine-month training periods. They went from shop to shop, mostly observing, and came back as steel men to run our plants. I encountered a group of them in America and gathered that they had done a poor job of learning. After joining the board of Hindustan Steel, I met them later at work in the shops and in groups socially in the evenings. They were generally a keen, bright-eyed lot, anxious to prove themselves, perhaps more so than to learn. Anxiety to please and impress is a fatal characteristic of ours at all ages and levels. I have always longed for but have seldom seen in an Indian subordinate a steadfast gaze, open and direct, combined with a capacity to listen intently and appreciatively, to agree without ingratiation, or to disagree with courage, politely but firmly. During their training abroad they were full of euphoria, straining at the leash, raring to prove themselves. I found this attitude disquieting, for it foreboded neglect of training that would create problems at the coalface. Moreover, I heard reports that they combined this longing to return with a characteristic capacity for travel—constantly visiting friends or relations among the vast numbers who live or travel abroad. Given affluence and freedom to travel, no Indian stays at home long. He is always visiting holy places or friends and relations, and today of course, "going foreign." I could well believe that with the discovery of the long weekend, easily extended on request, some took their training in a relaxed way. I doubt if they learned much in Britain. In West Germany things must have been a bit better, but the best job was done by the Russians, who put them to work as soon as possible, while the instructors stood by, taught, and watched. There was nowhere to go in the Soviet Union anyway.

I met many of them at the club in the evening at Rourkela, and they displayed a touching desire for opportunities to show their paces, held back by the presence of so many German technicians. If only the foreigners could be sent back, they said, they would get on with the job and show what they could do independently. The Germans were "experts" away from home, the boys argued, and not among the best; for why should the best, who had their chance at home, be sent abroad? In any case, no outsider could have the feel they had for their own plants in their own country. Although they talked with great fervour and conviction and I liked their enthusiasm, the rest left me unimpressed. No matter how keen our own young Lever trainees—a far more carefully picked and trained lot—I would have felt alarmed at the idea of their taking things over at so immature a stage. The irony was that here everyone was inexperienced, from top to bottom; no one had ever made steel before. But what bothered me more than their inexperience was their xenophobia in combination with a lack of the desire to learn. Their confidence did not impress one as much as a becoming diffidence would have done.

The German superintendent told me in answer to my question about the plant and the boys, "It is a fine plant, the latest in world steel technology, the LD process, one of the first outside Europe. It is a very sensitive process, fast and economical, and with it goes the rest of the mill, which specializes in flat products—not simple billets, bars, and rails—which of course makes it the more profitable. It therefore has to be run with great skill, and its most important demand is maintenance. Both these are matters of experience and care. The boys are a fine lot, keen and intelligent, and I have no doubt that in years to come they will make good steelmen, but you need more than a few months' training. They need to work hard at it. Steelmaking is an exacting task. A little neglect and there can be a snarl up, and a whole line has to be switched off. The workmen, too, are new and they also have learned their skills in this plant. Many are not far removed from the village, and their familiarity with machines is recent. In the skilled trades especially, we have some fine Punjabi Sikhs and Malayalis, but the labour from the neighbourhood is unskilled. The boys therefore have a double job, of learning themselves and of teaching others."

He knew the feelings of his Indian colleagues and anticipated my next question. "Yes, they can do the job, even now if they like. We shall be gone soon; sooner, if they wish; and even sooner if we had our way," he added with a tinge of sarcasm. "Rourkela is not a place that we are enamoured of. We are comfortable here,

CHAPTER ELEVEN

but our wives are lonely. There is nothing for them to do all day—the same movie house, the same club, the same swimming pool, the same faces. Of course they do manage to keep busy; German women will not remain idle. They have organized some activities, and run a school for our children, but they miss home. We do too, though work keeps us busy, sometimes round the clock. Yes, we will soon leave, because jobs are easy to get at home—in fact all of us were tempted out of our jobs because Mr. Krupp personally regarded this as one of the first major prestige projects abroad. It was good for the new Germany's image, and I think we have done a good job. Now it will be up to your people to show that they can complete it by making the plant run well and produce the items you so badly need for your development."

The German showed neither unease about remaining nor impatience to return home. He seemed imbued with only one idea—to leave behind a job well done. The Indian engineers began to collect around us, but he spoke on unperturbed. He had no complaints, no blame to apportion. One could, however, sense a little sadness at the lack of appreciation and the desire to see them go, which also carried the implication that they held plush jobs with nothing to offer that the locals could not do. To the German steelmen, with a dedication to work and generations of skill behind them, this must indeed have been gall to swallow. Three years earlier I had paid a fortnight's sponsored visit to Germany, starting at Frankfurt, going through the dense industrial belt, and ending at Hamburg. Because of their Indian connection at Rourkela, Krupp paid special attention to their Indian visitors. In Hamburg I stayed behind for a few days at the Unilever headquarters for West Germany, the largest and most prosperous in the Unilever group in Western Europe. In December 1960, Germany was fully recovered and affluent. While in Italy, France, and especially England the new prosperity had brought frequent strikes and a growing desire to take it easy, in German factories and offices work was still worship—Nehru's slogan that remained only a slogan in India, hardly ever practised. At Unilever's Hamburg office the working day was from eight in the morning till six in the evening. "Lunch break—no, we eat our sandwiches at the desk," they told me.

The German superintendent at Rourkela saw no signs of hard work, often not even a moderate amount. In the early sixties we were already taking it easy. When did we not, in fact, except during the three fortnights of the Chinese and Pakistan wars? Offices opened at ten, officials strolled in as late as half-past ten, and clerks slightly later. Then came the cups of tea and coffee. In the afternoon the exodus began soon after four. The workmen emulated this pattern.

The Russians at Bhilai, their biggest prestige project abroad, were different. To meet the board and local management, they arranged a party that began in the Swedish style with a single drink as we congregated at seven, followed by five hours at the table, so unlike the habit we had picked up from the British, and improved upon, of drinking on an empty stomach for so many hours that most people say goodbye as soon as they have finished dinner. At Bhilai, as in Sweden, you did not drink alone; someone toasted you. As is customary among Russians, it was a stag party, and the drinking was perhaps unusually heavy. But with food it did not appear burdensome; both time and liquor flowed smoothly and fast. The conversation was mainly through interpreters. Some of our men had picked up some fluency in Russian, but the hosts preferred to use their own interpreters, among them a particularly charming girl, the only slim Russian woman I have met. Someone told me that she used to joke about it: "What Russian will ever marry me? I am not even 140 pounds."

The Russian superintendent was not unlike his German counterpart, large, bluff, competent looking, but with no conversation. Here our men did not talk leave-us-to-do-the-job or express anxiety to take over. The number of Russians was large and remained so. I believe they deem this necessary even today. They did not attempt to mix, certainly not to fraternize. They mostly lived at Bhilai Hotel, which belonged to the plant, one family per room, keeping entirely to themselves. No questions were asked, no answers given, and there was no discussion. They took their own decisions. Neither were there any interpersonal problems. The Russians had come to do a job of work, and would stay as long as they considered necessary. This still seemed to be the case fifteen years later. And as for production, Bhilai has been the most successful of all the plants, notwithstanding its simple technology.

At Durgapur very few British remained after the construction stage. They lived a life apart, like their governing predecessors before them, which meant some recrudescence of the old problem of real and imaginary affronts, an aloofness misunderstood all over again—though I gathered that the fault partly lay with a

CHAPTER ELEVEN

pompous and status-obsessed man we had appointed from our side. The British, like the Germans, decided to leave as soon as possible, not to overstay their welcome, and to escape operational recriminations, of which there had been enough already. Oddly, when C. Subramaniam took over the ministry, he made the bold decision to keep on Douglas Bell as general manager at Durgapur for two years longer. Bell was given two men to groom, and was asked to recommend one of them to succeed him. Of course we chose the one he had not recommended, and when the plant ran down, Bell was roundly blamed for having flogged it to achieve near-capacity production during his own tenure. This I could hardly believe of him, for he shared the feelings of his Russian and German counterparts about steel mills. He was a Scot, born and bred in steel, handpicked for the job by the British consortium, and knighted after he left—small consolation for the criticism we gave him gratuitously and in good measure. I talked more freely with Douglas Bell than with the formal German; with the Russian one had no contact. They all represented a fine dedication to steel and to their respective plants. The successors we hastily turned out were naturally of a different type, but I wish I could have found in them the basic quality of steadfastness and strength that living with steel had instilled in their foreign counterparts. In any case, none of our three plant managers was a technician.

I went carefully prepared to my first board meeting at Hindustan Steel, ploughing through the voluminous agenda that kept pouring in. It began in Bombay; then there were the papers waiting at the Hindustan Steel guest house in Calcutta, more on the company plane waiting at Dum Dum airport to pick up the visiting directors, another lot in the car waiting at Ranchi airfield, more at the Ranchi guest house, and the final instalments in the boardroom, where papers kept arriving throughout the meeting and last-minute supplements were placed on the table after the agenda had been dealt with. It all showed a tremendous, but suspect, keenness to finish as much business as possible in anticipation of the following month's meeting. After a while I saw in this enthusiasm a bad habit, and came to the conclusion that whether the board met weekly or annually, the agenda papers would still have flowed down like the irregular and ever-swelling current of a mountain stream. The agenda itself consisted of papers of varying sizes—quarto, foolscap, double foolscap, some pages folded upwards, others sideways, and yet others folded

HINDUSTAN STEEL

both upwards, sideways, and at the corners. And then I wondered whether there was not a method to this madness, and a degree of gamesmanship involved in submitting the agenda in inverse order of importance, so that some important items were placed on the table last, after the meeting.

The text of the agenda was typed downwards, but the statements and tables read in all directions. The mass of facts and figures was truly breathtaking. The introduction to each case reached as far back in time as possible and pursued its slow course down to the present. References, cross-references, correspondence with the ministries, state governments, contractors, management, and others—all was carefully reproduced. Dozens of columns and hundreds of figures filled the statements, but there was nowhere an attempt at evaluation, assessment, statement of alternatives, or recommendation. At the end came the charming euphemism for indecision, "The Board may kindly decide." The board always had to do everything with kindness—kindly be informed, kindly consider—and the ultimate in kindness was to give a decision. It was the same comical circumlocution one found with Indian Airlines, where everything, including frequent delays, was announced for the "kind" information of the passengers. Thus, too, the East India Company, literally translating a customary courtesy from Persianized Urdu, used to refer to itself as kind, generous, honourable, gracious, the fount of everything, *bahadur*—the brave. The same spirit still endured in generous references to the Hindustan Steel board. The board would kindly recall that they had been pleased to consider this matter, and that they had kindly decided and directed, etc. The directors were, however, addressed as plain "Shri," with no reference to our personal courage, achievements, or attributes.

As a classic touch, the agenda's several hundred pages were pierced and joined with a candy-striped string, and the whole thing tied on a flat board with side flaps, grey-white tapes replacing imperial red. I was not surprised when, the next year, I began to receive similar agendas from the venerable Reserve Bank of India; but coming from Hindustan Steel in relation to the LD steel-making process, R&D, or the purchase of a new executive airplane, it looked anachronistic. Besides its antiquated appearance, the agenda's wealth of facts and figures was more than I could assimilate, despite my love of and familiarity with figures. As was only to be expected, the agenda set the tone for the board meetings, which

CHAPTER ELEVEN

could seldom rise above matters of detail. There was little chance for policy discussion.

What puzzled me, in my first experience of a government undertaking, was the whole new world of non-management. Brought up on systems and predictable behaviour patterns, I was astonished to encounter a world of non-systems. The agenda served as an introduction, but what followed was sometimes downright bizarre. At one meeting the chairman read out a letter from the secretary in the steel ministry suggesting that the board might consider passing a resolution along certain lines, but adding that it was not the government's intention to lay down what the board should decide, nor did they wish to direct it in any manner. Without treating this letter as a directive, it would nevertheless be advisable for the board to act in the manner suggested, naturally exercising its own judgment and prerogative to decide. The chairman explained that the government actually had powers to issue directives in the name of the principal shareholder, the president of India, but it appeared in this case and many others that the government would rather tell us what to do than formally direct us. The secretary wanted us to treat his letter as advice and not as a directive, but to act as if it were the latter, so that, while we decided in our own best judgment, it should be in the way the government had determined. The letter concluded with a request that the chairman should let him know that we had done so. I asked the chairman to tell the secretary formally that we had indeed done so; and also to assure him that we appreciated his concern for our autonomy as a board. The chairman laughed wryly, and said, "Join the public sector—you will enjoy it hugely." It was the secretary who received his just reward by being elevated to a highly decorative post in which nothing he did was ever right and nothing ever wrong; he simply did not do anything.

The chairman and the board could not do much without consulting the ministry, which took an all-pervading interest in the company. It was always argued by the men from the ministries that, as they were responsible to Parliament, they had to know what went on to guide the board in a way that prevented trouble with the legislature. Parliament, of course, treated the ministry and the company alike. The company was therefore at the receiving end of both, and both were as free with advice as with criticism. The legislators could as easily deal directly with Hindustan

HINDUSTAN STEEL

Steel's units, sub-units, and individuals. They made recommendations for jobs and contracts, demanded information and facilities, and generally acted in a privileged manner.

I became quite engrossed in Hindustan Steel, and was asked to draw up plans for a management information system and a new corporate plan. I suggested that the three main steel plants be made into subsidiaries of a holding company to be formed out of the head office at Ranchi. Each plant-company would be a corporate profit centre, responsible to its own board, whose chairman would be the plant manager. The latter would also be a member of the holding company board. Finance, research and development, senior personnel, dealing with the central government, buying abroad, and such matters would be handled by Ranchi. The scheme was received with great enthusiasm, but while the chairman was sympathetic, it somehow got nowhere. I realized that to them, bred in their administrative systems, it made no sense. It was perhaps regarded as fanciful; such a system might work in private industry and suit international companies, but here they were up against local circumstances—and auditing. And how would it help produce more steel or solve labour problems?

As someone new to the administration's psychology, I could not understand how they expected an industrial undertaking run wholly on bureaucratic lines ever to produce results. The two outlooks were quite different. Outdated enough in its own sphere, the administration was a worse misfit in the job the new enterprises were set up to do. The railwaymen, the civil servants, the audit and accounts men, competent in their own fields, all brought their own manuals, forms, and systems of filing and notation—evolved a century earlier as a foundation for the relationship between the districts and the centre—to the steel mills. Hindustan Steel thus became two worlds, the one that operated the new technology, and the other that controlled everything through an antiquated system not suited to industry. The two worlds blamed each other for their respective failings. The managers felt they were always being thwarted, while the administrators disapproved of the liberties taken and the corners cut in the name of increased production. Both were right in their own way. This difference in psychology manifested itself at board meetings in mutual recriminations. If the finance men had ever had a point, it had been lost long ago. If the production men had one, they never seemed to make it; they merely argued like the young engineers at Rourkela—leave us

CHAPTER ELEVEN

alone! That financial controls and freedom of production could be made to work jointly never occurred to anyone. Each fought the battle for his own base line. The only victim of this permanent schism was Hindustan Steel and any risk taking or venturesomeness that it might otherwise have exhibited.

With the sudden departure of Subramaniam, the minister who had been infusing some life into Hindustan Steel, to the Ministry of Food and Agriculture, where his drive was equally needed and where he did indeed give a boost to the introduction of the new varieties of wheat, the company began to sag. With characteristic imaginativeness, the minister, the secretary, the chairman, and the plant managers were all changed at the same time. This was not a conscious clean sweep, simply a coincidental routine change, to which no one gave any thought. And once again, the new men were not steelmen. They put in Banerji, the plant manager from Rourkela, as vice-chairman, to act as chairman indefinitely. He didn't know whether he would be confirmed as chairman or sent to the New Delhi secretariats. I called on the new minister to offer my services in case he wanted to consult me on anything. I suggested that he visit Ranchi and meet the board to acquaint himself with our problems. His eyes lit up for the first time, and he said he would very much like to visit a plant and address the workers. As for the board, yes, he might meet them too—but he showed no enthusiasm.

I wondered later whether I had been right in not accepting the Subramaniam offer. As I outlined my plans for reorganizing Hindustan Steel, he had listened with interest and had asked me if I would take over the company. I felt embarrassed because I did not wish my interest to be misunderstood. In any case, I explained, it was too soon for me to leave Lever. As their first national chairman, I had the task of grooming an Indian successor who was being moved up by stages to prepare him for the top post. To leave at this juncture would compel Unilever to send out an expatriate chairman, which both they and I would consider a pity. Subramaniam understood, though he asked me later if I would take over the Bokaro project, the largest steel plant, which was going to be built with Russian help after American collaboration had failed to materialize.

It was sad to see Hindustan Steel—this great dream of Nehru's, an international venture with so many industrial partners in the developed world—shrink into a sick and limping entity. In 1968

HINDUSTAN STEEL

Chandy became chairman of Hindustan Steel. He faced the accumulated problems of nearly four years of neglect, a minimally cooperative administration, a restive Parliament, and a hostile Left that one would have imagined to be close to him emotionally and ideologically—something that must have pained him more than the rest. Labour problems became acute as a consequence of bitter inter-union rivalries. Management was demoralized by constant political and labour pressures, which became truly cruel at one stage. No one helped; many hindered. Each time I met him, Chandy looked sadder, and his ulcers seemed worse. Ultimately, after three years of heroic effort, he threw in the sponge and left. There was no inquiring why had he failed, what had gone wrong, what could have been avoided. Though there was another reshuffle at the top, things were no better. In 1961, the first year of Hindustan Steel's operations, India produced a total of 3.1 million tons of steel; in 1970, 6.1 million tons; and in 1975, 6.4 million tons. Based on this progress, a minister made a statement in 1975, brave even for him, that India would manufacture 100 million tons of steel annually by the year 2000!

A simplistic solution caught everyone's imagination in 1971 as a panacea for the ills of the company. One evening over dinner the new minister, Mohan Kumaramangalam, outlined his plan for a holding company, the Steel Authority of India, whose chairman would also be secretary in the Ministry of Steel. It would hold shares in Hindustan Steel and its subsidiaries, and also in the two private steel companies to the extent that government financial institutions had given them loans. I thought the Steel Authority a good, bold concept—provided the system's weaknesses were done away with and not allowed to bedevil the new setup, as had been the case with each reorganization in the past. I had doubts, though, about his second idea. Combining chairmanship and secretaryship would doubtless shorten the organizational links, but while solving one problem, it would create another. A secretary in a ministry is a permanent civil servant who guides and serves the minister in his dealings with the public, Parliament, and the cabinet, and also coordinates tasks that concern other ministries, which in the case of steel were many. Directly and indirectly, he has to deal with the ministers of finance, home affairs, petroleum and chemicals, labour, planning, foreign trade and commerce, supplies, railways, and transport; in fact, with almost every portfolio except those of health and family planning. Looking after the

CHAPTER ELEVEN

minister through three sessions of Parliament lasting nearly seven months, each with an avalanche of questions; attending the many parliamentary committees; coordinating matters with other ministries both at the centre and in the states; attending numerous meetings—would all this leave the secretary-chairman any time to run the vast agglomerate that was India's largest holding company? Whether he was chairman or secretary-chairman, what mattered in the end was the freedom of action he enjoyed.

I suggested that the secretary might fall between two stools, and make neither a good chairman nor a good secretary. Besides, the two jobs called for rather different skills—one of industrial management and the other of administration in a political setup. And if the idea was to stop interference by the secretariat, this could easily be done by just stopping it. An understanding could be reached that the chairman would consult the secretary and seek his help, but that he should have direct access to the minister. In fact, the three of them—minister, secretary, and chairman—could work as a team. However, I wished him luck. Whether or not the idea worked well, Kumaramangalam's successor unceremoniously dismantled the whole arrangement without review or analysis because he did not like the secretary-chairman. And his successor changed everything again.

Chapter Twelve

A NEW BUSINESS SCHOOL

AS A result of the deep personal relationship that I developed both with the city and with two remarkable intellectuals, Vikram Sarabhai and Kamla Chowdry, Ahmedabad played quite an unexpected role in my life. It began in 1956, with an invitation from them to the annual conference on human relations sponsored by the Ahmedabad textile industry's research association (ATIRA). This was the first of its kind in India, I believe, and provided an opportunity to meet interesting personalities in the teaching and practice of management, human relations, and the social sciences, from India, the United Kingdom, and the United States.

ATIRA, which Vikram had founded, was the first institution in India to marry industry with science and had the additional novelty of being interdisciplinary. Besides research and development in the textile industry, its purview included statistical quality control, marketing research, industrial relations, and financial management. Vikram was perhaps the first institution builder in India to look beyond the single dimension of the core of activity and its disciplines. Where others saw things on a single, flat plane, he made them multidimensional. In fact, I sometimes had to remind myself that he was basically a physicist. The physical research laboratory which he had founded at Ahmedabad was the only place where one recognized him as such. Elsewhere one saw in him a manager, a humanist, a new type of world citizen.

He was of medium height, unusually light-skinned and grey-eyed for an Indian; what attracted you right away when you met him were his large head and boyish face, and a sincerity and openness of a rare kind that shone through. He at once engaged in animated conversation, making whatever you said seem interesting to him. Whatever the subject, his interest was genuine and deep, and if it was unfamiliar he listened avidly in order to learn. At the same time he was rather naive, especially about people as

CHAPTER TWELVE

people. He judged them as he did himself. He lived only for whatever he had taken up; his world was his own world, to which no one was barred but which few entered deeply—perhaps only Mrinal, his wife, a dancer, and Kamla, an academic. For the rest, Vikram's life was full of his own activity, an antechamber always crowded with people from all over the world.

Vikram was so essentially an institution builder that I wondered if he could really have been a researcher—unless it was that, like so many of our real researchers, he, too, had gone the way of administration. His interest in research had overflowed into creating an institution to encourage the growth of knowledge about the subject rather than into making a personal contribution to it. I do not think he added anything himself to physics, industrial research, or management—he did not have the time—but he widened the horizons of the men who trained and did research in those fields. It is significant that, of the plethora of institutions we have built in India since independence, his were among the exceptions that flourished: textiles, management, space. Whatever he built conveyed his characteristic refinement and sense of excellence. Whether it was a personal relationship, a building, or its landscaping, one could see his hallmark. Vikram was a restless man: his mind and body never stood still. Instead they raced together towards a rendezvous with fate until his body could keep up the pace no longer, and both came to a stop. He died young and suddenly, but to me not unexpectedly.

Over a period of, say, three weeks, Vikram's schedule might not untypically take him to New Delhi, Boston, Berkeley, Paris, Vienna, New Dehli again, Srinagar, Gulmarg, Bombay, Ahmedabad, and Cochin, in what was virtually a single itinerary, attending conferences, seminars, lectures, and negotiations. I would see him in a huddle with his assistants at an Indian airport, in between a domestic and an international flight, receiving reports and giving instructions, with his secretary taking notes. At a management program in Srinagar, Kamla would receive a call from him late at night to say that he had just arrived from Boston and was on his way to Ahmedabad; he was thinking of flying over to Srinagar for a day to discuss what the Harvard Business School faculty had suggested and what Ken Rice had to convey to her from the Tavistock Institute in London. Eminent in their own fields of physics and psychology respectively, Vikram and Kamla together pioneered the nascent area of management in India, which owes

A NEW BUSINESS SCHOOL

much to them. But they were yet more remarkable in their mutual empathy, a refinement of sensitivity which was rare then in India and probably always will be.

Vikram and Kamla fitted together perfectly, like the tenons and mortises of a dovetail. Together they helped build India's first institution of management education. He spoke freely and projected easily; she had to define her thoughts carefully before she expressed them, and then did so only hesitatingly, as though shrinking from each answer. He could think on his feet, while her voice dropped when faced with an audience of more than two. He advanced, while she withdrew. She had to feel wholly at ease, almost at a level of intimacy, before she would speak out; he was at home anywhere.

Kamla, a Punjabi Khatri from Lahore, was a product of Shantiniketan, the sylvan university founded by Tagore, which she attended at a time when Punjabi middle-class girls traditionally went to McLagen, Queen Mary, or Kinnaird of Lahore, all Christian and British Colleges, and never ventured into coeducation. Only a few girls of a daring, nationalist, artistic bent had begun to go to Shantiniketan. There, instead of learning to play the harmonium and sing as a qualification for matrimony like other Punjabi girls, Kamla learned sensitivity and aesthetics, with singing, dancing, and flute playing. From there she went on to Calcutta University to study mathematics, and at twenty married a young civil servant of her own choice.

Thence she would have slipped into a placid life of children, relatives, affluence, and domesticity, ending up as a secretary's wife in New Dehli, in a cream-coloured bungalow with a large unkempt garden on Akbar Road, but for the tragedy that befell the couple only three months after their wedding. It was one of those senseless killings typical of West Punjab. Her husband, in his first spell as a magistrate, was trying a man who, when he realized that he might be convicted, naively imagined that by removing the judge he would put an end to his trial. So, their honeymoon barely over, Kamla's husband was murdered, and she returned to Lahore and lifelong widowhood, not yet twenty-one. Slowly she picked up the threads of her life. Convinced that there would always be tears in her eyes—an old woman had prophesied this—she determined never to remarry and instead launch a career in her own right, an unusual decision in those days. From mathematics, she turned to psychology, obtaining a master's degree,

CHAPTER TWELVE

and decided to take her Ph.D. at the University of Michigan. The war had just ended, and she made the long journey, her first abroad, on an American troopship. Her stay in America, and the subject she studied, moulded her into a new and unusual personality. Living in a world of men, with a subject that developed an intense maturity of mind, but one that was rarely studied by women in India at that time, she had neither small talk nor time for any but serious company. Yet with it all she was deeply feminine, and wanted always and only to be treated as a woman, even when one might understandably have treated her as a man. If, in an argument, one failed to make the customary allowances, she would withdraw in hurt. Working among men on equal terms, she still demanded the conventional privileges she was entitled to as a woman. She wanted, as it were, an unequal equality.

I saw Vikram and Kamla together at conferences, and there always appeared to be a perfect rapport between them professionally—an aura of deep relationship. His colleagues in science, in India and abroad, accepted Kamla, as her colleagues in human relations and organizational behaviour accepted him. They dreamed of founding and nurturing the new institution of management at Ahmedabad together, and watching it grow. Their conversation always centered on human relations and management, seldom on current affairs or people, except when they were discussing individuals in their respective fields.

When, on the death of Homi Bhaba, the eminent pioneer in the atomic-energy field, Vikram succeeded him, Kamla began to study Bhaba's contribution to the organizational growth and structure of the Atomic Energy Establishment. She argued that, unlike others in India who first built institutes and then manned them, Bhaba had created institutions around men. If he found a man to be outstanding in a discipline, he gave him a new department, with freedom to build and develop it as he liked, and left him to recruit his own subordinates. This is how she and Vikram had built, too.

At my first ATIRA gathering in 1957, I was vaguely conscious of Kamla, flitting like an apparition along the aisles but nonetheless seeming an important part of the conference. I recognized her name from what I had heard about her husband's tragic death. With one shoulder bent, her head at an angle, bag and papers under her arm, she moved around organizing the conference as though by remote control. The only time she appeared openly

A NEW BUSINESS SCHOOL

was when she nervously climbed the steps to the platform and made an announcement. In the afternoon, the conference broke up into study groups, and at one of them I saw her with Vikram and a small group discussing their experiences on a recent visit by a textile team to Japan. She sat with her leg folded on her chair, listening intently, while he talked freely. Although never categorical, he was always pleasantly sure of himself. She sometimes endorsed what he had said, and would occasionally steer him in a different direction, which he seemed to like. Vikram's face would soften into that rare smile, when he was at his handsomest, and he would look approvingly at her and pursue the new line. She seemed to be his monitor, and so long as she listened silently, he felt he was on the right track. He would see her on his way home, and together they would go over the day's discussions and decisions, and plan the next. When in Ahmedabad, he would drop in at Kamla's for coffee in the morning before he began his day.

The Indian Institute of Management was Vikram's brainchild, supported by Douglas Ensminger, the director of the Ford Foundation in India, who had first mooted the idea of management education in India. He had suggested to the Indian and U.S. governments that two institutes of management along the lines of American business schools be formed in India. Two professors, one from Harvard and the other from Chicago, came out to survey the scene. They were an odd pair, with an odd music-hall combination of names, Miriam and Thurlby. I was invited to a meeting in Bombay in 1957, where they met a number of executive and academics. I was not surprised when Douglas Ensminger later told me the gist of their report—that what India needed at this stage was not business-management education, but plain education. They were right in their own way, but they ignored the simple fact that the process of growth is not orderly and logical or for that matter sequential. Indian Airlines, for example, could not have waited on our prefecting the bullock cart.

In the next year Dick Miriam taught me at the Harvard Business School. Undoubtedly brilliant, he was staid in contrast with the other professors, some of whom were colourful and taught the ordinary, prosaic subjects of management vividly and with verve. One incident memorably illustrated for me the reputation he had acquired, which had given him the affectionate nickname "the Iron Duke," well justified by his austere exterior. We were discussing the case of the president of a medium-sized company

CHAPTER TWELVE

that had gone badly wrong. These case studies were post-mortems of past situations from which we drew lessons for the future. What had ultimately happened to the president or company involved was not considered relevant. In this particular case, hardly any of us could see anything right with the president. At the end of the class, one enthusiast, whose sense of justice had been outraged by this unanimous criticism, began to plead for the man. The president was no fool, he said; he knew what he was doing, and although his first failures were obvious, they were merely the teething troubles of the change he was introducing. We must not judge him conventionally; events were bound to have proved him right. The president's lone supporter stopped us in our tracks, and many of us began to retrace our steps. Perhaps there was something in what he said after all; perhaps we had gone too far. We all began to atone for our harsh judgment.

As the Iron Duke was leaving the class, the enthusiast called after him, "Professor"—Miriam was the only one who was never called by his first name; to call him Dick would have been unthinkable—"as this firm appears to have been from the Boston area, do you know what happened to it?" This was a bold departure, as it had been made clear to us that the identity and the fate of the companies that chose to remain anonymous should not be asked. Large corporations were nearly always identified, and everyone knew their fate, but smaller companies usually chose anonymity. Miriam turned around with a look of surprise and with more than his usual severity, but then gave a faint smile. "Oh, yes, I knew the man," he said. "As the case showed, things became so bad that the firm had to wind up." Here he paused dramatically. "The president couldn't take it—he shot himself." And with this the Duke walked away.

No wonder Miriam felt that we in India were not ready for the sophistications of management theory and its teaching. Vikram Sarabhai and Douglas Ensminger persevered, however, and brought out a very enthusiastic person, Dean Robbins of the University of California, Los Angeles, on the strength of whose glowing report Ensminger and Vikram approached Harvard. Harvard sent out a team consisting of Dean Fox, of its foreign operations section; an equally remarkable personality, Robert Austin; and Harry Hansen, who was later to undertake the India Project concerned with helping to establish the new business school at Ahmedabad. Vikram and Kamla asked me to join them in the discus-

A NEW BUSINESS SCHOOL

sions, as I had spent three months at Harvard's Advanced Management Program. I had become rather attached to the school, and in return came to be liked by the faculty. Meeting some of them so soon again, and in India, was a happy reunion. While they were attentive and formal with Vikram and Kamla, they felt free with me. They were impressed by a lot of what they saw, and recommended the India Project, but mentioned some of their reservations to me.

Vikram and Kamla worked feverishly together on the new project, drawing me closer to them as I, too, became involved. In 1963 Kamla went to Harvard to participate in the Advanced Management Program to learn something about American business theory. Harvard asked me to come for discussions after Kamla had finished her course in May 1963. In the wake of the Chinese war, and the hard budget that was its aftermath, I accepted the invitation readily as a break between past problems and the new crop that was coming up thick and fast. The fortnight I spent at the Harvard Business School campus, where I had stayed five years earlier, turned out to be a watershed.

My first visit to Harvard and the United States in 1958, followed by the publication of *Punjabi Century* in 1961, with three editions coming out in quick succession, had left me slightly puzzled. Reasonably at ease with marketing, having first helped build up Dalda and then been entrusted with Hindustan Lever, I had nonetheless always been diffident about my intellectual capacities, which I rated as no better than ordinary. Nothing in my academic record had ever pointed to more. At Harvard I had done well, but that I attributed to my being an exotic presence among the hard-headed American executives, and one who mixed easily and held his own equally in class discussions in the morning and in the bars in the evening. That many reviewers in England, the United States, and India considered the book worthwhile was something I could as little understand as the readiness with which Vikram, Kamla, and now the Harvard faculty, took me up. Academic acceptance inspired me, but made me uneasy. Nevertheless, I looked forward to visiting Harvard again, especially because Maurice Zinkin also was attending the course, and in "Brides' Week"—the last week of the course, when the wives joined in—Taya was sure to turn up.

As I flew over the Atlantic on a mid-May afternoon, the Boeing travelling into the sun at half the speed at which the sun receded, the afternoon nearly stood still, sandwiched between the sky and

CHAPTER TWELVE

the sea, both intensely blue. Hindustan Lever, the government of India, licences, permits, budgets, dashes by air to Delhi, in and out of the pseudo Man Singh-Lutyens-Le Corbusier government *bhawans* with their pompous exteriors and unkempt interiors, where files moved like snails, and "sheep in sheep's clothing" flitted from meeting to meeting—all these nightmares dissolved as the Boeing flew on in clear, sunlit, silent space, and I made good use of the bar.

Many years later, when I joined a bank whose operations were confined to India, I realized how much these international academic and business contacts had helped me to maintain the optimism and determination with which I tackled things in so discouraging an environment. Through the years, these connections had given me an interesting life, pleasantly alternating business and study. The day they stopped I would scarcely be able to breathe, though in the end fate unexpectedly made me into a full-time academic.

In New York I spent a couple of days visiting Levers and meeting Burkhart, the chairman of the American company, and his wife Fran, who had visited India the autumn before and been caught there in the midst of the Chinese invasion. Of all the buildings wrapped around in glass on Park Avenue, Lever House, the first of its kind in America, built by a Unilever whizz kid, was the only one I found attractive. Those that followed it spent more money with less taste.

Arriving on a sunny spring afternoon, I drove from Boston airport to the Harvard Business School, which had thoughtfully provided me with a room in Hamilton Hall, where I had stayed five years before while attending the Advanced Management Program, and where the current session was just finishing. No sooner had I finished unpacking than Maurice Zinkin arrived.

Unilever's decision to enroll Maurice in the program interested me because, as some of the professors were to tell me, he ought to have joined the business school as an instructor. One of them told me they had been learning more from Maurice than they could ever have hoped to teach anyone. And yet Maurice was always humble and insisted that he had learned a lot. He now told me something he thought would interest me and might prove useful in India. Harvard, he said, set out to teach you to shun soft options and to take the hard choices. He referred to the method of study, in which one analyzed a situation that was once live, often

A NEW BUSINESS SCHOOL

one where an organization or its head had gone wrong because they had taken the soft option, sometimes in respect to change and innovation. "In India," said Maurice, "you do it all the time. But what is worse, you make a virtue out of a soft option. Worse still, you then pursue it with unction and get involved in proving your point, instead of dropping it when you realize that it does not work."

It was typical of Maurice that, though we had not met for quite some time, he was off on his fascinating thesis before we had even exchanged the usual commonplaces about our families. He could engage in earnest discussion at any time, oblivious to circumstances. As I always enjoyed listening to him on any topic, he warmed up quickly.

"Of course, we are no better than you. We share your unctuousness and the urge to compromise. But there is a difference. We were not always like that. In our pioneering days in Britain we took the harder choices, almost with perversity. You can't afford the soft options, and God knows we can't either, anymore. Nehru was a product of early European liberalism and, later, Fabian socialism. He got carried away by hard words but soft actions. Your well-ordered society, assuring a place for everyone, has a gentleness about it. I wish you could learn that to be a little cruel is sometimes to be a lot kinder."

Maurice suddenly remembered that some of the participants in the program were having a party. He and Kamla asked me to join them. They would be gathering in the lounge for the Happy Hour. Maurice introduced me to the group, which was much the same as my 1958 class—executives, defence officers, some Europeans, Latin Americans, and Asians, all friendly, earnest, and relaxed. In the midst of it all, Kamla arrived in a sari the colour of old bronze, and a simple silver medallion. Excited and flushed, she ran up to embrace me.

"So you have arrived! Here have I been telling all my friends that one of our directors was coming, my boss, also a friend, and you never even wrote, not a line, not a word, not a sign—but how typically male, you write to Maurice, not to me!" They all gathered round Kamla. I looked her up and down. She was impeccably clad in well-ordered elegance. I had never seen her so sure of herself, so confident, as she basked in the adulatory gaze of the rugged, middle-aged American executives around her, for whom her novelty appeared not to have palled even after three

CHAPTER TWELVE

months' familiarity. They had not, it seemed, seen this side of Kamla before—the self-conscious, gay abandon of a dancer walking on to the stage, expecting applause. She took off her glasses and looked at the ring of men fetchingly, with the intent stare of the nearsighted. They were all intrigued by her new vivacity. Someone asked her what she would have to drink. "No," she said categorically. "Mr. Tandon is going to mix my drink, and he knows the exact proportions." This was the gimlet, to which I had once introduced her.

The AMP party was typical of American executives on an evening out. Cheerful but restrained, and in expensive good taste, it finished early. I walked back with Kamla, who alone had the honour of having a small apartment to herself. She spoke at length about the course and her colleagues, the professors, the case-study teaching method, and also of her problems with one or two of the men whom she liked, for whom she was something different and new. As a psychologist, Kamla was sensitive and understanding. People got close to her quickly, and she let them, though she would repel them firmly but gently if they came too near. She was the only woman among a hundred and fifty men leading a monastic campus life, mature but at a watershed age, and many were drawn to her. In the case of one at least she had had to be firm with herself too, she explained, and tell him not to be carried away by her novelty. In the forty-three such programs that Harvard had held since the war began, originally to familiarize selected defence officers with business administration, she was the first woman. She spoke far into the evening. Having been cooped up on the campus for three months, she had a lot to talk about. Although Vikram had been there a week earlier, she seemed to want to unburden herself in a different way.

On the next morning we began talks with the faculty about our new school at Ahmedabad and its first program, which we hoped to organize in January 1964, followed by the first two-year postgraduate program in July. Kamla and Vikram had already recruited some Indian faculty, who were to join the school when it opened. I was very impressed with the amount of preparation Vikram, helped of course by Kamla, had been able to manage during his few brief visits, with his usual capacity for getting things started.

An interesting problem that I mentioned in our discussions was the general feeling I had gained from junior and middle-level managers in India that the enthusiasm with which they welcomed new ideas and techniques they had learned abroad or in courses in India was soon dampened by the attitudes of their seniors. The enthusiasts were told to get back to their jobs and forget these newfangled notions, which might work in business abroad but certainly not in India. This was true of private firms as well as of public undertakings—the former because control lay with the family, and the latter because control and auditing in the all-powerful system put a straitjacket on innovation and change.

This resistance to change was a problem then and still is in a society that desires change with expectancy, resists it when it comes, and yet in its ambivalence remains convinced that the fruits of progress are withheld by all else but itself. I have sometimes wondered whether there is not a death wish in us. As Patrick Moynihan was to put it many years later, when U.S. ambassador in New Dehli, "I think, given all your talent and capacity, that you have just taken a vow of poverty." But these contradictions in our society were then just dawning upon me.

From the perception of this common problem of Indian managers, we evolved a new training concept, the three-tier program to which we would invite middle, senior, and top managers from an organization, and, if the organization was large enough, from one particular division. This was to become Kamla's famous Ahmedabad three-tier program at Agra, to which a hundred managers have gone each year over the past fifteen years.

The Harvard campus was now closed, and I spent a peaceful fortnight in the glory of a New England spring, mostly in the company of Kamla and the faculty, with meetings during the day and invitations at night to the homes of some of the innumerable people whom Kamla knew, both in her own right and through Vikram. She appeared well thought of in her field of human relations, and I had the chance of meeting some well-known personalities. I listened intently to their discussions of the latest thinking and techniques in the study of organizational behaviour and the behavioral sciences in general, an area that I had of late begun to explore as a novice. Kamla had already begun to discern a pupil in me, and to give me confidence she began to tell me that if I lacked theory I had something not unvaluable to offer—namely experience, of which, she felt, I had made some intuitive use. I had, of course, read texts on psychology, personnel theory, and management, but when I listened to Kamla and her colleagues I was

CHAPTER TWELVE

enthralled by a discipline that was new to me. Perhaps my modesty in theory, combined with confidence in practice, made an unusual and attractive combination for Kamla, because I found her increasingly interested in me and conveying this interest to her colleagues. Now and again she would become impatient when I defended a practice that she questioned. "Don't be afraid of exposing your experience to an academic examination; it helps you and it helps us to separate the grain from the chaff," she said. "And please believe me, you have some grain! Vikram, who began as a physicist, has developed great insights and, I would say, competence in this field, to which he was new not so long ago."

I left Kamla reluctantly, wondering what it would be like to meet her at Ahmedabad, far from Boston spring, the mirror-calm Charles River, the ivy-covered halls, the stimulating evenings with the faculty, and walks home in the light-green nights through the peaceful campus.

We met again some weeks later. Travelling on the early morning Viscount flight to attend the institute's board meeting at Ahmedabad, I heard a tired voice say, "Hullo." Kamla had just arrived on the connecting Air India flight from Europe and looked as travel-worn and crumpled as only she could; just as no one else could look quite as fresh and crisp.

"See you at the board meeting," I said.

"Yes, sir."

Kamla organized the first three-tier program at Jaipur early in 1964. Its participants came from medium and large private and public enterprises, with a few also from the central and state governments. Kamla asked me to give a talk, and the theme I chose came from an earlier discussion at the Planning Commission of India. The Commission's new head, Asoka Mehta, had invited me, along with a number of others, to participate in a free and frank discussion on how to accelerate expansion in the economy. Many views were expressed at the meeting, centering mainly on freedom from the many restrictions on growth, the complex and cumbersome licensing procedures that not only took years to grant permission but always tried to whittle down requests. It seemed that if one was willing to accept reduced expansion or a smaller new venture, one stood a better chance, and one's application was also likely to be dealt with more quickly. One got the impression that the processors and recommenders of a case made

A NEW BUSINESS SCHOOL

it a point in the applicant's favour, and their own, that he had been persuaded to accept less. Encouragement that should have been poured out in ladles was doled out grudgingly in spoonfuls. I added that profit was fundamentally a dirty word to the government. Asoka Mehta reacted to this, and in a public lecture shortly afterwards denied that profit was a dirty word to New Delhi.

I pursued this topic at Kamla's program. "Service to the public, not just making a profit," was the constantly preached motto of our leadership; but service out of what? We needed surplus capital to plough into new growth, which inevitably led to size—and we did not like surplus and we did not like size. They added up to success, which to us was always suspect. Profit honestly earned was as much frowned upon as that dishonestly come by. Profit had become synonymous with profiteering, size with exploitation, and success with something anti-social. With such anti-growth attitudes, how could there be expansion? Even the existing small growth had begun to decline and would soon disappear, giving way to a stagnant economy in a context of rapidly increasing population. We needed not only a positive pro-growth attitude but an intolerance of anti-growth attitudes. The proper distribution of growth was a matter for the nation's leaders; its creation was the task of the managers.

On the flight back from Jaipur to Bombay, I saw a headline in a financial daily analyzing the performance of a hundred large companies. Hindustan Lever was named the most efficient user of capital, leading in its return on investments. The irony of this struck me immediately. The previous year's budget had already introduced a new tax which in a capital-scarce country hit those who made higher profits on a given amount of capital harder than those who made less. The least efficient got away altogether. I expressed my worry in a letter to Andrew Knox. On the face of it, I wrote, this might be considered a great compliment, but I feared it would be the beginning of new troubles. We had been singled out; our size and success were already held against us. Now our profitability would make us a still bigger target. In fact, though the headline talked about giants in industry, the biggest of them would not even then have figured among the top five hundred firms in the world. Interesting, I thought, that at Hindustan Steel I had felt sad because we made no profits, while at Hindustan Lever I was sad because we made profits.

One day Vikram made me a proposition. The first chairman of

CHAPTER TWELVE

the board of the Institute of Management, Dr. Jivraj Mehta, recently displaced from the first chief ministership of Gujarat, was going to London as Indian high commissioner, and had therefore resigned. Would I accept the chairmanship?

By tradition such posts belonged to chief ministers and politicians. Why pick on me? I was neither a public figure nor a politician, nor at the helm of a large family business. I had none of the usual qualifications. "We need a professional manager," Vikram explained. When I counsulted her, Kalma said, "Accept it—you will like it, and you have something to offer."

The institute's early problems were many. Among the earliest was the need to lay down certain academic workload standards for the first group of students, who were used to an academic laxity that bore no relationship to the rigours of the Harvard Business School standards that we were trying to establish. Used to earning a good second-class degree with a light workload of barely twenty hours a week, with a short spurt as examinations approached, and now subjected to a seventy-hour week with regular assignments and tests, they broke down soon after the first term began. They struck. The assignments were too many, the examinations too hard, the questions did not stick to the books, the professors were heartless and unsympathetic. The whole system was unfair and should be changed. This attitude which did not have anything to do with principles, was becoming the new style at the universities and was tolerated in the name of justice and freedom and cynically supported by some political parties. It struck at the roots of the academic system, and was to reach a stage when the right to pass examinations became, as it were, one of the fundamental rights conferred on every citizen by the Constitution.

At Ahmedabad there were a large number of subjects, both compulsory and optional, and their study was based on understanding rather than on learning by rote. This meant a level of concentration and discipline to which the students had not been used. They expressed their resentment by boycotting classes, as well as by demonstrations, shouting, and generally disruptive behavior along the lines of the students' protest strikes during the early days of the freedom movement. I wondered whether Gandhiji had realized what he was doing when he taught my generation to refuse to receive education at the hands of the British. Did he visualize the time when a few ill-prepared students would rise from their seats in the examination halls and shout for justice,

A NEW BUSINESS SCHOOL

disrupting the examination, and causing other, serious students to lose valuable months of work; when for one English professor shot during the Indian independence movement there would be countless Indian teachers stabbed; when protest on patriotic grounds turned into blatant attempts to pass examinations through intimidation?

I suppose Gandhiji had hoped that protest, as a weapon, would like the proverbial sword be hung up or beaten into ploughshares. Instead it turned arid and destructive, and became an almost daily affair at schools and colleges as well as in factories, offices and the streets. One of the striking students' demands at an engineering college in the North was to be given a degree automatically at the third attempt to graduate!

Fortunately, the faculty at Ahmedabad held firm. Gradually the students, too, saw the meaning of the new system and came to realize that one did well if one worked steadily and intelligently. The case-study method was in itself a new and absorbing experience in collaboration between the teacher and the taught—one was tested while one was learning. After the first tantrums of the kind they had indulged in at their old colleges, the students settled down to hard work, frequent examinations, and the academic disciplines of a peaceful campus. This was not mere luck; many factors contributed to it.

Industry, too, was beginning to take notice of Ahmedabad, and personnel recruitment teams began visiting the institute to get a feel of the calibre of the teaching and of the students, a new breed of potential managers. The latter became conscious of the demand and of the higher-than-usual starting salaries that were beginning to be offered to them. They therefore concentrated on their studies, and once the first batch had been snapped up at premium salaries, their successors needed no further urging to make the best of their two years. Their inhibitions dissolved, rough edges were soon knocked off, and work become their avid and only pursuit. With careful guidance from the faculty and good teaching, they settled down to their task.

A problem that loomed large was the appointment of a permanent director in place of Vikram, who was honorary and part-time, and Kamla, who deputized for him without holding office in her own right. It was a weak arrangement altogether. The board was divided over it, and Harvard was rather unhappy. Some thought Kamla should be the permanent director; others

CHAPTER TWELVE

were opposed. I was surprised at Harvard's opposition in principle to having a woman director. They were quite clear that a woman would not be able to run an organization that needed not only academic stature, which they conceded she possessed, but administrative authority, which they felt neither she nor, probably, any other woman would be able to wield. I felt they were prejudiced on this point, although I did concede that Kamla was not outgoing enough and did not have the kind of firmness she would need to deal with a young and ambitious faculty, several hundred very lively students, industry and donors (especially the Ahmedabad group), and government. Each one would be supportive to the extent that the director was clear and firm in pursuing the institute's objectives. There was, besides, an extensive building program for the new campus, involving large sums, many hard decisions, and much fund raising. The whole enterprise was literally a man-sized job.

When I first went to Harvard I had been surprised how rare it was to see a woman student or faculty member at the business school; and their answer was that business management and its teaching were not a woman's job. There had never been a woman among the three thousand or so alumni of their Advanced Management Program for senior business, defence, and government executives until Kamla attended it in 1963. Kamla was as feminine as could be, withdrawn and shy, confident only with the few with whom she felt completely at ease, and with no flair or visible liking for administration, but she had her point of view.

Business was a man's world, in which the allegedly male quality of firmness was at a premium. When applied to an institute, this quality had little meaning, however, especially if it took precedence over academic qualities. Nonetheless, the selectors would consider it quite proper to appoint a retired civil servant, who was weak academically as they were wont to do in India, rather than to choose a woman academic who was weak administratively.

Through all this, Vikram felt acutely unhappy. I think he had almost built the institution around Kamla. In the Textile Research Institute, where they had worked together before, she had made a contribution by introducing the social sciences into a purely technical research atmosphere, thereby giving it a refreshing new slant on human relations, and also on marketing and consumer research. Here at Ahmedabad they would work together to build India's first business school. He had great faith in her capacity to

A NEW BUSINESS SCHOOL

give this institution a business-education approach, as opposed to the usual family-business psychology of private industry and the administrative psychology of the nascent public sector. They had discussed this goal at length between themselves, and with their many academic friends at Harvard, MIT, and Stanford, but now that their dream was taking shape, a wall of prejudice was rising against Kamla. She was a woman, and one whom he admired. This consideration was enough for those who did not believe that Vikram could be objective in regard to her. He dutifully carried out the board's desire to look for another director, and even contacted an ICS man, then an ambassador, who, being at the end of his posting and uncertain as to what sort of offer the government might make him next, showed interest. Vikram asked me to talk to the board about him, and they were immediately impressed by a name of such administrative distinction. We corresponded, but the offer of the governorship of a state decided him, and he wrote to express perfunctory regret. The challenge of an academic assignment that he had talked about evaporated quickly. I was relieved, for if there could be a choice for him between a governorship and the chance of a lifetime of building a new institution of this kind, his refusal would only be to the institute's advantage.

Others sought the position, many of them retired administrators and generals who felt that their experience fitted them for business administration. As I resisted in each case, word went around that Vikram and I were stonewalling for Kamla's sake. Comparisons were made in favour of the sister institute at Calcutta, where Chandy had been appointed director two years before. Vikram became discouraged and lost interest, feeling mistrusted and unwanted. He also felt he had let Kamla down by not resigning from the board. She felt the same way about both of us. Whatever I thought of her administrative capacity, I rated her high enough academically to accept her as director; and if the board could accept a civil servant whose only merit was administrative experience, surely they could accept someone with only academic qualifications. But she felt that neither Vikram nor I was willing to make an issue of the matter. Only through a display of strength could the principle have been established. Vikram withdrew. I felt I had to see the matter through, but it was a duty that had ceased to be a pleasure, and I began to think of leaving as soon as the appointment was made.

Ravi Matthai now appeared on the horizon. He was young,

CHAPTER TWELVE

only thirty-eight, had worked in industry, and under Chandy's influence had moved from industry to teaching at Calcutta. With a clear, forceful mind, he was a good leader, and his high standards assured me that there would be no compromising with the institute's growth. Matthai took more than a year's persuasion. His heart, he said, was in teaching and research, not in administration; that was why he had left industry. While his integrity was apparent, I think he was mistaken about his desire to teach and do research, for when he was in a position to do both, he did neither. He was too restless, and lacked the necessary perseverance, at least for research.

Matthai was really an institution builder, and that is where we were lucky. He made two conditions clear—that he would not remain as director for more than seven years, and that I should stay on for another two years, at least till I had completed my five-year term. Leaving administration from time to time to go back to teaching was, I felt, a sound principle in academic life. As for the second condition, I was reluctant to stay any longer than he needed to find his feet, which should not be much more than a year. I was prepared to leave even earlier, and did not want to breathe down his neck. Used to being an active chairman, I did not relish playing a purely decorative role. Once the groundwork was laid, I would prefer to fade out. Ravi seemed genuinely eager to have me stay, however, and besides there was one delicate task to accomplish—to build a bridge between him and Kamla and get them to work together.

Ravi doubted whether Kamla would accept him as director and give him the help he so much needed. He would, he said, understand if she kept aloof, though that would make things difficult for him. Kamla, on her side, was a reluctant partner. I was afraid she would withdraw and that Ravi, finding her uncooperative, might throw in the sponge. Both, in fact, expressed to me in similar vein their wish to leave if the new arrangement was not to their liking. The prospect of both of them resigning, and my thus being left stranded, was a nightmare. Instead, what I least expected happened. I managed to bring them so close together that I could soon tell that I was needed no longer, and felt uncomfortable staying on. They worked like the team that she and Vikram had been at ATIRA. While the Calcutta Institute now began to develop its own problems of politicization, Ahmedabad, once established in its new course, went from strength to strength. Presently it could afford to shed its pioneering generation and take the change in its stride.

I stayed on a while, because the board insisted that we establish the convention of a five-year term. In due course, when he felt that his task was done, Ravi stepped down, but remained to teach. His succession must have pleased Harvard's keen desire for academic democracy. The faculty were asked to choose their next director themselves and picked someone quite young. The connection with Harvard had matured, and was shed. The institute turned to wherever it had something to learn.

Vikram's end came suddenly. I was staying in Bangalore with Air Marshal Mehra, head of Hindustan Aeronautics, who told me that he was going next morning to meet Vikram at the airport. I said I would like to go too, as it had been a long time since I had met him. At the airport, we were told by the station manager that the special air-force plane bringing Dr. Sarabhai was due in another hour. "Is he not coming by the ordinary flight?" Mehra asked in surprise. "No, sir, a special plane is taking his body to Ahmedabad." It was a strange way to get the news of a friend's death.

A new generation took over the reins competently and securely, a rarity in Indian institutions. In my last year, I watched Ravi Matthai deliver the valediction at the graduation ceremony, and while he was speaking with his characteristic youthful verve, I passed a little note to our chief guest: "In a small way I feel I have achieved something—to have left behind me a young successor, first at Hindustan Lever and now at Ahmedabad, both barely forty years old." She smiled knowingly; for she was herself a young prime minister.

Chapter Thirteen

LOS ANGELES

LOS ANGELES, where I spent the spring quarter of 1967 on a University of California Regents lectureship, teaching a course in international management, was quite an experience, especially as a continuation of my work at Ahmedabad, which had in fact emboldened me to accept a teaching post. In the post-war period, multinational firms were assuming considerable importance in business schools. My personal contribution might perhaps lie in the leavening of experience I had acquired in one of the oldest and biggest of them.

My class was mostly from the United States, with a sprinkling of foreigners—a Mexican, a Chilean, and one or two others. I had always been impressed by the industriousness of American students, and Anant Negandhi, an Indian member of the faculty, had told me to load them with work without compunction from the very beginning. I found that they worked assiduously both at home and in the library. They expressed their keenness in an air of almost studied informality that took some adjustment to, however. Their clothes always casual and sometimes bizarre; their language a leisurely drawl; a foot dangling over the seat, a paper cup of coffee, and two little mountains of buns on the desk—all this made one wonder when one entered the classroom whether one had not perhaps by mistake come to a football club meeting. The scene certainly held no future promise of well-groomed international executives in dark suits occupying air-conditioned offices with wall-to-wall carpeting. Addressed to the chairman of Hindustan Lever, the greeting, "Hi!" would have delighted a hundred young managers back in India.

The class never lacked interest. In the first week, when we were discussing the reactions of an executive of an international company to a foreign culture, the question arose whether he had any right to pass judgement on it or try to alter it. An American student reacted strongly, and said that if the man did not try, he had no right to be there. He was there only because he had something to offer, mainly in the way of change, the need for which he was able to see better than a local could. If, in the name of tact, courtesy, or respect for local mores, he shied away from his duty, he was of no use to that country. And as an illustration he concluded, "If I am thinking about a new idea the whole morning and I get steamed up enough to rush into the boss's room at midday to work it out with him, and then I am told that the boss is out to lunch for four hours—well, I have a right to get mad and to want to change the working hours."

At this apparent reference to a Latin American country, the Mexican reacted immediately and violently. "Hell," he said, "this is the damned Ugly American we don't want! What right has he to change our long lunch break? We work long enough. What if we do enjoy our lunch and siesta in a leisurely way instead of this son of a so-and-so's sandwich and coke?" The class approved uproariously, but the American protested loudly that the days of siestas and mañanas were over; they certainly didn't go with business schools.

The first rumblings of an overture to the coming student problem were already in the air, and were noted by the sensitive. They were of particular interest to me as a comparison to our own student unrest. Doubts were being openly cast on the Vietnam war, and there was a story in the press about CIA infiltration of the Peace Corps in India. Student informality was already testing the outer edges of tolerance. When the spring rains were over and the sun shone, I saw a weird chaos of colour and sound on the lawns at midday. There was a band of youths dressed in anything they could think of, each with an instrument that he thought would make some sound—kettles, cans, and pots. The result was a cacophony to whose underlying rhythm they swung and swayed, despite the protests of some teachers.

I was introduced to Punjabi families whose fathers and grandfathers had immigrated early in the century. They mostly grew vegetables or fruit, preserved the ways they had brought with them. At a party one night, I sat next to a Punjabi lady whose dress and every gesture remained unchanged from the day she had left her village in East Punjab. She talked quietly, with the hem of her diaphanous *dupatta* drawn discreetly across her face, in a gesture that even the girls in her ancestral village no longer practised.

CHAPTER THIRTEEN

Her *salwar kamiz* and black *gurgabi* shoes were in harmony with everything else, and must have been imported from home. A widow, she told me her story.

When she was a girl in her early teens, Sardarji—following custom, she could not use his first name—had come to her village. She was produced before him, and as he approved was given to him in marriage. They told her later that he was a big farmer in California, In Amreeka, where his father, the elder Sardarji, had settled many years ago, which of course meant nothing to her. She went with him on a big ship, and they settled on the farm, where she looked after the kitchen in Punjabi style. They had no children. Sardarji was a bit old, but she was otherwise quite happy because it was a plentiful life, and she never had to be economical—not that she wasn't. Some years later, Sardarji died. After the mourning was over, she had to decide whether to return to her village or stay on and run the farm. It was a big farm of two hundred and fifty acres, many times bigger than was to be found in the Punjab. There were two Mexican helpers, who had their cottages on the property. She knew no English, and they no Punjabi. For some years now she had been running the farm. California had become her home, and she had never been back to India.

I asked only one question. "How did you manage to get work out of the men without their understanding you?"

"There was no difficulty," she said. "I put them to work and they worked. And now they understand a little Punjabi."

She turned away and pulled the *dupatta* across her face in the self-conscious gesture I had not seen for years. I looked at her still handsome head in unconcealed admiration. What a people!

Towards the end of my stay in Los Angeles, a message came from Moddie to telephone K.B. Lall, secretary in the Ministry of Foreign Trade, in Delhi. I could not understand what he wanted of me, 15,000 miles away; he could be droll, but this was incomprehensible. I managed to reach him, and he came to the point via a gentle detour. He was glad I had now had the experience of teaching, having done my job with Lever, he said. Six years of the Lever chairmanship meant that it was perhaps time to do something else. My precious dollars were ticking away rapidly, but he seemed in no hurry to get to the point. Having served the private sector for so many years, he went on, it was perhaps time I thought of something else, such as the public sector. Having barely touched the subject, he flew off at a tangent, and wondered whether after manufacturing I might consider planning as a possible area—though of course there were steel and heavy engineering, fertilizers and chemicals, even food. And if I did not feel interested in planning, there was international trade—the STC, for instance. And there he stopped, having pointed to the perch he had chosen for me.

My heart sank. The STC, the State Trading Corporation of India, was always under fire from both industry and government, and was now in trouble with Parliament. Accusations were perpetual. Incompetence at buying and selling and corruption were among the milder charges. A more serious one, of late, was breach of parliamentary privilege, for which the chairman was going to be arraigned before the privileges committee of the House. Planning, however ineffectual it might have become, was at least peaceful. International trade was risky, if exciting.

The STC had been in trouble ever since its inception. It dealt in the scarcest, most sensitive commodity in India, foreign exchange, whose open-market rate was way above the official rate. Companies wanted it to import plant and raw materials; the public wanted it for luxuries—gold and diamonds, liquor and gadgets, trips round the world, from which they brought back trunkfuls of nylons, georgette, cosmetics, cuckoo clocks, Dresden shepherdesses, prints, anything that could be had at home more cheaply and in better taste, had they the discernment of those who came to India to buy its traditional products. The junk that covered the walls and shelves of newly rich homes was always a sign of well-financed travel abroad. The STC was the gateway to foreign exchange for the many who sought it by under-invoicing their exports and over-invoicing their imports, as well as for those who genuinely needed it and earned it by exporting in order to pay for their imports.

My mind raced along as Lall spoke, now and then with the high-pitched laugh that was his own commentary on his humour. I said I was returning to Bombay shortly, and would come to Delhi for a chat. Yes, that was a good idea, he observed—his characteristic response whenever he wanted something his way—and rang off. I rang the operator to find out what the charge was because I had put the call through from a friend's house. It was not small. The STC seemed to have already begun to exact its toll of me.

Their tests over, the students relaxed and came by more often

CHAPTER THIRTEEN

to chat about what they were proposing to do in life. Their interest in the subject of international management had marked most of them for a career in American multinationals, and indeed some had already been invited to interviews. They were reluctant to join large corporations, preferring some international service agency and work in India, Africa, or South America. They were averse to the very idea of large corporations and to their exploitative methods in vulnerable countries. They did not even relish the thought of working for their government, whether at home or abroad.

A refrain common among the young was their growing mistrust of their elders, to whom they no longer looked for advice. Their professors, they felt, did not devote enough time to them and their problems; they were too busy producing and consulting. The senior men sought calls to Washington, Taipeh, New Delhi, Tokyo, depriving the students of the attention that they felt should have been devoted to them. Wherever the young turned, from their homes to the larger society and now to the universities, there was a lack of concern—at least so they thought. I was particularly interested in this disaffection because the problems of our own young—so highly politicized—were so dissimilar. As a stranger, I could only ask a question here and there, more perhaps to satisfy my own interest than to help them. Not understanding fully, my advice might do more harm than good.

My last evening was spent at the home of Professor Anant Negandhi and his German wife. They had invited a number of young Indians from the university and elsewhere, and a discussion began on a subject that was to recur on my subsequent visits—the prospect of their return home and their attitudes towards the United States. They all expected to go home one day; the question was when and to what. Some were assistant professors, some held fellowships, others were working with firms in the area. Many had been home to bring back brides from their own communities. These they often found through advertisements in the daily newspapers, sometimes completing the whole operation in less than a fortnight's leave from work. The parents must have short-listed the girls, with details of their education, dowry, family, and whatever precise specifications the American-educated young man had laid down as the minimum. One sees such couples on Air India planes, the young man unmistakably Indian-American and his self-assured bride looking forward to her new, gadget-filled home, their acquaintance developing over the long flight. Some of these marriages fail, especially if the boy has been attached to an American girl and has succumbed to parental pressure, but mostly they settle down to a comfortable Indian life abroad. On Air India flights one now also sees old parents and widowed mothers travelling abroad to visit their sons. In due course, the boys send for their younger brothers for advanced education in the United States, having already helped them with their university education at home. The brothers, too, sometimes settle down, and I even came across a father who liked America so much that he settled there himself and developed a good business in Indian condiments and spices.

I felt that few of them seriously intended to return home. Some, of course, would try, but they would be back again. Those who had married American girls sounded keener, but they were also quicker to return to the United States. At the Institute of Management at Ahmedabad, although we offered the working environment they had hoped for and comfortable houses, those with American wives all went back, perhaps because their links with America remained unbroken.

It is not without significance that while, after a connection lasting two centuries, the British have in the last twenty-five years taken from India many hundreds of thousands of semi-skilled and semi-literate workers to do menial chores, the Americans have during the same period selected many thousands of the best from among those we sent to them for advanced education. They were not simple Indians who had left home looking only for a living, but the cream of the universities. It was said at one time that the top ten of those who graduated annually from an Indian institute of technology went straight to American universities and remained in the United States. Each one of them was a potential catalyst for growth lost to India. Those comfortably ensconced in India, especially the politicians, sometimes talked of a spirit of sacrifice that should make these men return home to develop a truly Indian science and technology, and at other times spoke menacingly of cancelling their passports. But there was no discussion of what we had to offer them, or of how we could quicken their interest with academic challenges and opportunities instead of frustrating them with administrative obstacles.

No, I said to these young Indians in the end, they should try to feel comfortable with whatever they decided to do. If they de-

CHAPTER THIRTEEN

cided to return, then they should accept India as it was and stop making unfavourable comparisons. They would soon fit in. If they did not find the opportunity they were looking for, on the other hand, then they should make up their minds to stay in America—but in that case they should regard it as their home. They oughtn't to criticize America to prove that it was not its attractions that made them stay. For their own peace of mind, and in fairness to the country, they should accept it with grace and realism. America had given them everything and held back nothing; it had in fact served them better than it had its native minorities. They should give it credit for frank appreciation of their talent. In return they owed their country of adoption loyalty at least—something which, interestingly enough, they withheld from India also. To justify their not going back to India, they ran it down more than it deserved, and they certainly never gave America its due. Anant Negandhi was a rare example among them of one who had made up his mind to stay, and I seldom heard him talk against either India or America; the one had given him his first chance, the other his second. By all means let Indians in America keep their roots fresh; many of them would visit India periodically, but America was their home, and if emotionally not quite theirs, certainly their children's. I laughed self-consciously and said that I had delivered the Gettysburg Address that one of them should have made. I admitted that I was only too conscious of how easily one could be drawn into this society. Nowhere else are you assimilated so quickly—provided, of course, that you don't hold back, but give yourself to it.

Chapter Fourteen

LEAVING LEVER

ON MY return to Bombay, I plunged into the Hindustan Lever five-year plan. Prepared mostly in my absence, it was a thorough and polished effort that laid down only one major premise for fulfilling its ambitious targets—that the company be permitted to grow. It made minimal demands on public funds, foreign exchange, or Unilever help; rather the accent was on research and development and import substitution. The new research and development laboratory, the recent reorganization, and the growing cost-consciousness would assure a high rate of growth despite all constraints—if only they became no worse. Research was led by an able young scientist whose rare passion was the profitable application of science to industry.

I went to talk with K. B. Lall, who remembered how I had called on him to discuss our plans six years before. He lost no opportunity to press his point and said, "Ah, this is the time you should leave! Don't have the vanity to attempt two plans. Leave your successor with something to do, as your predecessor did." I explained that I had no one ready, though we had someone in mind. Rajadhyaksha was going to be made vice-chairman in the following year, and would be groomed to take over on my retirement three years later, in 1971. It would not be fair to leave at this stage and force them to bring in an expatriate chairman. I offered to help the STC with advice, however. At this Lall laughed and said that might work with Lever but not with the STC, because government psychology was different. Advice from outside would have no effect. They would listen but go on as they were, with the possible danger that they might even turn the situation to their advantage to do what they wanted but ought not to do. And yet, if I was in the chairman's seat, they would do as I bid, for if there was one thing they did understand, it was orders. I saw his point from my experience with Hindustan Steel. Officialdom

CHAPTER FOURTEEN

seemed as incapable of utilizing advice as of arguing with an order, good, bad, or perverse. It was an interesting mentality, one of total deference to authority.

On my next visit Lall suggested that I talk to the STC about their organizational structure. The minister had plans which he could not implement because they both doubted the STC's capacity to carry a much bigger burden. He had therefore made an appointment for me to meet the chairman of the STC.

I would not have been surprised to discover that he had deliberately sent me to drive his point home, so ludicrously abortive was my visit. A clerk met me to say that the chairman had been called away to a meeting, but had left word that I might meet one of the managers. I was therefore going to be taken to the head of their economics division. My disappointment lightened somewhat at the thought that at least they had such a division. The important gentleman who received me began by describing himself, a barrister-at-law who had held various important posts in government and now headed this big department. I discovered, however, that despite its name, it consisted of nothing but a large number of clerks and managers. The head of the economics section was a graduate in chemistry. Their only economist had left in disgust soon after joining. The department assisted the chairman in answering parliamentary questions, and currently in his problems with Parliament itself. It also controlled foreign offices and their postings. The ultimate prize in the corporation as a reward for good service was an important division, however unrelated to one's past experience, or a posting abroad, which this gentleman was hoping to obtain the following year in return for his preceding three years of service. Instead of being utilized to send younger men abroad so that they might bring back their experience to headquarters, a posting abroad was usually a prelude to retirement.

He looked blankly at me when I asked about their plans and what changes they had in mind. Why should they want to reorganize or change? As for planning, the government made their decisions for them, so really it was the government that should plan. He turned happily to describing his job, and brought out a pile of studies of various countries that he had prepared for exporters. I thumbed through some, and found them to be simple accounts of geography, people, production, imports and exports. He told me that they had been found so useful that they were going to be reprinted. As he seemed quite uninterested in the purpose of my visit, I thanked him and left, and subsequently complimented K. B. Lall for understanding his STC so well. Having persuaded him and some others that, while glad to be of help to the public sector, I was not—at least not yet—ready to join it, I returned to my own problems.

India experienced two difficult years of bad monsoons in 1966 and 1967, and the economic situation worsened in the wake of a big devaluation of the rupee in 1966. The first of a series of recessions set in. The government promptly introduced tight controls, and as a result our profitability dropped. Unilever appeared to feel that my growing involvement with the government, while it might initially have had some limited value, was resulting in my handling our own problems with the government with less directness and vigour. I was spending too much time with government enterprises and committees, and I was thought to be too close to them to press our claims at the risk of upsetting them. My three months' absence in Los Angeles, which had no direct relationship with their business, also seemed an indication of my diminishing interest. Hoskyns-Abrahall, in charge of India, once asked how much of my time I spent with government, and was surprised when I said about a quarter of it, because they were under the impression that it was more than half.

A small but interesting problem, which delicacy prevented me from discussing with them, was my sense of the diminishing interest among younger Unilever personnel in working in the Indian business. Two foreign directors, and the odd specialist we might need for starting something of which we had no experience, was all we required. In fifteen years, during which the business had grown greatly in size and complexity, the number of expatriates had dropped from more than fifty to a mere four or five. Unilever was keen to have a couple of their promising men on our board, but it was becoming increasingly difficult to bring out men who were interested in the country and who would regard India as more than an interlude that furthered their careers. At their level, they had not only to be able but to demonstrate their leadership of men nearly always older, and usually no less able. They also had to be liked, and to be liked they had visibly to like working in India. We made it easier for them to go home every year on leave, and there was, of course, the spreading knowledge in Unilever that those who made it in India had a good chance of making the home board. Somehow this practice

CHAPTER FOURTEEN

seemed to add to the intolerance of at least some for having to work in an environment they did not like. The congestion and climate of Bombay, the unfamiliar and seemingly unnecessary problems of business there, the perpetual struggle with raw-material shortages and production constraints, were enough to fray an Indian's nerves, and to the expatriate even the greater glory of Unilever scarcely seemed a sufficient motive.

At the beginning, Unilever would arrange for me to meet the man and his wife, and usually an ex-India hand would have done some gentle selling beforehand. The process frequently went in reverse, however, with the couple, especially the wife, interviewing me instead. Some took a chance and decided against India straight off, secure perhaps in the feeling that if they were good enough to be tried in India they would still be tried somewhere else notwithstanding their decision. I got the feeling that these were areas that Unilever was not willing to discuss. In fairness, though, it was more likely that they had not given much thought to the matter. In any case, they never discussed the subject with me, and I left it alone.

Seven years' stewardship of the company was also perhaps long enough in itself. A change was needed for Hindustan Lever's sake, for the parent company's sake, and for my own sake. I was becoming increasingly conscious of how easily answers came to me, of the temptation to repeat what had worked before. I remembered the remark of a professor at Harvard that management will tend to do in the future what it thinks it has done well in the past, and that in this lies a danger. If I stayed longer there was the danger both of my getting stale, if I had not already become so, and of my building up resentment of Unilever, which had always been supportive and constructive. Besides, there was the danger of my justifying these feelings in a way unfair to both sides. The more I thought about it, the more I definitely came to the conclusion that the time had come for me to go. On the other hand, there was the insistent call of the public sector, which I no longer seemed willing or able to resist. Though knowing that it was not going to be an easy master to serve, I was forming an attachment that was pulling me towards it. K. B. Lall had guessed well.

Just then a small incident of no particular consequence conveyed to me that Unilever was becoming edgy, and in retrospect perhaps I was too. On an impulse at a Board of Trade meeting in Dehli in January 1968, I sent a scribbled note to K. B. Lall to say that the answer was yes. Back came a note from him saying that this was very good news—when? As I left the meeting before it closed, he followed me out and wanted to know more. I explained that I was going for a week's holiday to the Kulu Valley, where I would have an opportunity to think over the decision that I had made only a few minutes before. He readily agreed that we should discuss the matter further on my return.

It snowed all week at Kulu, so I had plenty of time to reflect. It seemed best, all things considered, to follow my instinct and to move on. Later that month I was to visit London on Andrew Knox's retirement, and that would give me the chance to talk things over with them. He was leaving the company after fifty years of service, and a great gathering had been arranged of all the chairmen of the companies that he had been associated with. As India had always been his first love, I was given the honour of making the farewell speech at the banquet. Before leaving I asked Lall if I could return via Moscow to get some feel of what it would be like to deal with the Soviet Union, the most important customer of the STC. He thought it would be a good idea to visit the STC office in Moscow and the commercial section of the embassy. This step, taken purely out of curiosity, moved me still further towards the final decision. News also came from London that with the departure of Andrew Knox there would be changes in the overseas committee, and that Hoskyns-Abrahall also would be retiring. In Hindustan Lever, the vice-chairman, who was also one of the directors, was due to retire two years ahead of time so as to make way for Rajadhyaksha to become vice-chairman. The year 1968 was picking up well after the previous bad years, both in the economy and for the firm, and this improvement was reflected in the first few months' results. Thus, wherever I looked, I saw signs that this was the best time to go. Let Rajadhyaksha take over as chairman and deal with the new overseas committee. He could launch the new corporate plan with assured good results in his own first year.

On the Monday in early February when the conference began in London, I wrote a brief note to John Hoskyns-Abrahall saying that in this year of so many changes it might be as well for Hindustan Lever, too, to have its own change and begin again with a new chief. This was perhaps the best time for me to make a fresh start; the government had been making repeated offers; I would like to accept one of them. I left the note on his desk. The

CHAPTER FOURTEEN

break came when I walked out of the room, not when I actually left the firm half a year later. I went back to the conference and joined my colleagues from many parts of the world, some of whom I had known over the years as our careers took their upward curves, meeting them on courses and at Unilever House, and reading about their achievements and the progress of their companies. As I sat among them, part of them and yet a part no longer, nostalgia came over me. But when I thought of Rajadhyaksha and his young board, whose average age would drop to below forty with the departure of Ramaswami and myself, the new chairman himself being barely forty, it seemed indeed the time to go. For many years I had been helping the young to rise, so that anyone who had merit got his first shot at senior responsibility in his early thirties and a chance to join the board in his late thirties or early forties. The logical consequence was for the old to retire voluntarily and early.

At lunch Hoskyns-Abrahall walked up to me and said, "Well, that was a surprise." Next morning he, Andrew Knox, and I spoke about the timing of my departure and the succession. I though how fitting it was that I should be discussing it with Hoskyns-Abrahall, who had been sent out to India over twenty years ago, soon after the war, to start the process of Indianization, with instructions, no doubt, to identify and train the first Indian chairman. The process was by now so well established that I had no hesitation in recommending Rajadhyaksha, even though it meant promoting him straight from being a director. Hoskyns-Abrahall wondered vaguely whether I would stay on for a period as president or something of the sort to see the transition through, but I told him that I thought it would be best to make a clean break, for both the government's and the firm's sakes. There was certainly no point, they agreed, in sending a chairman out for three years. Indianization at the top having started, there was no logic to even a temporary deviation. Rajadhyaksha would no doubt make as good a chairman now as he would three years later; he had the qualities that inspired us to trust him with the responsibility, which in itself would bring out the best in him. If ever I admired Unilever it was in such moments of trust and decisiveness. I reminded them of the succession plan that we had discussed seven years before; at least it had worked on this occasion, in its first major test.

I missed this more than any other aspect of the firm later in the public sector, where top positions could remain vacant for a year and more, the process of selection was long and vacillating, and the final choice sometimes incomprehensible, even perverse. Even the procedure for the appointment of a government selection committee did not work too well. Planned succession seemed alien to the bureaucratic mentality, and consequently the same was true of continuity in policy.

As the week of the conference progressed, I began to feel the excitement of a new career, with its unfamiliar challenges. From what little I knew about the public sector, I would miss the order and predictability of the system I was leaving behind. I had worked nowhere else, and the world of the firm was all I knew. I realized that the doubts I had lately begun to harbour about Unilever were merely my way of pushing myself into a decision to leave. I was now sure that in fact neither they nor I really felt that we had had too much of the other. But it was time for a change. K. B. Lall would have won anyway. Looking around at the group of chairmen at the conference, each one of them among the best executives in the world, meticulously selected and groomed, I wondered how much freedom one would enjoy in the government administration to develop such talent with care and consideration for the feelings of the person. This was one thing I was going to miss in the government. Aspi Moddie told me later, "You will find that the individual does not matter there. It's the designation, the rule, the file—everything but the man."

Chapter Fifteen

MOSCOW

I TOOK the Aeroflot flight to Moscow the next morning for a week's visit to a world quite unknown to me. With Unilever, and later with the STC, I travelled to many lands, in all continents. Of each new country I had some advance knowledge, culled from books, newspapers, films, and individuals, so that I knew to some extent what to expect, but not so with Russia. Outside of the Russian plant at Bhillai, and there too seldom, I had encountered fewer than a dozen Russians, I had spoken to one, and known none—and this for someone who had been brought up in Europe and had revisited it many times. Even in Sweden, which became my second home after I met Gärd, one never met a Russian, despite the fact that the two countries were neighbours. My total picture of modern Russia came from Soviet propaganda, a Unilever buyer who had been there to discuss business, Wendell Willkie's account in *One World* of his visit during the war, and some contemporary literature and music.

The air hostess gave me a monosyllabic reception, and when I asked if I could sit at the back, simply said, "No." I discovered that that was where she was going to sit herself much of the time. After we had taken off, I asked her if I could have a drink. Again she said no—and as an afterthought added, "Later." Much later, after she had served the crew and eaten herself, she asked, "You eat?" And added generously, "Drink?" I consoled myself with the thought that she and the crew were at work, while I was idle; perhaps she was right to serve the workers first. Besides, it was perhaps preferable to what I might have had to face with a friendly, voluble hostess on a long flight without other passengers in the forward cabin. There was the same democratic reluctance to serve one at the hotel, an old-fashioned place called the Peking, which had the familiar quality of our own state-owned hotels and public service counters.

MOSCOW

As it was a Saturday, I asked the young man from the embassy who had met me at the airport if I could take a walk in the street, though it was past midnight. He offered to come with me and explain things. The night was cold—though I was informed that for the first time in weeks temperatures had risen to a mere minus twelve degrees—but there were a lot of well-muffled men and women walking in the streets with an air of nowhere to go. He explained that the government had recently declared a five-day work week, but as there were few private cars, no tradition of a weekend, and few restaurants and bars, people just walked about. The strong impression made on me during the days that followed was of a European city that lacks affluence and its concomitant nervous rush and bustle, noise, fumes, cars, neon signs, advertisements, and crammed shop-windows. The few shop-windows, the goods in them, the people and their figures and dresses, the few cars—everything had the functional look of a no-nonsense, no-frills, no-glut, no-waste society, whose decision makers thought in simple, austere terms.

On Sunday morning, I walked about the streets again, and later went to our commercial counsellor's home, in a block of flats built for embassy staff. At the entrance a Russian guard opened the gate into this privileged and protected enclave. A few blocks away a large building ran the entire length of Friendship Street, practically deserted since most of its inhabitants, the Chinese mission, had left. It had been built and the street specially named in the first euphoria of friendship, at the time when we also were "*bhai-bhai*" with the Chinese. Then it must have been bursting with activity, but now it stood silent.

On Monday I visited my first Russian public enterprise, which had recently bought its first consignment of detergent powder from us. The deal was interesting, because we had never met Russians before, and the negotiations that took place in New Dehli between the Indian Lever managers and the Russians, in the presence of government officials, resembled bargaining, with bids and counterbids, and new conditions introduced every now and again, sometimes quite incomprehensibly. We showed them our brands and asked them what brand name they would like—or did they not believe in such a bourgeois practice? No, they must have a brand name, "Umbrella." When we asked for its equivalent in Russian, they said simply "Umbrella." They wished the panel on the side in English to be retained, but not the Hindi on the oppo-

CHAPTER FIFTEEN

site side. They also wanted to retain the women pictured on the panels, one in a dress and one in a *sari*. It then dawned on us that they wanted to give the package an imported, exotic look which would help to make it a fast seller and fetch a good premium. The Russian text was to be featured only as a concession to explain the use of the product.

We were taken to a small room, where an elderly official and his interpreter met us. I did not know the ritual, so after exchanging greetings I asked whether he knew about our product, and if he would like to tell me about it—how it had reached them, the quality, packing, and so on. He said that their president was busy and could not see me, and that there was nothing he himself had to say about the product. I began to wonder whether he knew anything about us, but apparently he knew a lot, for he loosened up the moment I suggested that I would take it, then, that they had no problems. I had assumed that as this was the first consignment, they might have had some trouble.

At this his face lit up, and he started talking volubly. There was nothing right about the product, its quality, cartons, outer packaging, and delivery schedule. Apparently, as with us, the way to a Russian's heart was through an invitation to complain. I kept nodding my head as he went on, with the interpreter barely able to keep pace. At least I had got him to talk. I expected him to come forward with a big claim, to anticipate which, I apologized for all that had happened. Under the circumstances, it was as well for us not to accept another order, because we were short of the product in the home market and had only entered into the contract for our government's sake as a matter of good will. We could sell all of it and at a much better price than they were giving us. My advice was that they should buy detergent in Europe in future.

I do not think he was sufficiently senior; he had probably been sent because no one else's time was worth the meeting with me. At my unanticipated reaction, he seemed to take fright; excusing himself, he left the room. He returned with a smile, and informed me that the president unexpectedly found himself free, and would be glad to see me. They had made an excellent deal, at prices far below Europe's, and had paid in non-convertible rupees—while we had to spend valuable foreign exchange to import the raw materials.

From the small, bare, windowless room, he took me to a large handsome office, with a view over the city. The president was a youngish, well-dressed, impressive-looking man with several gold teeth. Expansive, he conversed easily and amiably through the interpreter about our product, western Europe, Unilever, and the current market situation. I was back in the familiar multinational world. He might have been an executive at Shell, Philips, Unilever, or Tata, but I found later that he was unusual. We did not discuss detergents much, and of course he let the little man go. Eventually he took me to the door, and remarked that we would be meeting later, as he was coming to our cocktail party. At the party he started an animated conversation, speaking freely in English without an interpreter. I was to discover subsequently that at parties only government ministers had interpreters.

After several illuminating discussions with Damodaran, our minister at the embassy, and some sightseeing through Air India, always a friendly outpost abroad—a look at Lenin, fresh-faced and roseate as if he had died yesterday; a ballet show at the Bolshoi; and a vodka-and-caviar dinner at the famous Workers' Restaurant, where couples danced sedately to a band literally out of the 1930s—I was put on the midnight Air India plane from London for the journey from the snows of Moscow to the summer heat of Bombay. Well muffled, in my new beaver hat, I climbed the gangway in a long queue and stood in the freezing wind while a much better muffled Russian policeman stood inside the warm cabin, examining each passport one last time with great care. I knew that I was going to return. There was the prospect of many things in common in dealing with Russians.

K. B. Lall was pleased with my visit. A satisfactory report on it had, of course, already reached him from Moscow. Together we began to plan the many details involved in bringing in someone from the private sector, and from a foreign firm at that, to join government administration at that time. His complex mind could not envisage anything simple; he had to devise a strategy. He had rightly expected the STC troubles to rise to a pitch during the budget session of Parliament, and he wanted to move with finesse. Just before his ministry's grants came up for discussion, he would announce the appointment of a committee to review the working of the STC, with me as its chairman. A hint would, of course, be thrown to the press that I was likely to take over the corporation later. He would thus be able to gauge Parliament's reaction, both to the committee and to the rumour of my appointment during the debates.

CHAPTER FIFTEEN

One morning I found a telex message on my desk: "The following message was received for the chairman this morning from T. T. Krishnamachari—'Prakash, please do not commit suicide. T.T.K.'" The message amused me, but coming from T.T.K. it intrigued me as well. As Nehru's finance minister, he had founded the STC. In fact, he had been the architect of the public sector, the instrument of Nehru's socialist dreams. He had once been Lever's agent for South India. That he should take so much notice of a three-line announcement in the press, and telephone our office from his home in the country, not with his characteristic half-congratulatory, half-deprecating message, but with something so sharp, disturbed me. I replied thanking him and referring to the slow death of the private sector that he had already ordained. But one day Krishnamachari's message was to pull me back from the brink of desperation.

The STC review committee's terms of reference were wide enough to give me the unusual experience of first suggesting all the changes I could think of, with an assurance of their being accepted, then going on to implement them myself, and, finally, being responsible for the results. K. B. Lall would certainly make it possible for me to do whatever I thought worthwhile. I decided to combine my own farewell visit to London in May with visits to the STC offices in Tehran, Beirut, and Rotterdam.

The Unilever farewell was a gracious affair, to which they had invited some whose acquaintance I had cherished over the years, many with whom I had worked in India, and others whom I knew on the Dutch side of the business at Rotterdam. Lord Cole, the chairman, gently stilled a past controversy by saying, "Prakash was a patriot to whom India's interests came first, but with whom Unilever's interests were always safe."

Back in Bombay, I said farewell to the company. There remained very few who had been on hand when I had joined it thirty-one years before. The next evening, I took the Frontier Mail to Delhi, a train journey that I had made so often in the past. I thought it would be relaxing to take the twenty-four-hour trip in air-conditioned luxury. As it turned out, we ran into floods, and the journey took three days and three nights.

In the enforced but relaxed idleness, I fell to thinking about Hindustan Lever. The picture was one of light and shadows, mingled into an experience that had been worth having. To be the first and to be sensitive had made it the more difficult, especially in a period of political transition, when to work for one's own was considered better than to work for our former rulers. Fortunately, I did not see it that way, because those of our own whom I had approached for a job over thirty years before had not been interested in anyone other than their own kith, kin, and caste.

Lever had continued the process of my maturation in England. The multinational firm was a comfortable extension of the Merseyside business world. I had been its first experiment in grooming a national head for one of its largest subsidiaries, and I had developed together with the business through the distinct stages of our mutual growth—from dependence through independence to interdependence. From the time in the 1930s when the traffic was all one-way—home mail, home policy, even home advertising material, and a "European signature" for all sanctions—we had moved to the stage when one felt we ought sometimes to disagree if only to assert ourselves; and finally to a well-balanced, though not always smooth, relationship. Moving from one stage to another had had its problems and conflicts, but somehow we had managed to get to the next stage, creating new relationships of a different texture, in which each unit did what it could do best. At the same time, we took advantage of the centre's world experience.

Chandy's earlier example and my leaving Hindustan Lever ahead of time to join the public sector set a kind of pattern that my successor, Vasant Rajadhyaksha, chief economist Nath, and director of research Varadarajan soon afterwards followed, as did many others. The system of training and sending out men in their own right as professional managers proved effective. The multinationals were generally more successful at providing managerial talent than the professionally managed Indian firms, and certainly more successful than the family firms, whose family men would not venture out and whose professional men were not encouraged to do so. Even today, fifty years after the process of family-founded firms being run by professional managers began in the West, there is scarcely a large firm in India which is not headed by someone whose name is also the name of the firm—Tata, Jain, Sarabhai, Kothari, Mafatlal, and several hundred others. And today most multinationals in India are headed by Indians.

I wondered how much trust the controlling ministries would give one in a public enterprise. Would they appreciate independent thought and action, divergent from their own? Would I be

CHAPTER FIFTEEN

allowed to mould the new organization as I wished, and would the environment be, if not permissive, at least tolerant? Would it permit me to derive the satisfaction I had had from my previous assignment? At Lever—more important than all the problems of change I managed to cope with—I was able to leave a successor who, while improving and filling the gaps, would not proceed in desperate atavism to demolish everything in trying to prove himself. So often I had seen new brooms in public enterprises sweep out much good and bring in nothing better. Rajadhyaksha was a different type, possessing that personal warmth which the organization would need after my coldly impersonal drive for efficiency. I had also to welcome back one of the up and coming men, Thomas, who had left the company a few years earlier to join his family's business, and then predictably returned. Someone had asked me how Thomas's colleagues would react to his return, because normally when once you left Lever you had left it for good; badly at first, I said, but the company would gain a likely chairman. In fact, he not only succeeded Rajadhyaksha, but went further and was ultimately appointed to the Unilever board, which in the past had been mainly Anglo-Dutch.

Chapter Sixteen

STATE TRADING CORPORATION

THE STC, India's first international trading corporation, was set up by the government of India in 1956 at the request first of the Chinese government and later of the Russians when they entered into bilateral trade agreements with us. These were based on unconvertible currency accounts, and known as the rupee trade; in fact, a system of barter. Both Russia and China felt that their state enterprises would feel more at ease dealing with a state enterprise in India than with private business. A running balance was maintained and the surpluses on either side could not be converted into free foreign exchange; instead they were carried forward and offset by further trading. The Chinese agreements came to an end with the war of 1962, but bilateral trade with Russia continued, considerably reinforced by the participation of other Eastern European countries, till it has come to form a substantial part of Indian imports and exports.

We imported whole plants for new public enterprises, defence equipment, chemicals and pharmaceutical products, ships, and power plants, but no consumer goods. In exchange we exported commodities, tea, coffee, cashews, jute, textiles, shoes, railway wagons, and light engineering goods. Both sides benefitted. The communist countries sold products which were not sophisticated enough to gain access to European markets, and in return bought our products without having to use their hard-earned foreign exchange, which they could spend on more sophisticated imports from the West. The benefit to us lay in access to plant and equipment for which we did not have sufficient free foreign exchange, a good part of which was spent in importing foodgrains from the United States. Though mutually beneficial, the trade resulted in perhaps greater gains to the Eastern Europeans, if only because of their superior trading strength, abetted by a touch of euphoria on our part and the naiveté of our administrators turned traders—a class which at home they traditionally scorned.

CHAPTER SIXTEEN

In time the Russians were to hold it against us that we had "forced" them to trade through the STC and not allowed them to buy and sell freely through private enterprise, as did the United States, Western Europe, Japan, and others. When I pointed out that they in turn channelled all our trade through their state corporations in Moscow and did not allow us to deal separately with the constituent republics of the Soviet Union, they simply argued that that was their system. We had to deal with their monopoly enterprises in Moscow, but they wanted the benefits of competition in our open markets. In due course even though they dealt on a state-to-state basis with us, they nevertheless appointed their own Indian special agents in India, whom they paid commissions for services not readily apparent to us.

Like the Russians, large foreign corporations and consortiums also employed a system of Indian agents. This was especially true of the aid-giving, developed countries, the more so when their aid was tied. Being weak economically and possessing little bargaining power, we were always vulnerable when receiving aid from developed countries. Their "cartels," sometimes functioning only when dealing with aid-receiving countries, exerted influence around the globe, so that no matter where in the world we made a bid, we came across "understandings" on prices. These cartels argued that they were forced into this practice because they were obliged to deal with a state monopoly. Whichever way we looked at it, competition was only for the strong and equal. The Indian lobbies of these capitalist monopolies were as extensive as those of the socialist countries, but with a difference. The Indian "intermediaries" of the developed countries were usually a very sophisticated lot, often retired defence officers, whose influence was quite visible in the lavish parties they threw, with a bevy of those who mattered invited, and in the telephone calls they could arrange from above at the opportune moment. By contrast the agents of the Eastern Europeans usually lacked standing.

Placed in such a sensitive position, and often dealing with the seamier side of international trade, the STC could please no one. It was criticized by private industry, public enterprises, the press, government, Parliament, the audit, foreign intermediaries, and the state enterprises and cartels abroad. It was never in the right. Ill-equipped professionally, its administrative and financial system archaic, the STC had much to be blamed for, and it was understandable that paranoia and perversity had penetrated its soul. I

STATE TRADING CORPORATION

entered its office, if it could be called that, one monsoon morning, anxious and unsure about what lay in store for me.

B. P. Patel, the man I was replacing, was relieved when I arrived. He hoped to take some leave, and the next parliamentary session, starting soon, would now not be his worry. The breach-of-privilege issue had been settled, and the committee had absolved him. He looked embarrassed when I asked him if I could drop in the next morning. Could I make it after midday? I gladly agreed and suggested that, if it suited him better, I would take over on the following day. He jumped at the idea. I thought no more about it till I was informed by Dr. Alexander, the joint-secretary, to whom K. B. Lall had entrusted the task of inducting me into the STC and of keeping an eye on my private-sector ways, that Patel had obviously consulted his astrologer about the right hour. He had had too much trouble with the STC to risk more through an ill-starred departure, though I suppose some astrologer must also have predicted the right hour for him to join the corporation. Alexander told me that everyone in Delhi—cabinet ministers, even prime ministers, politicians, administrators, and businessmen—kept in touch with their astrologers, and that no major decisions were taken without consulting them. He had earlier negotiated my terms of employment, with instructions from K. B. Lall that the government would be willing to consider a salary higher than 4,000 rupees, the maximum for civil servants. We agreed that it was not worth making the exception. Paradoxically, in fact, on my STC salary, after paying personal tax (which then went as high as 97 percent), rent, provident fund and other deductions, I actually owed money every month for the privilege of working for this public enterprise. And my total personal income was of no great magnitude.

Next morning, Patel, looking well pleased, formally handed over charge, a ritual surviving from British days, and we both signed a statement to the effect that he was handing over and I was taking over. As a modern touch, there was a photographer present, who made us shake hands.

I looked around the room, and at the Muslim graveyard outside the window, the one more depressing than the other. The main office, through which I was formally taken around on another ritual, the inspection tour, was a slum of dirt, disorder, and unbelievable chaos, with stacks of floppy files piled to the ceiling, rickety glass-and-wood-partitioned private offices, ink-stained

CHAPTER SIXTEEN

desks, and collapsing chairs. The whole office reverberated with the noise of people talking loudly across their desks or standing around in groups, and of bells ringing to call peons, who took their own time to respond, as they, too, were busy conversing and doing nothing somewhere else. I was at one end, secluded from the rest by a vestibule and a small office for my staff of eight, two peons on morning duty and two in the afternoon, a personal assistant, a personal secretary, a stenographer, and a filing clerk. My office was enormous compared with the small pigeonholes outside, and it was full of furniture: a large horseshoe desk and swivel chair, a conference enclave, and walls lined with shelves and covered with charts, all with ascending coloured lines and bars that grew taller. On the floor was a wall-to-wall carpet, with many smaller ones on top of it. In one corner a screen hid a basin, a bucket of water and a jug, a towel stand, and a soap dish—another distinctly British touch from an earlier century.

I called for the peons and sent them out loaded with books, files, charts, furniture, rugs, and pictures of presidents and prime ministers. They asked me what they should do with it all, and I told them to take it wherever they liked. An hour later my room was sparsely furnished, its walls bare, and I sat back exhausted. I vowed to give the STC a new modern office, fit for people to work in. My office would be quite small, with no desk, just a few low chairs; no carpets or raw silk curtains to fade and gather dust, but instead grass mats and bamboo *chiks,* handloom tapestries and hangings with simple themes. The last touch would be to panel the walls with strips of stained wood to prevent dirt marks. This eventually was to become the style of all STC offices in India. It was simple, cheap, and of a purely Indian decor.

The curiosity aroused by the mounds of furniture on the landing was fanned into utter disbelief when I declared that I would need a staff of no more than one, a good stenographer, and the staff saw me carry my papers to another room, take my own telephone calls, and make my own coffee from a thermos flask of hot water and a jar of instant-coffee powder. I announced that anyone wishing to see me could walk in without an appointment, and that I did not wish to receive a file but only a note stating a problem or a proposition, the alternatives and the recommendations. I was determined to do away with the anachronistic remains of the Moghul-British style, so carefully woven into our own.

There were certain expressions of basic equality that I missed in

STATE TRADING CORPORATION

this environment, such as a senior manager saying to me on the telephone, "Yes, I will be over, but could it be in about fifteen minutes because I have a visitor with me?" No, in this world even a director would drop everything and leave the most important visitor on his own to come running. And for someone to say, "Well, I am not so sure that I agree with you on that," was unimaginable. The disagreement always came though, and in good measure, but only after one had left the organization. Then everyone would hasten to assure one's successor that he had never agreed with your policy, how boldly he had disagreed, and how he had been made to suffer and pay a price. While one was on hand, there was an atmosphere of total agreement and deference, in which people went wrong with fatal ease while assuming infallibility.

In the organization all matters for decision went up in a straight line to the apex that was the chairman. Down the line powers were delegated to different levels and always jealously guarded by those who possessed them. Yet when it came to the decision itself, they somehow always managed to bring in someone else, preferably their senior, to share the burden, just in case anything went wrong. Any decision might be questioned one day, and examined in retrospect a quick bold choice could prove fatal. I was shown a circular which among other things advised decision makers to look carefully at a decision taken faster than normally. Many patently suspect decisions were taken, but were so well camouflaged in rule and precedent that one could do nothing but in frustration admire the ingenuity involved. The new head of administration, I discovered, distinguished himself in interpretation of the rule. Describing the library, consisting of a few thousand volumes, mainly government publications and fiction, he mentioned proudly that it had a staff of four: a senior and a junior librarian, a clerk, and a peon. I asked about the volume of work, and found that on an average eighteen books were issued and received back in a day. "I suppose," I said, "the work of your library had increased so much that you had to add a junior librarian?"

"No, sir, we had to recruit a senior librarian, for there was already a junior librarian."

Asked how he could justify this action, he proudly brought a file and showed me the pages that made a case for strengthening the library staff. Corporations require books for reference by their staff, to enable them to keep up to date with the growing knowledge in their areas . . . at the same time it was necessary to

CHAPTER SIXTEEN

provide the staff with general reading matter to improve their minds . . . the library had been started with a meagre few hundred volumes, but now it had grown to several thousand, an increase of many hundred percent, which was expected to continue . . . therefore, in prudent anticipation of yet further progress, it was recommended that the library staff be strengthened. . . .

"But you must have had someone in mind for whom you wanted to provide a job," I hazarded.

He grinned knowingly. "But, sir, all posts are created and filled in accordance with proper procedure. I know my rules," he answered. He seemed proud of his capacity to legitimize an unjustifiable request while refusing to budge a hair's breadth from the rule when it suited him or a protégé.

How well they manipulated things, I discovered later. There was a system, for instance, for providing for substandard and unqualified protégés by hiring them temporarily, in which cases a separate rule relaxed the qualifications required for permanent employees. Both rules were perfectly valid and could be used as one wished. There was, however, no limit to how long a person could remain in temporary employment, and justification could be made from time to time for continuing the appointment—but only on a temporary basis. The person was given excellent reports for two or three years, and then, with equal insistence, it was recommended that a permanent post be created. The temporary appointment was thus made permanent on the strength of length of temporary service and good reports. Another person, who lacked influence and was hired temporarily merely to circumvent the need to justify a permanent post and seek the necessary sanction, might remain forgotten for years.

We decided that in future no temporary posts should be created. People should be hired only on the basis of justifiable need and through a proper selection procedure of qualifications and tests. In any case we were grossly overstaffed, especially at the clerical and peon levels. As for the existing temporaries, we decided to waive the entrance qualifications, which none possessed, but to subject them to tests, though of a standard lower than the normal. As a further concession we gave them three chances. One by one, almost all those who took the tests passed; some preferred not to take the test and to leave. Ultimately we were left with a girl who had failed each time. There was pressure from all quarters, including a minister, to confirm her. I spoke to the personnel manager about her case, and what I discovered shook me.

"Can't you do something to close the chapter on the temporaries?" I said. "There is only this one girl left. Can't you give her some simple test that she could pass?"

"No," he said, looking acutely embarrassed.

"Why not?" I pressed.

"Well, I will tell you the truth. The girl is barely literate. She cannot pass any test. She can read and write a little Urdu, but even in that I doubt if she could pass a test. For the past two years she has been coming to the office and spending her time knitting and talking. Everyone likes her, they understand her position, and she has been receiving good reports, so that in the normal course she would have been confirmed on the strength of the reports."

The place was full of people placed by someone, somehow. It was a haven for those who could not qualify for entrance into the government service, where quite high standards prevailed and the competition was stiff. It also proved a temporary haven at all levels for men who were on deputation (i.e., fixed tenure) from one of the ministries and awaiting their turn for promotion in their parent department. In the STC they could get a deputation allowance and good reports; there was, besides, the much coveted perquisite of foreign travel. I was reminded of a story that Bhagwan Sahay, who was then governor of Kashmir, had told me. He asked me if it was true that I was joining the STC. When I said yes, there was some talk of it, he said that it needed cleaning up, because it had become the refuge of those with influence who could not get in anywhere else. He had met someone at the Delhi airport who was anxious to shift from a distant post in Rajasthan to a more congenial place like Delhi or Srinagar. Bhagwan Sahay tried to put him off, as he considered the man useless. When the man realized that Sahay would not help, he said in disgust that if there was no other place, then he would have to get into the STC; and he did.

In the course of time, those who came in through the back door developed their own vested interests, and demanded that subsequent deputationists be sent back to their ministries and that we accept no one from outside. The most strident, not unexpectedly, were those who owed their own entry to influence, including a woman who later led them. There was also a demand, at almost

CHAPTER SIXTEEN

my first meeting with the staff, that I introduce merit as a policy in place of seniority, as they assumed must have been the case in my old company. I agreed that I had been brought up that way, but asked whether they were ready for a merit system. Though they protested loudly that they were all in favour of merit, a senior man, who was retiring soon, disagreed. He said they were not at all ready to accept merit in reality, for with them it would be a case of merit when they had it and of seniority when the other man had merit. He was right, I was to discover.

Upon my joining the STC, it was suggested by the cabinet secretary that I should call on the prime minister. In the brief audience she gave me, she received little notes and scribbled answers to them. This was a habit she shared with other important persons in India, who usually go on with their work when they receive one, taking telephone calls, reading files, consulting with their staff, and asking one to go on with what one has to say—which in my case was very little. The prime minister expressed the hope, as I was leaving, that I would introduce promotion by merit in the corporation, but she added that I would not find it easy to do so. She recalled an incident that characterized one approach to merit. When appointing someone whom everyone considered suited to and deserving of the job, she was quite earnestly told by a senior colleague, "Madam, there could be other more important considerations in life than merit." She added with a smile, "One does not even know where to begin answering something like that."

I discovered that it was always the case of the rule when it was in their favour, and of the exception when the rule went against them. This would have been understandable—had it not been for the protests that always followed when someone else gained in the way they had tried to do themselves. Their pragmatic acceptance of really big influence was interesting, however. Those who had it were envied, for the sources and power of influence were known to all. Curiously, it was tolerated better when it came from outside and especially from a high quarter; exercise of influence from inside was regarded as unfair. That you might not be able to resist pressure from outside was understandable—and there was always a give-and-take—but that you should try to exercise it yourself when no such pressure had been brought to bear was not acceptable.

K. B. Lall kept a close eye on me, and made Alexander my wet nurse. He was to see to it that my private-sector training did not cause me to leave my decisions unrecorded and unguarded, so that they might be questioned years later. If there was no record to show how a particular decision had been taken, the issue could go by default. The noting system could cover even a perverse decision with a lengthy recitation that at its weakest must at least admit some argument, whereas a good, bold decision, poorly or simply recorded, stood no chance. I found, too, that notes were made with such precision that they might, for example, begin with "The meeting was called by the secretary in the Ministry of Foreign Trade on Monday, 1st July 19.., at 4 P.M., in the office of the secretary at Udyog Bhavan, New Delhi, at which were present the following persons. . . . The secretary opened the meeting by stating. . . . " I was told that someone had gotten into trouble because he had been unable to prove in his defence that his action had been decided on at a meeting, because no time and place of the meeting were indicated in the note he had prepared.

My first experience of "audit" was instructive. Of the numerous checks made on an enterprise, audit was much feared, and yet the situation was not without its humour, if you could rise above your suffering. The audit men would arrive and begin a minute examination of all actions taken, decisions made to buy and sell, contracts entered into; and as the audit usually took place three to five years after the actions, sufficient time had elapsed to enable the auditors to show in retrospect that some at least of the myriad decisions taken were either wrong or could have been improved on. After the war between India and Pakistan in September 1965, when the field of action was Kashmir, civilian road traffic between Srinagar and Jammu had been disrupted at a time when the autumn walnut crop was ready for shipment. Someone decided that to help the farmers, who usually owned only a few trees each, the STC, the only government commercial organization available, should buy up as much of the crop as possible and sell it on the Indian market. To give the maximum help to farmers, a high price was set. The corporation was therefore left with large stocks that it had to sell cheap, and thus lost money on the purchase. That the main purposes of providing timely help had been served was of no concern to the young audit team leader. Why had the crop been bought? Was it bought in the ordinary course of the STC's commercial operations? Was the price paid and that at which the walnuts were sold commercially sound? In each case the

CHAPTER SIXTEEN

answer was an emphatic and honest no. Then why was it done? I explained that it must have been done on instructions from above. Had the instructions been received in writing, and, if so, had the commercial unsoundness of the operation been pointed out in writing to the authorities concerned before taking action, and had clear instructions been obtained to proceed nevertheless? Was it made clear, in writing, that there was going to be a loss, and the nature and likely extent of the loss, and was written sanction sought for it, and received? The STC was an autonomous corporation, and its management must surely be expected either to act on sound commercial principles, or to seek clear instructions to ignore them.

I put myself in the shoes of the man who had authorized the purchase. If he had dotted all the i's and crossed all the t's so meticulously pointed out by audit now, it would have taken months and he would have been regarded as a pretty poor specimen of trader besides. And I was amused, too, at the idea of an administrator committing himself in writing to buying and selling with such patent commercial unsoundness, losing money, and himself risking the very audit questions that the STC was now facing. Whoever it was must have been wise enough to ring up someone in the STC and possibly to follow up the call with a letter that left it to the corporation to decide—of course in the way that he meant it to. I remembered the letter of the secretary to Hindustan Steel.

"Tell me," I asked the auditor, "during the wartime emergency, is this the way you would have acted?"

He tried to equivocate. "Your question is theoretical. My task is only to point out the facts. It is for management to send in its own explanation. I am not passing final judgment."

"But you are exposing the management to the risk of being questioned by Parliament. Do you think the STC will ever succeed like this as a modern, international trading concern that will have to buy and sell on snap decisions and risk buying badly if the market should go wrong?"

He was unmoved, though he did admit to me naively that he had to think of his career; objections sustained would be marked to his credit and, if not sustained, at least to his watchfulness. And as for us—well, he implied, you manage to explain things away; don't take it too seriously.

Some years later, the STC was caught doing in Andhra just

STATE TRADING CORPORATION

what the young auditor had suggested it ought to have done in Kashmir. During my absence abroad, it was asked to buy the unsalable leftover varieties of a tobacco crop in sufficiently large quantities to make a big impact on prices, in order to please the local electorate in the forthcoming elections, and to start doing so in a big way in three days' time. The exercise was meant not so much to favour the farmers, who had sold their crop already, as the politically influential tobacco traders, who wanted the STC to buy at inflated prices. Someone in the STC agreed, but asked for written instructions, because commercially it was not a sound proposition. He added that at the quickest it would take a week or so to send men to that distant part of India and organize the operation, which covered a large area and involved many crores. There he went wrong. Did he mistrust those who gave him the orders, to want them in writing? Was this the speed at which the premier trading organization of the country moved? Could he not act first and ask for instructions later? He did, in fact, act. The crop was bought, the "situation was saved"; but the instructions never came, and the man was called uncooperative and unimaginative and was transferred from the STC. As we rued our fate, I remembered the young auditor.

I discovered that the questions audit asked paled beside the questions that poured in daily when Parliament was in session, and for which a manager and a small staff were specially appointed. These covered almost the entire range of STC activities, and certainly kept the corporation and its management on their toes, though at some cost. Many of the questions were directed at me personally: my educational qualifications; my private-sector past; my travelling abroad, its cost, and the export orders I brought back; my relations with the ministry and its secretary; and the names of the foreign journals to which the corporation had subscribed since my joining it—these were some of the milder and easiest ones to answer.

A few months after joining the STC, I submitted the review committee's interim report and, some months later, the final report. K. B. Lall said that the government would accept all its thirty-eight recommendations, but not the proposal to appoint a vice-chairman, who, apart from taking much routine work off my hands, would provide for succession, the bane of most public undertakings. Lall was certain that this particular recommendation, logical though it was, would not find acceptance. When I

CHAPTER SIXTEEN

pressed him, he said that no minister with power to do so would let slip the opportunity to appoint a chairman of his choice. Whatever the reason, the STC took a year to find a chairman after I had left. It was common for public enterprises to leave board and chairman's posts vacant for long periods of time despite the fact that retirements had been anticipated years in advance.

Soon after joining the STC in 1968, I outlined to the ministry my plan to leave the corporation for three months in 1970 in order to accept a teaching invitation at Berkeley, California. It would be useful to let the corporation run on its own momentum, and on my return I would be ready to start grooming someone to take over from me. In any case I wished to leave at the end of four years instead of the contracted five, and preferably earlier.

Before I left for California early in October 1970, a problem arose in connection with the new system of hiring a dozen or so management trainees every year to provide new blood. Added to this, that anathema of Indian labour, the computer, reared its head. Our growing volume of contracts had to be computerized to process the large amount of data generated. To this departure there were violent objections. As these were being resolved, the newly active officers' association became involved, and so did the issues.

The officers' associations, comprising the junior and middle-rank managers, were a new phenomenon, peculiar to the public sector and originating perhaps in the ICS Association (the main activity of which was, however, a gentlemanly annual get-together, rather like a regimental reunion dinner, at which some reference was made to the state of the service). The managerial staff felt under increasing pressure from the growing belligerence and violent demonstrations of the labour unions. The unions were encouraged by the political parties and so always won their point, no action ever being taken against them for their misdeeds. Unsupported from above, the officers felt isolated. They were often humiliated by the workers, and senior management could not help them, since after each strike the agreement forbade victimization, which in effect meant that no action could be taken for the most flagrant breach of discipline or insults to officers. The officers' leadership was usually helpless, either because it was weak or because it was under pressure from the top to settle, since it was a foregone conclusion that management must surrender in the name of justice.

STATE TRADING CORPORATION

Corporation officers therefore began to seek protection in organizing. They, too, turned to the politicians for support; and soon they also were demanding and protesting much as their subordinates did. There were enough men in their ranks who had been promoted from below with experience in demanding and protesting. There was some hesitation at first among the directly recruited officers about whether and how to protest, but soon those who had come up from the ranks took the lead in establishing new methods of demanding and protesting, till some of the officers' "charters of demands" read like the workmen's union manifestoes, and also did their protest slogans and their method of delivery.

The STC had been simmering for some months, the officers not knowing what they wanted except "justice and fairness"—generally meaning more and quicker promotions, with as little induction of officers from outside as possible, and automatic promotion based on length of service. They were led by a redoubtable lady, quick, intelligent, and a natural leader. We would often have chats about merit, on which we agreed; but pressed for the seniority system by her followers, she had to support this too. She suggested that I should follow the example of an earlier chairman, whom she regarded the best the STC had ever had. He had believed simultaneously in both seniority and merit. If he felt that the tenth person on the seniority list was the one with most merit, he would promote all ten. The nine senior officers were happy to get the promotion, eight of them unexpectedly, and the tenth the chairman placed where merit was needed, thus making everybody happy. She waited expectantly for my approbation; instead I made some trite remark like, "What about the organization?"

Leaders of the staff association and the union decided to throw in their lot with each other, and as this was the week before I was to leave for Berkeley, both sides must have felt that it was the right time to act. All hell was let loose, both at the office and upon my house.

In the same week our younger son, Gautam, a young cavalry captain, was married, and we held a small reception at our house. The union men arrived in several hired trucks just before the guests were due, and lined up in front, complete with the large, lugubrious-sounding Punjabi drum that is slung from the shoulder and beaten on the sides with two sticks. With great Punjabi lustiness they beat the drum to the rhythm of a dirge invoking my death,

CHAPTER SIXTEEN

followed by rhythmic beating of their breasts in a Punjabi *siapa,* as though their wish had already been fulfilled. Whereupon the invocation of my death would start once more, again followed by the dirge, thus adding their funereal contribution to the felicitations that the young newly-weds were expecting from the guests. In between there would be passages of protest about management trainees and the computer before they switched to English, lacing it with much abuse and invective.

My wife and I came out to present ourselves, because there had been a telephone call from their president, a member of Parliament, to warn me of the demonstration. He had genuinely protested, he told me, when he learned about the wedding reception, and had made the unionists agree to disperse as soon as the guests arrived. It might, however, be helpful, he suggested, if I went out and met them for a moment so that they would feel rewarded by being noticed, but of course I must ring back if they did not keep their promise. He had also taken the precaution of asking the nearby police station to send an officer and men just in case things got out of hand.

As we appeared, there was a shout that rose to a crescendo. Happy, laughing, transformed in a moment from demons to children, they broke off. Their cheer leader came forward to shake hands and offered congratulations to the young couple, after having so earnestly wished Gautam semi-orphaned. At the office there was much shouting and yelling, with musical instruments and drums, and muck dumped on the boardroom floor, all of which puzzled our foreign visitors, particularly those from communist countries.

Everybody had made his point. The next day an agreement, in large part saving the union's face, was signed, and the incident was over. When I reached the office, the whole place had been cleaned up; the broken plant pots had been replaced, and the dignified calm of an international trading corporation had returned. The victorious lady gave me a disarming smile. The union leadership had proved itself once again by successfully bringing them through a struggle to the end, including a *morcha*—they had led a sortie, after all, and had invested my house.

I went to say farewell to K. B. Lall, who asked me what had happened. I explained that the protest had been against me alone, a consequence of the two years of strain that the organization had been through, the changes I had introduced, and the pace I had accelerated before going away for three months. The protesters had accepted it all with more willingness and grace than I would have expected, but a point had to be made and they had made it. The organization could now freewheel for a time, and I did not think he would have any problems in my absence.

Berkeley was a moratorium and a recharging experience. The student unrest whose first signs I had seen at Los Angeles three years earlier had reached its peak in the spring quarter of 1970. In the autumn quarter, when I arrived, the campus was quiet.

Berkeley's rise in the post-war world had had a special significance for India, because it had trained the most young Indians of any university abroad, especially in science, and the largest foreign contingent among its students still came from India. Many Berkeley scholars had worked in India with an interest that exceeded the interest the British had once displayed. If the latter had worked hard on their gazetteers, the Americans took up such narrow subjects as the growth of the families of a small Punjabi village as they spread all over the world. (I asked this particular young scholar why he had chosen this village, and he told me that he had married one of its Sikh girls, who was also doing research.) Another American was doing research on the Gadar independence movement before the First World War, a topic little worked on in India, and he had built up a whole library on the subject. A third spent his young life, which ended abruptly in the United Provinces, translating the works of Munshi Prem Chand into English. But this scholarly activity was now on the wane, because of new restrictions. When I visited Berkeley two years later, only a trickle of exchanges remained. American scholars were turning instead to Africa, China, and the Soviet Union. The British, French, and Germans had lost interest in India many years before, the Russians were never interested, the Chinese were cut off from us, and now we had decided we did not need American scholars.

There may have been political and rational reasons for our academic isolationism of the late 1960s, but to me of most interest was the envy of our own academics, who began to feel that the American scholars were intruding on their ground with vastly greater funds. But were many among our academics really interested in research? This question was never-examined. Few scholars in India publish because they usually need not do so. Much teaching is still from books published abroad, and the output of research and writing from our institutions of excellence is sadly small. When Indian

CHAPTER SIXTEEN

academics do publish, it is mainly collections of articles or readings. There must, of course, have been Americans who descended on India without much feel for their subjects, or much scholarship, but with ample funds. There were many more, however, whose contribution was substantial in fields that did not seem to interest our scholars, at least then. In the end, what brought the lid down firmly was, I believe, the rule that a student coming to India to do research for a degree from his own university abroad had to work under an Indian faculty, whose veto could prevent his own university from awarding him a degree. We also began to ban entry on one ground or another. There was much talk of the anti-Indian writings of American scholars, of their misrepresentation and of their lack of understanding of India, and naturally of the CIA, charged by the American press with infiltrating the Peace Corps. Was it conceivable that, having received so much aid over the years, India had somehow to compensate for the sheer weight of gratitude, and that perhaps we overcompensated?

Towards the end of my stay, young Indians began to drop in with the expected question, but this time there was a difference. Many had settled down or were in the process of doing so, and there was less talk of going back. Others who were planning to return, a much larger number this time, had decided to start their own businesses, and were saving capital and looking for some area of collaboration with firms in the United States to manufacture in India under license. What worried them, however, was talk, reports in the press, and speeches about delays and the graft needed to cope with the maze of permits and licenses. For a license to produce, to acquire land, to obtain power, water, telephone connections, finance, raw materials, for every step forward they would have to pay. But there was nevertheless great confidence among them, and they accepted these problems as so many challenges.

Chapter Seventeen

PORTRAIT OF A MINISTER

I WAS in Moscow in the summer of 1970, staying with D. P. Dhar, our ambassador, when news came of a major cabinet reshuffle, and I found that there had been a change in my own ministry, the third in two years. The new minister was L. N. Mishra, whom I had never met. I therefore asked Dhar how I would find him as my minister, with whose two predecessors, both predictable men, I had gotten on well. He smiled. "You will have no trouble with him at all. He will always have a big hug and a broad smile for you. There may be a message to give help here and there to someone interested in an import license or a job, and as long as you help you will have no problem. None at all," he added with emphasis.

It would be my first experience of dealing with a real politician. Not being a regular civil servant, and unused to dealing with political personalities, I was diffident at the thought of having to learn to deal with my third new minister in two years. I felt uneasy starting on the journey home, afraid that in my relations with the ministry I would now have to cope with political factors, something I found unfamiliar and distasteful. I had come to the STC to offer my managerial skills and not to cope with politics, for which I was plainly unsuited. As it turned out, while I found dealing with Mishra somewhat less difficult than I had expected, I was always in silent conflict with his in-group, whose lack of standards and unconcern for international trade were accompanied by some involute ways.

On return to Delhi there was a message asking me to meet Shri L. N. Mishra, the new minister for foreign trade, for which I should make an appointment through his personal assistant. In this environment, no one at a level senior to you would ring up and introduce himself, or send a short note with a word of welcome; the custom was to leave it to the personal assistants to arrange

CHAPTER SEVENTEEN

things. "The honourable minister will speak to you," would be the peremptory demand of his secretary over the telephone.

Early next morning, I rang up Harish Sarin, secretary in the defence ministry. I asked him what he thought of his old minister, and he described the man and his style with characteristic clarity and forthrightness. Harish had learnt something about me from his younger brother, Mahesh, who after a particularly rough passage in two public enterprises had joined as one of the directors of the STC, and seemed to have settled in well. Harish told me I was not going to find the going familiar or easy, for of all the ministers he had worked under in his long years in Delhi, even including Krishna Menon, Mishra was the only one with whom he had not known how to build a connection. "I don't think I ever satisfied him," said Harish. "I wonder if I would even know how to. He is warm, effusive; but don't let that worry you. With your lack of understanding of our administrative and political ways, with your sensitiveness and your management style—well, you will find it, let us say, interesting. I wish you luck."

Apprehensive, I walked into the minister's room, where I had so often breezed in confidently in the past, both during and before my time with the STC. Mishra was of medium height, round, with a short, thick neck accentuated by a Nehru jacket, and a toothbrush moustache. He gave me a wan smile as he half rose to offer a soft, limp hand. Having received me without any special warmth, he began to question me perfunctorily and absently, while he talked to his deputy minister. I explained a little about my background—that I had only been in the STC for two years and was not a regular public-sector man. He cut me short; he knew all about that, he said. How was the STC doing?

"Doing reasonably well," I said. "It could do better, but of course it has been growing fast."

"Have you any problems?"

"Not particularly; and if I did I would try not to trouble you with them."

"Oh. Why not?"

"Well, they would be for me to solve, and I would not like to worry you."

This seemed to puzzle him.

The conversation continued in desultory fashion for a few minutes, and then he waved me out and continued to talk with his deputy. It was one of the very few business conversations we had of such length. I walked out with the same sick feeling in my stomach with which I had walked in, bracing myself for the unfamiliar experience ahead.

I went into K. B. Lall's room, and with his usual cheeriness he asked me how the first meeting had gone. Badly, I said. I had left Mishra unimpressed. I didn't think he needed a manager; he needed a minion, a tool for I didn't know what purpose. Lall said he could guess how we had reacted to each other, but one had to realize that here we had a new sort of person to deal with, someone who would be determined to have things his own way. He added that things would undoubtedly be different, but that we must wait and see, and jump to no conclusions. If I was depressed, my curiosity was also aroused by this new public-sector challenge.

A few days later, Lall told me, with a touch of seriousness instead of his customary facetiousness, that I had been right. My first meeting had gone badly, and I had certainly not impressed the minister. I was not alone in this; he, too, was having problems. The minister wanted Lall's additional secretary transferred, right away. K. B. had tried to explain that an official could always be transferred—it was the prerogative of a minister—but that when a man had a good record a hasty transfer could cast an undeserved shadow over his reputation, apart from leaving him discouraged. One should find a suitable place for him first and then make the change, rather then removing him from his job summarily. The desired end could be achieved without causing harm to the individual. But, as Lall had expected, this argument did not work and the man was transferred.

Although he put on a brave face over the loss of his secretary, I knew that Lall was hurt and disappointed, particularly as a new group was emerging in the ministry who had begun whispering that it would be his turn next to move, and that it was now the turn of the Brahmins to displace the Mathurs. This indeed happened. A number of departmental secretaries also were moved around at that time, on the ground that they had been in the same ministry for too long. Lall had been in the ministry for over ten years, except for a three-year break as ambassador at Brussels to Belgium and the increasingly important Common Market. In the defence ministry, to which he was now moved, he succeeded Harish Sarin, who had been there for over twenty years. It made sense to introduce new blood, given good administrative reasons, but many would not see it in that light.

CHAPTER SEVENTEEN

When I suggested to Lall that perhaps the minister might want to shorten my tenure in favor of a person of his own choice, he replied, "No, although I do see your point. The organization needs you for some time yet. In any case, it is best not to suggest it, because he will most likely take advantage of your offer. He must already have someone in mind. Let us leave it over till after you return from Berkeley, and I will support your other suggestion to test out Praxy Fernandes as acting chairman." I was informed that the minister did have someone in mind and felt thwarted because the recommendation of Fernandes, one of the STC's directors, had already been made. I believe Mishra wanted this withdrawn so that he could make his own recommendation. There was an impasse, but, through Lall's insistence, Fernandes acted as chairman from the outset, although official confirmation did not arrive till near the end of my absence. As his behaviour cannot have added to Lall's acceptability to Mishra, and must have been one more reason for his own departure, I was surprised and touched that he should have so persevered.

Upon my return from Berkeley, I found the STC in good shape. Despite some differences among the directors, the team and the systems had worked smoothly. Praxy had proved a good leader. Although in this, his first big command, his "up-guards-and-at-'em" approach had not been quite the style of the other directors, he was dynamic and well-meaning, and all went off satisfactorily. But just as we were starting my first management committee meeting, a telephone call came from the minister. After perfunctorily noticing my return, he told me that he was fed up with Fernandes, who had refused to do what he had asked him to. I said I would look into the matter and report back. The complaint involved a promotion sought by someone, and denied for good reason, but brought to the minister's attention as an injustice.

Praxy's problem with the minister during my absence was an interesting example of how one can be influenced by an allegation of injustice if one lacks all of the facts. A young man in the STC had approached the army chief of staff, under whom he had served, and asked him to speak to the minister about a grave injustice done to him, an opportunity denied him because of a bad annual report, which had been given deliberately after the good one he had received the year before. General Manekshaw must have spoken to the minister, who spoke to Praxy. The latter tried

PORTRAIT OF A MINISTER

to explain, but no one was interested. Since no action was taken, the young man must have reminded the general, who in turn prodded the minister, apparently adding that the latter's writ did not seem to run very far in his own corporation. Praxy contacted the general personally and tried to explain, but again with no success. Everyone was convinced that there had been an injustice, and that it had to be put right. By now the young man, the chief of staff, and the minister were all feeling frustrated. When I took the telephone call from the minister, I must have arrived at the flash point. I told Praxy not to worry. I would see the general myself. He grinned with relief.

It was strange, I thought, that so small a matter could grow so big. Praxy was generous to a fault. Through a man of clear likes and dislikes, he was just and fair, and had in this case gone out of his way to help. And yet no one believed him, the acting chairman of one of the largest corporations of India, or even asked him for the facts, so convinced were they of the injustice.

Manekshaw, soon to be the hero of the third Pakistan war of 1971, was fresh and trim and immaculately uniformed. He received me openly, without condescension. I said I had come to see him because Fernandes did not seem to have been able to convince him that the young man had not been unfairly dealt with. The general declared himself convinced that an injustice had been done, because he knew the young man was good material. The same man who had given a good report the previous year had now given a bad report, which looked like deliberate downgrading. He spoke crisply and confidently, in no doubt about the only version he had heard. I said I could appreciate how he felt about injustice to others, since he had once himself been unjustly treated. If this surprised him, he did not show it. As it happened, my heart had gone out to him when, during Krishna Menon's defence administration, he had nearly been asked to leave the army on the spurious and naive grounds that he was overly British and therefore of dubious loyalty to India as a soldier. I suggested to Manekshaw that I would send him the confidential reports about the man for the last two years. I would then come back, and accept his judgment. "Fine," said the general. "That is good of you."

I had read the two reports, written by the same official, and had found them entirely fair, consistent, and sympathetic, bringing out both the strengths and weakness of the subject. The earlier

CHAPTER SEVENTEEN

report had, in fact, also touched upon the weakness in question. When I saw Manekshaw again a few days later, he received me with much warmth and said he had read the file and agreed with us. He was sorry that the young man had not responded to what we had tried to do for him. He would say no more. I thanked him for his generosity. I would still help the young man because he was indeed good material. "With all the regard and respect he has for you, it might help if you spoke to him," I suggested. "You bet I will," replied Manekshaw.

As I shook hands with him, I added that he had acted just as I had hoped. I had a young son in the army, and I felt reassured. At this he seemed surprised and pleased. It was encouraging to think how little it took to change the scene. Far too often the judgment was handed out with the charge.

I explained to the minister that I had spoken to Manekshaw, who was now satisfied. Mishra was satisfied too, so long as he did not have to be reminded about it. Soon he stopped sending men to me for favours because those he sent were usually not the kind who made the grade. He realized that I was not prone to ask or grant favours, though I don't know whether he appreciated such independence. It seemed out of place in an environment in which, as in a joint-family network, favours done and favours asked were a natural exercise of whatever power one possessed. He must have had demands on him all the time. Relations, friends, and others who needed little things, and increasingly the not-so-little, turned to whoever had the capacity to pull strings for jobs, promotions, transfers, withholding of retribution for misdeeds, and granting of contracts, licences, or permissions out of turn and at the expense of someone else. For a whole range of favours people looked to members of the power grid to put in a word with someone if that someone was higher than them; to speak to him if he was below them; simply to instruct him if he was well below; and if he was too far below, then to have him spoken to. There was a well-defined and demarcated heirarchy of approach, and the system had been refined into an art. The telephone call, the personal visit, and, if the matter was very important, sometimes even a dinner invitation, were all well timed to be neither too soon nor too late. The message would come just as the file dealing with the case reached the table. Persuasion was equally well balanced between a hint and a demand, sometimes a feather touch and sometimes the sledge hammer. In such cases, the help of someone lower down had, of course, already been invoked to create the coincidence. The personal assistant of one would ask the personal assistant of the other when the file was to be sent up, and on the tip-off would arrange the phone call. It was not unknown for a senior minister to ring one up in connection with the appointment of a peon or watchman.

There were usually two styles of approach, the simple and the sophisticated, the direct and the indirect. The simple, direct approach, common among politicians high or low, could be utterly straightforward, depending upon the power it commanded, and consisted of just asking for something to be done, exactly in a certain way, with no quarter given, and no reasons accepted for inability to do it. The sophisticated approach exercised by some, usually the administrators, was to leave you to decide—but, of course, their way. In between the two were a variety of personal styles and nuances, but in the end they all added up to a plain give-and-take, a mutuality of interests, a candid sharing of the fruits of power. That was Mishra's in-group; if one joined it, pressure did not need to be brought to bear on one, because one was a part of it and had accepted it as a way of life. One did what one was asked to do and in return asked for what they could do, each to the best of his ability, which meant to the outermost circumference of power, and even in the penumbral region beyond.

There were exceptions. When leaving on a trip to the East and Australia, I said farewell to Dinesh Singh, the former minister of foreign trade. He was on the point of being transferred, though I did not know it. Singh asked me if I would have a look at a young man in the ministry, whose chances in the government setup were limited. "Yes, we would be glad to look at him and do what we can, but I hope we will not be made to feel bad if we are unable to help," I replied. Dinesh never sent him or anyone else.

On the other hand, there was a member of Parliament who kept ringing me up, always before I was awake, about a young man who had applied for a job. He flared up when I told him that a thousand others had also applied for it, and were taking the tests; all had a right to be considered. What more than *his* right was this boy asking for? he thundered. In a free country, did he not have the fundamental right to employment, which even the constitution assured everyone; was he not merely demanding his right to a job; was he not qualified for it; by what justice, could I deny him that right? Men like me had no sense of fairness, na-

CHAPTER SEVENTEEN

tional feeling—and he enumerated all that he felt I lacked. Men like me should not be where we were. We still clung to an antiquated, slavish past. I had no answer to this kind of logic; besides he was privileged, I was not. And his patience seemed exhausted, while mine could not afford to be.

In the midst of our launching a new selection scheme for management trainees, Mishra rang up Mahesh Sarin, who was in charge of it, and said, "What is this newfangled scheme you have introduced? What do you need—first-class graduates, sportsmen, with extra-curricular activities? How many do you need—a dozen? I will send you ten with all those qualifications. No, I will send you twenty, so that you even have a choice. What more do you want? I don't see the point of all this fuss and expense!"

The way a favour was asked certainly had its own irrefutable logic. There was of course the lighter side too, as when a minister, not known to me, rang up most affably.

"Ah, Mr. Tandon, how are you?" he said.

"Well, sir, and you too, I hope."

"No, haven't you read in the papers? I had a severe heart attack, very severe, and I only came out of the hospital yesterday."

I politely apologized and lied suitably.

"Yes, and as I left the hospital, the doctor told me to be more careful in every way."

I was now beginning to guess.

"He told me to ride in a very smooth car, not our Ambassador—its jolting would not be good for me."

I now knew just what was coming.

"A friend has therefore advised me to go in for an imported car—what is its name? Mercedes or something. Will you please see to it that the STC releases a good recent model?"

To politicians and businessmen of a certain kind, Mercedes symbolized power and success. Politicians got it through the exchequer at a special price; businessmen bid for it though their firms at our auctions and paid lakhs of rupees. As it happened, in this case the poor man died soon afterwards, despite his well-sprung car.

Lalit Narain Mishra, my minister, a middle-class village brahmin whose upbringing and education had bequeathed him directness but not cultivation, was purely political, suffering few inhibitions. Placed in a job next only to foreign affairs in sophistication, his likes and dislikes were never half-hearted. His foreign trade

PORTRAIT OF A MINISTER

portfolio demanded an understanding of the world of business and international commerce, while his own horizon extended from provincial politics in Patna to national politics in Delhi, and beyond to the commerce and industry of Coimbatore, Surat, Ludihiana, and Kanpur; Bombay and Calcutta he did not care for. Into his world, as to the depths of the seabed, no light from the universe beyond penetrated. He was elemental and earthy. It was as interesting to see him at a meeting with politicians from his home base as with a foreign ministerial delegation on international trade. At the ballet in Moscow, he yawned through Swan Lake and left before the interval. He was essentially a country type from Bihar, now drawn into international trade, with no concessions made to anything that was not Bihari. A man all of a piece, his grain ran consistently and predictably one way. He was truer, though, than some other, more sophisticated politicians.

Slowly he granted me familiarity. I would see him with or without an appointment, but we did not discuss the intricacies of foreign trade. Looking back I cannot even recall whether we discussed trade at all. The meetings were usually held to communicate information or to explain something. He seldom sought my advice but always listened. I would occasionally tell him about our results, and he was content to know that everything was going well. Above all, he wanted no problems in the STC, and once when we had staff trouble and I wanted to take firm action, he told me to go ahead so long as I could contain it. "Bhai Tandon, peace buy, *karo*," was his simple advice to me. "Make sure they don't take a procession to Parliament or to her house." He seemed, however, to like his relationship with me, and in the presence of colleagues showed pride in my partly familiar but impeccably correct and circumspect manner, implying both respect and equality. It was an unfamiliar combination to him, and he seemed to like it.

But there was a court. Mishra's bulky, soft figure, especially when he sat with his legs drawn up on the sofa, dressed in loose starched *kurta* and *dhoti,* resembled that of a *zamindar rajah*—an interesting contrast to Dinesh Singh, who was a *zamindar rajah* but played an altered role. Having lived as a boy in an Indian princely state, Bahawalpur, that was medieval except for the ruler's Rolls Royces, I could understand court society, where one moved in convolutions which mostly achieved so little that they appeared to be indulged in for their own sake.

CHAPTER SEVENTEEN

Mishra seemed by nature to put more trust in luck and omens, and in lesser men, than in a confident, self-reliant course. In themselves, his clique of supporters were a disparate lot, with talents that could have been used to help him grow into a bigger man; his abrupt, early end might have been avoided. These men practised the old art of statecraft, in which the world of international trade played no role except to provide a good life at home and abroad. The trusting way in which Mishra let himself be influenced, and even moulded, puzzled me. According to what may have been an apocryphal story, he was once asked to cut someone down to size. He obliged, and afterwards asked if they were satisfied. They assured him that he had handled the matter extremely well. "But what had the man done?" he enquired naively. In my own presence he once remarked, as if tutored, "Yes, yes, we will have to provide for some direct control over STC, for the time when Mr. Tandon is there no longer." It was a hint I was supposed to take while I was still there.

Strangely, Mishra was a good friend of Manekshaw, a relationship presumably dating back to his days in the defence ministry, and they had an easy familiarity with each other that superficially lacked logic. It was a case of opposites reconciled, something common among us. Mishra seemed to like calling the general Sam, and Manekshaw's calling him Lalit, both slightly mispronouncing the names. The trim, moustachioed, heavily British-accented soldier, who could have fought at Balaclava, Omdurman, Amiens, or Chhamb, and the soft Maithili politician, on first-name, back-slapping terms, made a combination not easy to understand. Mishra was an old type in a new situation, Manekshaw a new type in an old situation. The two were so utterly different that they hardly seemed to belong to the same country—examples of a kind of contradiction common among our public men, whose behaviour often gave the lie to their language. We Indians have a propensity towards synthesizing our differences. I was reminded of what a Yugoslav had once said to a young man at the Indian embassy in Belgrade. He wondered whether in India we had two different kinds of people. "They don't dress like you, they don't look like you, they don't talk like you, they don't eat like you, and yet they are Indians and so are you," he observed in puzzlement.

The pressure mounted perceptibly on the STC, and I could feel the growing effect needed to resist it. The attack began with a whispering campaign hinting that the corporation was becoming too big and complex, and that its autonomy ought to be curbed for its own sake. The government should have a greater say in its day-to-day affairs. A plan was prepared to effectively control the corporation. All contracts of substantial size were to be negotiated with the concurrence of the ministry, whose representative was to be associated with all negotiations at all stages. This provision struck not only at the roots of the corporation's autonomy, but also at such speed and flexibility as it had lately acquired through reorganization, especially in its dealings abroad.

A New York oil-seed broker told me that the STC had in the past always paid more because foreign firms had to provide a cushion to allow for market movements during the fortnight it took the corporation to decide, whereas other traders acted promptly. "When the STC decides to buy 'quickly' on a Monday, by the time the office has prepared the note and cleared it through finance, it may be Thursday at the earliest," he said. "Then the message is sent by telegram, because the STC does not even possess a telex. We receive it on Friday, when again no broker will readily quote without a cushion, because he does not know how the markets will open after the weekend. And add a little more, because there are still other procedures to go through."

Since then the STC had acquired a telex, a speedy decision-making system, and a branch office in New York. To have now to refer every transaction to the ministry and to bring in its man, who for his own safety would understandably take all the precautions he considered necessary, would mean an even slower buying process than the one that had prevailed previously.

A question that someone had asked me at an early stage of my association with the STC, at a managers' conference at Srinagar, came to mind. How much of what I built would last? I began to wonder now whether anything one built or grew that the soil and environment would not accept could endure. And what could the STC alone do in face of such opposition to change? This question was often asked me as an early agent of innovation in the public sector. Some were convinced my effort was hopeless, others wished me well; few indeed shared my optimism, certainly not those who proclaimed their faith in progress.

Late one evening, out of the blue, I received a phone call to the effect that orders had been signed to relieve me of two of my directors because they had not exercised their option to stay per-

CHAPTER SEVENTEEN

manently in the STC or return to their government departments. A third was slated to go. The fourth, Praxy Fernandes, had already wisely decided to return to government. Thus I would be picked clean of my team, so carefully built up, and in return would have one not of my choosing imposed upon me.

I rang Mishra up immediately, and said I was coming over to see him. He replied, uncertainly, that he hoped not over this matter. I said that it was, and in a few minutes I was in his office. He did not quite seem to know how to cope with a situation that I was convinced was not of his making, nor perhaps to his liking, though he disliked some of my directors. I talked to him several times that week before he decided to say yes to me. The directors were permitted to remain on the STC board. I think we were both defeated in our own ways. I certainly felt defeated and was convinced that I was needed no longer.

In the next week, the crisis over for the time being, I wrote him a short letter in my own hand, addressing him for the first time by his first name, to say that I had tried hard to satisfy but had failed; I had done my best by the STC and by him; I would appreciate it if he would now let me go. There was no rancour in my resignation, only a touch of deep sadness. I wished him well in the future and in his own career. I do not know if he referred the letter to someone higher up and was told to stay his hand, or whether he felt it to be in his own interest that my departure should not be sudden, but he rang me up with great effusiveness, anxious that I should stay a while longer. I said, yes, I would, for his sake, but only for another two months. He then wrote a warm letter to thank me, also addressing me by my first name. I warmed towards him, too; he had risen in my estimation.

Two months later, after turning in the year's results, seemingly to his satisfaction, I stepped down. Mishra arranged one of his weekly officers' meetings for the day of my departure, and made a warm reference at the end of it to my leaving, for which I thanked him. Both within his ministry and outside it, he asked people to suggest a "new chairman like Tandon."

Curiously, despite its seeming irrationality, I found the faith to persevere in the public sector. It was there, it had a future, and someone had to serve it; otherwise it would have no future, or even exist. The early days of Indianization in a multinational corporation had not been easy; now we were experiencing the early days for professional management in the public sector.

PORTRAIT OF A MINISTER

Despite the worst storm ever faced by a minister in Parliament, Mishra had in him the makings of something bigger than what some of his "well-wishers" would have had him be. He was essentially a gentle and superstitious man, but with the great asset of determination. Unshakable faith and fidelity were what he had to offer. His ambition was to serve. And who knew what the future might have held? So long as his patron saints and the astrologers were happy, he was content to wait, propitiating them and the gods, both of whom ultimately cast him aside. He moved on and moved up—and beyond! His violent death—one of the only two political assassinations in India since independence, Gandhi's and his—brought surprisingly little comment that understood the man. Beyond some trite sympathy and condemnation of violence, no contribution was recalled, as if none was to be found. Some recognition came later, in the changed ambience of the Emergency, when an attempt was made to place the mantle of martyrdom on him. He left behind a big question mark, and on my mind he left more than a scratch.

On my return to Bombay from Berkeley in January 1971, I called on Ravi Hazari, deputy governor of the Reserve Bank, one of many excellent new government nominations from academia. He asked if I had had enough of the STC and would consider moving to banking? I laughed with surprise and replied that the answer was a clear yes. He said he wanted me for the Punjab National Bank, not because I knew anything about banking, but because it was time for a manager to enter banking, or at least to try it.

Looking back, the vivid patches at the STC were varied. Contrary to my experience at the bank later, its problems had all been across the boundary; within, it depended entirely on whatever momentum it could generate. As my first experience of moulding an Indian company, it gave me the feeling of having been raised like one of those venturesome horse regiments of the eighteenth and nineteenth centuries—Probyn's, Hodson's, Skinner's—to do a frontier job. Both in the years before and after me, the STC received little praise from Parliament and the press. Praxy Fernandes, who stayed in it the longest, a student of Karnataka history, and biographer of Tipu Sultan, who could himself have played the parts of Tipu, Dupleix, or Clive to perfection, summed up its spirit. B. P. Patel, my predecessor, a Gujarati Patedar Patel, had given the

CHAPTER SEVENTEEN

organization founded by the Kayasth K. B. Lall the thrust it had needed. These two had been the outstanding personalities as chairmen, with some political and administrative interludes.

The STC's problems abroad were not small either. Friendly nations offered credit on easy terms, and received back through tied sales more than they could ever hope to receive on sales for cash. Being confined to buying within the country, the normally competitive bidders had "understandings" among themselves, and rigged prices, but even when one was free to buy internationally, cartels existed on all sides, whether the bid came from the East or the West, from a free or a controlled economy. The cost of aid was thus amply repaid. There were understandings even between the controlled and uncontrolled economies. A price had to be paid for being new and inexperienced in the world market, especially wherever aid was attached. As someone once quipped, if aid comes, can strings be far behind? As if all this was not enough, some private traders in India would fly abroad and undercut the STC's export quotations with suspicious abandon, or get themselves appointed representatives of foreign exporters, performing no service and merely adding to the cost of imports, but giving their principals the assurance that they were fixing things in India on their behalf. The ways of these intermediaries could be devious and unsavoury, and some at least showed signs of power and influence. The bevy of administrators and politicians they could muster at their parties had to be seen to be believed. Countries of different political hues were all grey in the dark of this world of international trade.

The public sector was an experiment worth something, though I could not have said what, at least then. Moreover, my experience, traumatic though it was, took me back to the Punjab, and later also to Ahmedabad, and gave me a spell at Boston to teach a course in the management of public enterprises.

Chapter Eighteen

THE PUNJAB NATIONAL BANK

WHEN I entered the dining room on my first day at the Punjab National Bank to meet my senior colleagues at lunch, I felt I was back in the Punjab of the 1920s. Here time had stood still. One man was addressed as Panditji, someone else as Lalaji; others were Sharma Sahib, Verma Sahib, Chopra Sahib, Kapur Sahib, Brara Sahib, Soneja Sahib, Prasher Sahib. All the Sharma, Verma, and Arora subcastes of the West Punjab were there. Men who had worked together at branches at Lahore, Amritsar, Sargodha, Khanewal, Hoshiarpur, and Phagwara since leaving college addressed each other with formal courtesy and gravity. An exception was the exotic presence of a Vora Sahib—but a Gujrati Vora, who after years there appeared still to feel a stranger. The food was the same simple, middle-class Punjabi food—Arya Samaj *priti bhojan,* not rich or too spiced, a *dal* and a vegetable, with the fruit of the season. They all ate heartily and were mostly overweight. One by one as they finished, before the toothpicks were passed around, they loudly expressed their appreciation as if saying grace. The thin one, Lalaji, bantered with the fat one, Khanna Sahib, in what sounded like a daily routine. The solitary variation from the daily Dayanand Anglo-Vedic college menu was fried fish—pomfret—for Panditji, his only concession to non-vegetarianism.

As I listened to this conversation, I felt myself back among the ghosts of my father and his friends, dressed, eating, and talking in a manner that had not changed in half a century. Seeking firmer ground, I inquired whether they went for a morning walk before getting ready for the office. They all did. Emboldened, I asked one, more austere looking than the others, whether he was out well before the sun? Yes, he replied, by six in the winter and five in the summer. Another made sounds of wanting to be asked, and said that by that hour he would be back from his walk. Then the conversation expectedly turned to their alimentary systems, whose

CHAPTER EIGHTEEN

functioning had last been discussed the day before, with much familiar advice exchanged. In their working methods and the whole institution, I gathered, there was also a timelessness, broken only when Walker Sahib had come from the old Imperial Bank for a few years and made some changes.

In the afternoon I took a walk around the office, and felt as depressed as I had on my first day at the STC. The place was full of desks, files, cupboards, peons, and clerks; a milling crowd stood on the landings and the staircase on the way to the canteen, from which ill-clad boys rushed up and down the stairs all day long, precariously balancing trays of food and spilling tea and gravy. The canteen and the conveniences next door to it emitted mixed odours. In the stairwell of the building a steady volume of sound reverberated round the walls. From this cheerful chaos, I walked into my office, a large, pompous room with grease-stained upholstery, a carpet that harboured the dust of many a chairman's feet, and a big kidney-shaped table piled high with files, masses of paper strung together on thick thread with steel ends piercing each piece. This time I knew where to start.

I sent for the architect and suggested that he cut my room in half and ask the STC to sell my old furniture to the bank at its written-down value, because no future chairman of theirs would ever use it. We reorganized the executive wing into smaller offices, and refurnished them in my STC Indian style. The change left the general manager (known respectfully as Lalaji) untouched, however. He still had his large office, horseshoe-shaped desk, buzzer for the peon, and other symbols of his position, including his late hour of arrival at the office and a peon to open his car door and carry his slim briefcase. I found these old-fashioned symbols charming, since they appealed to my sense of the past and also constituted a cushion against change. In an old institution it was useful to leave at least one familiar landmark, a rallying point if the winds of change should blow too hard, and something to revive after I left.

Starting in 1895 as the premier Punjabi commercial institution, the bank had been founded by the nascent Hindu reformist movement Arya Samaj, and later became part of the new nationalism. It withstood many crises, especially the failure of a locally owned British bank, the Alliance Bank of Simla, in the middle twenties. With Punjabi sturdiness it grew stronger with each crisis, as if to demonstrate the economic strength of nationalism. It was one of the three pillars of Punjabi middle-class society, the other two being the Dayal Singh Majithia Trust, which ran a college and a famed English-language daily, the *Tribune;* and the Dayanand Anglo-Vedic chain of schools and colleges, especially those for girls. Interestingly enough, the one sprang from the Brahmo Samaj, a nineteenth-century Hindu reformist movement, a Bengali import, and the other from the Arya Samaj, also a Hindu reformist movement, which had come from Kathiawar. The Punjab National Bank and the *Tribune,* the first North Indian-owned English-language newspaper, belonged to my earliest memories. My coming as chairman to the bank of Lala Lajpat Rai and Mahatma Hansraj provided a satisfaction of its own, different from what I had known at the STC and Hindustan Lever, and with it the familiar feeling of the Punjab.

I had had my first introduction to the bank in the week I joined Lever in Bombay in 1937. Its branch manager had rung me up and asked me to drop in. Impressed by such flatteringly early recognition of my prospects, I discovered that what he had in mind was something totally unexpected—an offer of matrimony with the daughter of a respectable, affluent customer, on whose behalf he was approaching me. Considering one disappointment enough for him, I opened an account.

More than half of the bank's assets had been wiped out in the Partition, but its chairman had shrewdly moved the head office from Lahore to Delhi in good time, over the opposition of the Muslim-dominated government of the Punjab, and then only by appealing to the High Court. As if reinvigorated by the shock of Partition, the bank grew stronger and began to penetrate every part of India, changing from a Punjabi to a national institution.

At my very first board meeting, which was to be the last meeting under my predecessor, I realized the remarkable inherent strength of the PNB. A weighty discussion did justice to a massive agenda of hundreds of pages, so typical of the public sector, and the directors, Punjabi and non-Punjabi, argued with familiar Punjabi vigour, and took the management to task with great Arya Samajist rectitude. As the only member of the board from the bank, the chairman tried heroically to defend the management but, mild by nature, stood his ground with insufficient firmness. There was much iteration and reiteration of lapses that continued despite the chairman's assurances, one particular director taking the lead. Occasionally one of the managers in attendance would

CHAPTER EIGHTEEN

try to explain a point, unavailingly. With such thorough discussion of its faults each month, one might have thought that management would have little chance of going astray. Yet the discussion gave the impression that despite the board's assiduous efforts nothing had been learned. I also gathered that each member of the board specialized in some area, in which his criticism made a particular contribution.

I was interested to see how, after the chairman's hectic last meeting, his colleagues were going to bid him farewell, but they thoughtfully spared him. The party was an austere affair, which after two soft drinks and a buffet meal ended at an early hour. I had served on many boards, but had never seen such severity or lack of colour in an evening's entertainment, where even public enterprises were learning fast.

The bank's internal systems, and non-systems, were reminiscent of the STC: the chairman-may-kindly-decide kind of decision making, the board-may-kindly-recall approach. A loan proposal might originate in a distant branch and end up before the board months, sometimes as much as a year, later. The decision then took as leisurely a pace in percolating down, unless the customer was influential, when things moved fast. There was little modern planning, budgeting, or appraisal, mainly a reliance on accumulated experience and wisdom. As far as planning was concerned, the organization was left to sort out the uncertainties of its own creation. There was, expectedly, no telex. Before nationalization, the institution had worked well in the interests of the owners and those close to them, irrespective of the quality of service to the general public.

With little knowledge of the workings of commercial banking, I was puzzled at first by the number of customers who made losses or at best poor profits in industries known to be profitable. When I shared with my senior colleagues my apprehensions that our money could not be trusted with such companies, I was assured that it was perfectly safe, that they would never let us down. One had, of course, to take a "practical view" of how they arrived at their losses; that was their business. In time I was to discover why. It was not uncommon, for instance, for customers to borrow money from banks for a business that was doing poorly while the directors made personal gains which they invested elsewhere. A remarkable example was a small concern whose capital and reserves were wiped out by accumulated losses, and one of whose directors had taken a loan from the company equivalent to twice its total capital, repayable after thirty years, in the year 2001, at an annual interest of 2½ percent when the going bank-loan rate was around 15 percent! Equally common were boards packed with father, wife, sons, and daughters, including minors and near relations. One understood why when one saw them flying *en masse* to stay in luxury hotels at holiday resorts to hold their board meetings.

Bank nationalization sought to bolster up the small man instead. Small farmers, artisans, and rickshaw pullers, and even very poor workers on the edge of subsistence were all to be helped with credit, on easy terms and with no emphasis on security—a much harder assignment. The first problem for the banks was to seek such clients and to offer them credit, not to be mistaken for charity, which was to be spent on building up assets and creating an income rather than on ceremonials. Such potential customers had to be coaxed to enter a bank and to face its multifarious forms and signatures or thumb impressions, when the local money lender lent on trust at any time of day and night—though, of course, at his own rates.

There were two schools of thought in the bank about the innovations I attempted. The many, with a Punjabi resignation born of strife and change, felt that like others in the past, this too would blow over, and that it was best therefore to simulate interest. Those to whom change appealed, also a Punjabi characteristic, responded with genuine support. To the former, the new regime of discipline and initiative was irksome, for it deprived them of their comfortable world of give-and-take and flexibility at work, from which they derived personal power and patronage. To them, initiative lay in running private businesses and insurance agencies on the side, and to stop such activities infringed on their fundamental rights. I was told a story of a manager who hired a motor rickshaw and asked to be taken to the bank's head office. The driver said, "Yes, and to the fourth floor." "I suppose you even knew where I sit," said the manager. "Yes," replied the driver proudly, "I also work in the bank. I sign the muster roll every morning and then go to my own work."

Soon after I joined, I got an excellent opportunity to delve into the problems of banking. The National Institute of Bank Management, which I had already begun to cultivate as my academic mentor, called a conference of chairmen of the nationalized banks.

CHAPTER EIGHTEEN

Also invited were the finance minister, the governor of the Reserve Bank, and some of his deputies. Because nationalization called for far-reaching changes in the system, and Indian banks were not prepared for it, the finance minister was interested in hearing about their progress. The bank chairmen seemed preoccupied, however, with their major problem: the attitudes of the unions and the officers' associations, which were leading to deteriorating customer service, growing indiscipline, a poor day's work, and hence rising costs and falling profitability. The banks, they said, had indeed made much progress with their new tasks, but it would be limited unless they could cope with their staff problems. The minister asked what their suggestions were in this regard. They replied that he should talk to the union leaders and prevail upon them to be more cooperative now that the ownership of the banks had been taken out of private hands.

The bank chairmen were, in fact, competent, well-trained men who had built a banking system that was safe and solid and might have been envied by many developing countries. But though banking had been ahead of Indian industry in the 1930s, after the war industry modernized, while banking did not and fell back. The leading groups that controlled industry also controlled banking. Whereas in industry many innovated and diversified, introducing modern management and research and development, they left their banks alone—so long as these provided their own industries with the necessary money at rates that were among the cheapest in the world. When everything else was scarce and expensive, money was abundant and cheap. Banks continued to be run as before. Despite vast growth, they retained their simple, old methods of bulky ledgers and signatures and countersignatures. The Reserve Bank of India did not even have a spearate personnel division till the 1970s, and most commercial banks followed its example. The myriads of transactions continued to be dealt with manually. To move a paper from one desk to another in the same room, one relied on peons, while customers waited patiently. A cheque from another town would take three weeks to clear, though the mail moved in a day.

But if the banks did not change and modernize, their staffs did. They organized into strong unions, while the officers formed associations—a subtle social distinction. Both demanded modern benefits from the old-fashioned banks. The staff was well directed; the managements were not. And so while the unions, and in their wake the officers, won all the benefits they asked for, management got little in return except diminishing output at a rising cost. Instead of better terms resulting in modernization of bank operations, reduced costs, and improved service, the tendency was toward engaging more and more men and letting existing services deteriorate. Management became a mere holding operation. Soon the banks were charging customers more, giving them less, and paying a lower return to their new owners, the government. There was a familiar public-sector ring to it all.

After the conference, a bank chairman invited me to lunch to meet a great union leader, Prabhat Kar, the master of the All-India Bank Employees' Association. Our meeting was long and wordy. As soon as one problem was dealt with, another was posed. The union leader went on to explain in vivid terms that the main problem was management, or rather the lack of it in the system. The banking system in 1972, in some 15,000 branches, employed more than 250,000 people, of whom half were under thirty years of age and had joined since nationalization in 1969. The clerks were mostly college graduates and comprised the single largest graduate work-force in the country. These young people came from an environment of protest; they had often protested and demonstrated, and had always won, at home, in school and at the universities. Their demands had varied—to get a teacher removed, an examination postponed, a test made easier, results relaxed, and at one stage to have the whole system of testing scrapped, with freedom to attend classes or not, study or not, with a degree assured at the end. There was even a slogan, "No degrees, just jobs."

Against a background of vast unemployment, banking gave them well-paid jobs for a relatively easy work, backed by a very strong union, whose demands had gone far beyond the need-based wage to what Kar called a "fridge-based" wage. Making these young people work and training them to become useful, productive bankers, he regarded as being the job of management, a job that called for two things, management systems and management skills; and he was not sure that these existed. Most managers had risen from the ranks, with little special training; they were hardly in a position to guide and train others. What role his own powerful union could play, he did not touch upon.

"From what I have heard, you have come to your bank not just for a job but, to use your own language, as an agent of change,"

CHAPTER EIGHTEEN

he said to me. "You face a big problem; you must begin making changes at the top, and that is where you will meet with the most resistance. Those at the top are the no-change kind, otherwise there would have been no need to bring you in; managers could have done it. But they don't think they need you, and they are not going to be happy with you. You have been imposed upon them. They will join with the men below, with us, and try to sabotage everything you attempt; and whatever you manage to do they will try to undo after you leave. Let me assure you that we will not be your problem. It will be the managers. We would like changes, but we can't help you."

I very much wanted to ask why, but decided not to. He was enjoying the audience I provided, of a kind he probably did not often have, even among his peers. Between puffs at one of the cigars with which, he cynically observed, his friends the bank chairmen kept him provided, he watched me with interest and a benign smile. He had certainly guessed the problem, but offered no solutions. Nationalization to him was only a half-way solution, a stepping stone to the larger aims of his party, the Communist Party of India. I left him with mixed feelings. Here was another task to be performed in perpetual strife and confrontation, and with little help from either side.

I could soon see where Kar's strength lay. Walking through our largest branch in Delhi, on the ground floor of the head office itself, I found men happily playing games before four o'clock one afternoon. When asked, they said that it was customary to do so, and that in any case they had "finished their work for the day." This very branch had only a few days earlier asked for more staff to clear arrears that had accumulated over many years. Both men and managers accepted this situation as normal. The union leaders shrugged and said it was management's task to get work out of men—without, of course, adding to their already "heavy burden of workload."! The manager pleaded helplessness; at the slightest show of discipline, the men would shout and rave. In some branches men returned home in the early afternoon—having, of course, finished their allotted work and also collected their overtime for the day—and then went to afternoon film shows. Some came back from mythical sick beds, or annual leave, to collect overtime, euphemistically called "contractual" overtime.

But if there were many internal problems, there were few pressures from outside. Perhaps these were the early days of bank

PUNJAB NATIONAL BANK

nationalization, but I had never seen such permissiveness in the public sector. Parliament was benign, and dealt mainly with the ministry, and the ministry seldom bothered the banks. Nor did the customers often go to the government or members of Parliament for help. For once, all my problems were my own and the PNB's, for us to create or solve.

Reconstitution of the newly nationalized bank boards under the Act of Nationalization came at the end of 1972. All boards would have fourteen directors to represent the government, the Reserve Bank of India, the depositors, small industry, medium industry, big industry, the scheduled castes, economics, handicrafts, progressive farming, the officers' association, and the staff union. In the case of the PNB, there was also one who represented his own influence and was supposed to be connected with the highest powers in the land. The chairman and an executive director were the only employees of the bank representing management. The post of executive director was never filled in any bank. This omission was for the benefit of the chairman, sparing him the presence of an impatient crown prince. To this perfection of organization, my board sought to add a final touch. In order to provide adequate guidance and control over the day-to-day management of the bank, it wanted to divide itself by subject into subcommittees that would meet between and in addition to its regular meetings every three weeks. The board, consisting entirely of outsiders, would then decide policy, which its subcommittees would implement and manage. This I had to oppose, although many banks adopted it.

With nationalization, the officers' association flexed its muscles, and I perhaps helped it mature. It was management's own creation as a buffer between itself and the union. Its early presidents were amiable senior officers, and the chairman and senior managers were invited to its gentlemanly annual conventions to "give their blessings," until a pair of new leaders, one frankly political and ambitious and the other an idealist with a morbid concern for justice, took over. They overthrew the seniors and embarked on a tough line. Their first growls were misread in the wishful conviction that they were going to be overthrown by the rank-and-file, who would surely not approve of their belligerence. When the increasingly awkward spectre of militancy could not be wished away and these highly paid officers began to demonstrate and shout *"murdabads,"* the senior managers formed their own associa-

CHAPTER EIGHTEEN

tion, to which the officers' association at first reacted violently. Later, the latter saw an advantage in accepting it, provided the dividing line for membership was drawn in their favour. I was sandwiched between their leaders and their daily broadsides and broadsheets, directed first against each other and then against me. Each wanted my support and condemnation of the other, and when these were not forthcoming, both went for me at the same time as they went for each other. Thus only I knew where I stood—nowhere. The rest, including the top managers, had a sneaking sympathy for one association or the other. The senior association died a natural death, for the true answer to the problem posed by the officers lay in facing it and not in trying to circumvent it by creating a new force to oppose them.

I gently warned the officers' association that in its enthusiasm to strengthen their ranks and demolish a past disliked for its favouritism and nepotism, the leadership should not set itself up as the new fountainhead of power, offering patronage and protection to those who came under its wing. Its president rushed into my office one day asking for a transfer to be cancelled because the man concerned was his local organizer. When I refused to interfere, he stormed out. His favourite phrase with me was "cooperation or confrontation," both flexibly defined by him. But he was predictable, so long as one looked at his interests and not for consistency. He had an attractive smile, but whenever I saw it I knew I was being asked to concede, or had conceded, an unreasonable request. His frowns I found more reassuring.

The staff union was stronger and more confident. The staff could afford to leave me alone for a bit and let me get ahead, because the changes I was making would affect management first, while their own interests were secure, given their strength. Their president, unlike the officers' president, had no advice to offer me, nor any expression of fears, expectations, or support. To him I suggested what I had suggested to George Fernandes some years earlier, that we should let our personnel managers and his union officials negotiate and reach their conclusions, and ourselves meet occasionally to discuss policy issues and deal with any serious roadblocks. With him, as with Fernandes, both being generous, down-to-earth men, this system worked well.

The union president made the unusual proposal that the whole promotion process, then based on seniority alone, should be overhauled to give the young a chance to rise rapidly on merit, a suggestion I had never heard before or since from any union leadership in India. We worked on the proposal and arrived at a new promotion policy. Where it usually took clerks till their early fifties to become managers, under the new formula that we devised, they could compete for management posts within six years of entering service. That the president had the wisdom to recognize the impatience of the young, and got them to compete for self-improvement, was as remarkable as it was encouraging to me to press ahead with the change. There was opposition; someone took the matter to court, but nothing came of it. The policy survived until soon after I left, when it was abolished.

One day the union president asked me about my plans. I told him that I hoped to use the first of my three years for rapid change, the second to freewheel and consolidate, and the third, if the organization and the board had not built up too much resistance to me, to lay the foundations for a totally new style of management. He said he would wait and watch for the first year, which he scrupulously did. At one stage he asked whether I was not going too fast for a hidebound organization such as the PNB, but I assured him that I was keeping a finger on its pulse and trying to be both surgeon and anaesthetist. In the event, the bank developed so many problems in the second year, almost like antibodies to change, that there had to be forced freewheeling instead of the controlled one that I had hoped for. Perhaps, as in the STC, it was the consequence of too-rapid change. Everything happened at once, and I let it do so, in the hope that things would clear up in my final year. As luck would have it, they did.

The union president fell ill seriously, and was laid up for almost a year. Because of his dominant personality, his withdrawal from the scene created a vacuum both on the board and in the union; but out of it also came a remarkable experience for me, and a rare personal relationship. First out of courtesy, then out of curiosity, and later out of pure interest and a new involvement, I began to visit him in his sickbed. Initially he was courteous and wary, but slowly he began to talk about the bank's difficulties, the slackened pace of change lately, and how much of it would last after I left. In fact, he had heard that someone conservative and opposed to change was already making a bid to succeed me, and was behind the new problems. He and, as he put it with unconscious self-importance, the "progressive forces behind bank nationalization," had opposed this man successfully when he had last tried, and

CHAPTER EIGHTEEN

would oppose him again. He also talked about the banking system, and wondered what nationalization had achieved in reality. The union had begun with such high hopes of a new economic order, but now the system was reverting to type. The top men of the All-India Bank Employees' Association had met the minister and the prime minister, and she had asked for a note on the subject; but nothing came of it. He despaired of nationalization, and felt the more depressed in that what little the PNB had achieved lately might conceivably be wiped out.

One day, during one of my calls at his sick-bed, I asked him if I, too, might indulge in some thinking aloud. The director of the National Institute of Bank Management, and two of his PNB watchers were all present. I posed a large, open-ended question.

"You, as a union, are powerful, and I believe that your all-out support hastened nationalization, which might otherwise not have taken place, or at least would have been delayed," I said. "Since then you have gained more strength and more concessions for your men, who, for work that is relatively light, are now the highest paid in industry and government. No one can move one of your men, not even from one desk to another a foot away. Many build their own homes, after which it is impossible to transfer them even from one branch to another in the same town. In a small district town they get more money than the young civil servant, who is the pick of university graduates and is moved every three years, and much more than the young army officer, who is moved practically every year, and for years on end is posted at stations from which he visits his family only twice a year for two months. In the PNB I have had to ask Sam Manekshaw to recruit young, prematurely retired officers to open our new offices in distant mountain places to which everyone in the bank refused to go despite the generous pay and allowances. And your organization protects and cossets your man till he has lost the basic desire to work, even to advance up the ladder. Many refuse promotion to avoid transfer, and certainly any promotion that means responsibility. The system costs the customer more each year and gives him less, not even normal courtesy. He has no choice, either. When management protests, you regard it as victimization, transgression of rights, undemocratic. It is all rights and no obligations.

"Management cannot cope with the problem, I think, because they are themselves not trained as managers should be. They have risen from your ranks—but do you ever give even your own men a chance when they rise? While the officers seek to solve their problems by following in your footsteps and organizing in their own right, what will the senior managers do? Will they also organize themselves, as they have already tried to do? And will having three unions—staff, officers, managers—solve the problem? Or will it ultimately be left in the lap of the government, which you blame for inaction?

"But why always expect the government to do the something that you can but won't do yourselves? Government should ask you a question. Having got nationalization, what have you done about it? The banks are yours. You are on the boards, as staff or managers. It is for you to make what you want of banking; no one will stand in your way.

"Socialization of banking was necessary, but for it just to happen was not enough. It should be the means to some end—service to the society of a kind that it certainly has not been. Your senior colleague told me a year ago that change would only come when it was accepted at the top. The top says that it has yet to be accepted lower down. Each expects the other to change first, but resists when an attempt is made to do so. Yet where change is concerned, there is no top or bottom. It can begin anywhere, but it must be accepted by all who believe in it. At least in our bank it has started. If the top has not accepted it, have your men done so? They all—managers, officers, and men—say they want change, and they all fight it at each step."

There had obviously been a lot building up inside me. I laughed, and told the president that I had been waiting for a chance to express my feelings. They were in the nature of a protest. Everyone else protested; it was time I did so too. He looked thoughtful, and said I had given him an idea. For a man trained and brought up only on confrontation, on whose face I had seen pure hatred and venom when he was addressing a union meeting, a curious softness appeared.

Next time I called, he said he would like to pursue the subject. His union colleagues had often wondered what I meant by the change I talked so much about. Would I talk to some of them if he arranged a meeting? I reacted with alacrity. I would go further, and arrange a seminar, to which I would bring some of my senior colleagues. We would survey the bank's operations over the last few years, and have an open discussion about our strengths and

CHAPTER EIGHTEEN

weaknesses, where we were going and should go. Banking is unlike any other industry in India because its operations are so decentralized. Our 18,000 men were scattered over 1,100 branches, each an island entire to itself but no part of a main. No circulars could, for example, make the small group at the branch in Peo, the last town on our northern border, frozen for more than half the year, feel a part of the chain. We had to make each link feel that it had its own strength, though dependent upon all the others. If ever there was a case for a participatory movement, it is in banking.

We first held a seminar with our management; another, after some tantrums, took place with the officers' association, and then one with the union. After that problems suddenly descended thick and fast, to which all of us—I, the officers, and the union—contributed.

The government, and also my senior colleagues, had been urging the banks to do something about falling discipline and the rising cost of overtime. Overtime had become a "fixed" obligation of management; so much had to be paid every month for what was, in effect, a twenty-five hour week. Wherever this habit took root, it inevitably affected customer service and discipline. In my last year, I decided to deal with it, amidst immediate cries of injustice and violated rights, rights wholly irrational, which once established could not be waived. At the prospect of participation in management, moreover, deep inner personality conflicts within the union rose to the surface. The officers' leaders first tried to take advantage of the union's uncertainties, and then, as the staff turned upon them, backed away.

In Delhi a prolonged struggle lasted half a year. The familiar demonstrations were held; *gheraos* were made to build up pressure behind the demand to revert to the old overtime. At one particular "peaceful" *gherao* of a manager, more men than one would have thought possible pushed into his small room. Tightly surrounded, he had to listen to obscenities which were the mildest part of his ordeal. The men kept on in relays through the sweltering, suffocating May heat, till their "shocked" leader arrived at midnight to lift the siege. Then the victim was allowed his first drink of water and visit to the toilet in seven hours. Shades of Siraj-ud-Daula of Black Hole of Calcutta fame! The manager went home and next day was taken to hospital with a severe heart attack, his health shattered. Even so, he was luckier than one of his colleagues, who at his *gherao* earlier had slumped dead in his chair. My own *gherao* was a pale shadow in comparison, relying only on shouting imaginative accusations, with derisive references to my foreign car and my foreign wife, and praising the men's own courage, solidarity, and strength with much conviction. For months thereafter there could be no talks on participation. Whatever the cumulative past sins of management, and they must have been many, they were more than paid for by this hapless generation of managers in the years after the unions were formed and acquired strength. Gradually, after simmering for some months, the troubles began to subside and the problem was ultimately resolved.

As the time for me to leave came nearer, I made clear that I was not looking for an extension of my three-year contract. In December 1974 I asked my minister for permission to leave at the end of my contract in the following July. I had about three months' leave due to me, and this I asked to take before retiring. In this environment, this was something unheard of. Seeking extensions was a great pastime, and one at least tried to get one's accumulated leave refused. This gave the politicians, who could grant extension of service, power over men during the last few years of their service, when retirement began to cast its shadow. It tended to affect, sometimes even vitiate, men's powers of decision, and opened the way to an unhealthy exploitation of their gratitude. The men could not be blamed, for retirement at an early age of fifty-eight, when they were fit and able to work for many more years and family responsibilities were usually at their peak, at a pitiable superannuation of about one-quarter of their retiring salary, with all fringe benefits gone, posed quite a problem in an age of inflation.

With the union problems out of the way, the organization was now on a fairly even keel and showing signs of picking up its interrupted progress. As the time for my departure came closer, and my intention to leave became clearer, I detected a softer light in the eyes of the board, and even of the leadership of the officers' association. Suggestions came from both the union and the association leaders that I stay longer to complete the experiment. Things were at last running smoothly, and with a new wind in the sails we could all combine to achieve much more. I told them that these encouraging remarks were perhaps the very sign that it was time to leave. If they felt I should stay longer, then it was time to go. Who knew how long the welcome would last!

CHAPTER EIGHTEEN

The union and the association then suggested that we at least formalize the participation-in-management experiment. I agreed, and we organized a preliminary meeting of the three groups—union, officers, and managers—at which a steering committee was appointed to lay plans for a convention upon my return from leave, before I stepped down. We all realized that the experiment was so big and amorphous that we could do no more than make a show of courage by embarking upon it. There would doubtless be many problems, but at least the changed PNB was better placed to make the attempt.

We held a participation conference in Bombay at the National Institute of Bank Management, which had adopted us and our experiment. There were nearly a hundred people from all parts of India, representing the federation, the association, and the management. There was much hard discussion and questioning, but also general agreement on the need to experiment. As the conference drew to a close, all our differences seemed to dissolve, and there was reminiscing about the past three years and what we had all learned. Much irritation and needling I had caused when introducing change was remembered, but reconsidered in softer tones. My past was forgiven and their future welcomed. Three cheers were even raised, with a Punjabi lustiness. Many showed a bigheartedness and sentiment I had not suspected.

Alone in my room at the Delhi Gymkhana that night, I looked back over my last three years with the PNB. What had I received, what had I given? After four years of the STC, thirty-one with Lever, and eight in England before that, I had needed the three years at this Punjabi bank to bring me back from forty-three years of exile from the Punjab. I had gotten too far away from it. Staff, officers, managers, and directors had all restored my Punjabiness. Chadha, the union president, a Punjabi Khatri turned radical, had at last accepted that I had feelings for the bank. Ahluwalia, the association president, a cross-grained Jat, in the end editorialized in his association's journal that my leaving signaled the end of an era. Kahlon, the Dugar Jat Sikh Ph.D., an agricultural economist who said what he meant and usually a lot more besides, had looked straight at me and said he was going to miss it all, including me. Dutt, the civil servant representing the ministry, a support in my moments of despair and the most discreet of them all, had said nothing but conveyed much. Among the managers, however, some whom innovation had infected remained discreetly silent and at a distance, wondering whether they would soon be identified as agents of change. Kamla Chowdhry's words about my creating problems returned to me once again: no one is grateful to a problem maker.

Yes, I had gained a lot—but then, I felt, I had also, in return, given professionalism to an institution which for eighty years had been the personally managed domain of one or another family. Times were changing, and nationalization had given banking a new context. In introducing me into the bank, someone must have sought to cross its traditional sturdiness with a new, but nonetheless Punjabi, strain of management. Many of its systems and the ways of its men were antiquated. Charming though some were, they were out of tune with the times. A simple, old branch manager in a small town said to me, "Tandon Sahib, *Kamal kar ditta*—You have done wonders. You have even given us a new language. What we called a loan department, we now call the credit administration division. *Vaqia he kamal kar ditta!*—Really you have done wonders!" I laughed but saw his point, because with the new names came new demands and new ways. Credit had to be administered, not just loans given.

In the PNB one could identify the work of each of my predecessors. So why not a legacy from Tandon Sahib? I had begun to feel part of this history—a short period, but compressed and vivid. This brief, atavistic connection with a Punjabi institution had in its own way meant more to me than my time with the STC and Hindustan Lever, and the wrench of leaving was of an unfamiliar kind. Repelled by its nearly century-old crust, I yet came close to its core, which was alive and vital—its men.

And thus after three strenuous and seldom peaceful years, I left the bank. I knew there would be many changes, many rejections, much unctuous disassociating with the past by some to express fealty to the future. This was our Punjabi way. I remembered my father being transferred from Lyalpur when I was a boy. The new incumbent, an Englishman, had arrived the day before, and the whole staff had disappeared on a salaaming pilgrimage, some doubtless even conveying that fate and *sarkar* had been kind to have sent them a sahib again. As a people, we were good at adjustment. I chuckled over my experience in delegating authority with a very senior division head, whom I had made chairman of an important committee. Reading the minutes, I once asked him about the line of reasoning for the decision on an issue. He imme-

CHAPTER EIGHTEEN

diately said, "No, *huzoor,* I entirely disagreed with the committee. I entirely agree with your honour, but then the committee members would not listen to me. Now I will go and change the minutes and tell the members that both your honour and I disagree with them all. That will teach them to listen to me in future, and I will always consult you in future before the committee meets." I gave up.

As with Lever, on leaving the PNB, I refused to bow out with the customary *bharat darshan,* a formal visit to the main offices in India. On the last day, after my last board meeting, which Subramaniam, the finance minister, attended, I hastily emptied my room and asked them to sell the simple furniture they had bought from the STC—a few low chairs, but no desk—to my next employers in turn. The old furniture was moved back to the old general manager's large office, which had been kept vacant, in anticipation of the new chairman's joining the following day. There was a desultory farewell function, and a press conference to announce the half-yearly results. A seasoned journalist had asked me three years earlier, after I had joined the PNB, "Why don't you go and teach and write? Probably you will last even less time here than you did in the STC." At this press conference, he reminded me of it, and I told him that this time I was going to take his advice.

I said an apologetic and self-effacing farewell to the board, and the new chairman, a bustling, cheerful, moon-faced Punjabi, uttered a few words about my contribution and what I was leaving behind. I could only mumble, "Well, thanks, but please don't hold it against me." The point was missed.

Long into the windy monsoon night I relived my time with the PNB and my life in industry over nearly forty years. I remembered, too, my father's career, which had ended forty years earlier, after beginning at the end of the previous century. So varied in their different ways, they were yet so alike. He left as the shadows cast by the British were lengthening. I had started out when the sun of the Raj was setting and Indian independence was dawning again after a thousand years. Despite frustrations, our times were also full of interest and hope—if one's faith drew sustenance from the remote past and the distant future.

EPILOGUE

MY FRESH association with the Punjab became even stronger after I left the bank. I accepted an invitation to join Punjab state's new planning board, to head research projects on its development, and, what touched me most, to join the University of Punjab as a senator, professor, and dean of the faculty of management. This meant frequent visits that refreshed my roots. I discovered a new Punjab, its vitality and activity reminiscent of the early days of my father's career, nearly one hundred years before.

I wonder what my father would have thought of the new foreign dwarf wheat compared with the tall Punjabi wheat that waved so gracefully in the wind; or of the rice cultivation that has made the Punjab the largest rice-exporting state in India. How would he have reacted to the replacement of the musical sound of the well and its Persian wheel by the hum of the tubewell; to the complete disappearance of bullocks from cart, well, and plough; to the spluttering sounds of trucks and tractors instead of the affectionate swearing and cursing of bullock drivers; to mud houses giving way to houses of cement and plaster, with tall radio and television masts; to houses moving out of the village and into the farmers' fields; to the Jat's long *kurta,* turban, *tehmad,* and spurred *gamashahi* shoes exchanged for nylon bush shirts, trousers, and plastic *chappals?* Now, along the three hundred miles of the Delhi-Amritsar Grand Trunk Road one seldom saw a bullock cart, a plough, a horse, or a Jat walking.

So the Punjabi farmer, unconcerned with aesthetics, rushed ahead in his passion for productivity and prosperity. When he first saw the new wheat, he would pay fancy prices for the seed—and was equally willing to steal it—to have his fields flourishing with this visible symbol of progress and high yields. He educated himself in the balanced utilization of water, fertilizer, pesticides, and weeding. He learned how to price these elements, calculate the return, and alter his mix to maximize it. He learned to handle and maintain the tractor and farm equipment as if born to it. His appetite for life grew with his affluence, which he loved to display. On Sundays the town squares were full of the tractors and trailers of villagers visiting the cinemas. He would appear at the bars, his pockets bulging with hundred-rupee notes, order the most expensive scotch, and with a touch of contempt mix it with cheap beer. The farm labourers, too, had acquired expensive tastes. In addition to a relatively high daily wage, with full meals, they wanted a bottle of whiskey in the evening—though they were content with the Indian variety.

While the farmer produced and progressed, the planners and academics argued over what he should and should not do. The academics argued that the mechanization of agriculture reduced employment opportunities; the farmers countered that it improved crop yields. In some areas high yields and crop increases as a result of mechanization had created a greater demand for labour, as in the Punjab, while elsewhere mechanization had displaced labour. The more influential among the planners therefore insisted that mechanization should be discouraged, and persuaded the government to ban the import of combine harvesters. The ban mainly affected the successful Punjabi farmer, who had the highest yield and crop increases and was also the strongest magnet to "guest labour."

Father had witnessed and participated in the earlier miracle of the new canal colonies started by British revenue officers and engineers, which made men from East Punjab move to the former deserts of the West. Now one witnessed an even greater miracle, worked after Partition by displaced and broken men, who had brought with them only the bundles that those who drove them away had allowed them to carry. These men laboured hard, helped by equally dedicated district officers and engineers, who settled them and with feverish speed built roads, rail links, canals, and a new capital. The same government tried as hard to help the refugees in eastern India, but with different results.

My grandfather had seen the beginning of a new Punjab. My father saw its flowering and collapse. I witnessed its rebirth and new vitality. Within just a few years after Partition no one could be called a refugee. What will my father's twenty-five grandchildren and great-grandchildren see?

In Faridabad, a new township built specially for refugees and now the largest centre both of big and small industry in the Punjab, I decided to build a house. The inhabitants of Faridabad all came from the former, distant Frontier Province district of Dera

EPILOGUE

Ismail Khan. Distinctive in dress, language, and appearance, they were still quite uninterested in the local Punjabi population thirty years later. Their grandchildren, born in Faridabad, proud of their different origin, and their Pathan Punjabi accent still intact, referred to some of their playmates as "Punjabis." On the golf course they earned pocket money as caddies and *agewalas*, and it was a mark of shame among them to lose a ball. They would spend hours, sometimes days, to find a badly driven ball in the undergrowth. "Where is Langoori?" I asked one day of a boy nicknamed for his prowess at climbing trees like a monkey. "Oh, he dare not show his face, Sahibji. He still has not found Chadha Sahib's ball since yesterday," was the contemptuous reply. They still retained their violent temper. In a fight his brother cut Langoori's foot with a knife, so severely that it had to be amputated.

Punjab's politics reflect our vitality. After a succession of mild Hindu chief ministers, the state was firmly and well managed by a Sikh, reminiscent of Ranjit Singh, the last Punjabi king. A ruthless builder, he wanted only results, and got them. His education in the United States had made him into an exemplar of the early American builders. He developed agriculture, industry, and education, while his sons built lucrative cinema houses and, in the way of the sons of our public figures, proved his undoing. He was killed in revenge on the Grand Trunk Road by someone whom the sons had allegedly wronged. He went unmourned, but was remembered for his firmness, something the Punjabis admire. He was what they call a Male Man, *Nar Admi*.

The new city of Chandigarh, designed after the First World War by Le Corbusier, the father of futurist architecture, was a bold experiment both in founding a new city and in giving a foreigner a free hand. Next door, an American dam designer named Slocum, a self-taught man, was invited to build what was then the world's highest dam, from which water and power flowed to provide energy and nourishment for the new-ploughed land. The new University of Chandigarh, designed by a brother of Le Corbusier, Jeanneret, was perhaps the best endowed in the country. Nehru's vision was a great support to the Punjabi passion for building big—to build bigger than what *they* had left behind, as if in revenge.

Out of this vital chaos I came, and to it I returned.

GLOSSARY

Agewala	One who runs in front (*age*) to locate the golf ball
Amarnath Yatra	Pilgrimage (Yatra) to the holy cave of Amarnath
Arya Samaj	Aryan Society, a Hindu reformist movement started in the late nineteenth century
Bandh	Here meaning total strike
Besakhi	Festival before the harvest, celebrated by a river bank
Bhai	Brother
Bharat	India, its ancient name
Bharat Darshan	Sight of India, round trip
Bharat Yatra	Pilgrimage round India
Bhawan	House; government buildings are called *Bhawans*
Bhoj Patra	Birch bark which comes off in flakes
Bidi	Cigarette of crude tobacco
Bijli	Lightning, electricity
Brahmo Samaj	Reformist sect in Bengal, influenced by Christianity
Chapati	Unleavened bread like a pancake
Chappals	Flat sandals
Charpoys	Literally, "four-legs string-bed"
Chenar	Tree of the maple family
Chik	Curtain of split bamboo
Chowk	Open square
Chowkidar	Watchman
Crore	Ten million

GLOSSARY

Dak	Mail. Dak bungalow; rest house, originally a stopover for mail carriers
Dal	Lentils
Dalda	Brand name for vegetable fat
Darshan	Sight, appearance. A venerated religious leader gives *darshan* to his followers
Dayanand	Founder of the Arya Samaj
Dhak tree	Tree with very hard wood
Dhobi	Washerman
Dhoti	Men's nether garment of one length of white cloth
Dupatta	Veil worn with the Punjabi costume
Durbar	Royal audience
Dussehra	Festival celebrating Ram's return from exile
Falleti's Hotel	Old hotel in Lahore, for long the only Western hotel
Gadar movement	Early revolutionary movement
Gamashahi shoes	Punjabi men's leather shoes, open and unlaced, and with pointed leather spurs in front
Ghat	Steps down to a river; also a hill
Gherao	Literally, surround, not allowing a person to leave the room
Gurgabi shoes	Women's leather shoes of a European design, open and unlaced
Hansraj	A venerated leader; ji is a suffix denoting affection
Harijan	Children of God, name given by Gandhi to the untouchables
Havildar	Non-commissioned officer
Huzoor	Literally, your presence, Sir
ICS	Indian Civil Service; changed in 1947 to IAS (Indian Administrative Service)

GLOSSARY

Jat	Farming caste of North India
Johar	Rajput custom of immolating themselves when the fortress gates were opened in the face of defeat; women smeared saffron on the men's foreheads, and they marched out to be slain in a last charge; the women would put on their best clothes and, carrying trays of incense and earthenware lamps, march singing through the streets to throw themselves over the city wall
Kameez, kamiz	Tunic, from the French *chemise*, worn by women
Karo	Do
Kayasth	Urban caste of upper India
Khatri	Punjabi for Kashtriya, member of the warrior caste
Kirana merchant	Grocer and general merchant
Kleender	Literally, cleaner, mechanic's assistant
Kurta	Tunic worn by men over pyjamas
Lakh	One hundred thousand
Lajpat Rai	Punjabi leader in the freedom struggle
Lalaji	Customary polite address to a senior man
Langoor	Big monkey
Lungi	Men's nether garment of one length of coloured cloth
Maithili	From a part of Bihar
Mandi	Market
Mathur	Subcaste in Uttar Pradesh
Mohalla	Old word for residential parts of town
Morcha	Point of assault in a battle; now protest march
Mundu	A nether garment
Murdabad!	May he die!

GLOSSARY

Nagar	City, as in Ahmednagar. New suburbs are often given a name ending in *nagar*.
Neelgai	Literally, blue cow; a big deer
Neem	Tree whose leaves have antiseptic and medicinal properties
Oxford or Cambridge Blue	Holder of the highest sports award at these universities
Pan	Betal nut and condiments wrapped in a leaf, chewed after meals as a digestive aid
Pan-bidiwala	One who sells pan and bidis, rolled leaf cigarettes
Patedar	Warrant holder, a caste in Gujarat state
Pi dog	Pariah dog, mongrel
Priti Bhojan	Simple food served at Arya Samaj functions
Raksha Bandhan	Day of the August full moon, when sisters tie (*bandhna*) coloured thread (*Rakhi*) around the wrists of their brothers as a symbol of asking for their protection
Ravana	Ten-headed king of Lanka, defeated by the god-king Rama
Sadhu	Holy man
Salwar	Wide trousers
Sardarji	Title usually given to Sikh men (*Sadarniji* is the female equivalent)
Sarkar	Government
Satyagraha	Gandhi's "Firmness in the Truth," a non-violent demonstration
Sepoy	Office attendant, originally a soldier in the Company's army, from Persian *Sipahi*
Shlokas	Verse (couplets)
Shri	Mister
Siapa	A mourning ritual

GLOSSARY

Siraj-ud-Daula	King of Bengal, famous for the so-called Black Hole of Calcutta
Srivastava	Subcaste. In India names of subcastes are often used as family names
Swadeshi	Made within the country, indigenous
Tehmad	Coloured cloth tied round the waist and reaching to the ground, worn with the *kurta*
Tonga	Two-wheeled horse cart
Vanaspati	Vegetable cooking fat
Yatra	Pilgrimage
Zamindar	Landowner

Compositor: Huron Valley Graphics
Printer: Thomson-Shore, Inc.
Text: VIP Bembo
Display: VIP Bembo
Cloth: Holliston Roxite B 53561
Paper: 50 lb P&S Vellum B-32

LIBRARY OF DAVIDSON COLLEGE

Books on regular loan may be checked out for **two weeks**. Books must be presented at the Circulation Desk in order to be renewed.

A fine is charged after date due.

Special books are subject to special regulations at the discretion of the library staff.